access to history

Poverty and Welfare 1815–1950 SECOND EDITION

Peter Murray

HODDER
EDUCATION
AN HACHETTE UK COMPANY

The publishers would like to thank the following individuals, institutions and companies for permission to reproduce copyright illustrations in this book: © Bettmann/CORBIS, page 88; Centre for the Study of Cartoons and Caricature, University of Kent, page 3; © CORBIS, page 105; Getty Images, pages 55, 116, 145, 146; © Historical Picture Archive/CORBIS, page 22; © Hulton-Deutsch Collection/CORBIS, page 144; The Illustrated London News Picture Library, pages 12, 49, 84; The National Archives, ref: HO44/27 pt.2 (1), page 45; James Smith Noel Collection, Louisiana State University, Shreveport, page 18; © C. H. Park, pages 53, 107; By permission of People's History Museum, page 151; © Peter Higginbotham/www.workhouses.org.uk, pages 40, 64; Private Collection/Bridgeman Art Library, page 7; Reproduced with the permission of Punch, Ltd., pages 103, 117; Science Museum/Science & Society Picture Library, page 24.
The publishers would like to thank the following for permission to reproduce material in this book: Oxford, Cambridge and RSA (OCR) examinations for extracts used on pages 70, 128, 154, 180.
The publishers would also like to thank the following: Longman for an extract from *The Birth of Modern Britain 1780–1914* by Eric Evans, 1997; Palgrave Macmillan for an extract from *State, Society, and the Poor in Nineteenth-Century England* by Alan Kidd, 1999.

Every effort has been made to trace and acknowledge ownership of copyright. The publishers will be glad to make suitable arrangements with any copyright holders whom it has not been possible to contact.

Although every effort has been made to ensure that website addresses are correct at time of going to press, Hodder Murray cannot be held responsible for the content of any website mentioned in this book. It is sometimes possible to find a relocated web page by typing in the address of the home page for a website in the URL window of your browser.

Orders: please contact Bookpoint Ltd, 130 Milton Park, Abingdon, Oxon OX14 4SB. Telephone: (44) 01235 827720. Fax: (44) 01235 400454. Lines are open 9.00–5.00, Monday to Saturday, with a 24-hour message answering service. Visit our website at www.hoddereducation.co.uk

© Peter Murray 2006
First published in 2006 by
Hodder Education,
an Hachette UK Company,
338 Euston Road London NW1 3BH

Impression number   10 9 8 7 6 5 4
Year   2011 2010 2009

Cover photo © Royal Holloway, University of London/Bridgeman Art Library
Typeset in Baskerville 10/12pt and produced by Gray Publishing, Tunbridge Wells
Printed in Malta

A catalogue record for this title is available from the British Library

ISBN: 978 0 340 88900 8

Contents

Dedication

Keith Randell (1943–2002)

The *Access to History* series was conceived and developed by Keith, who created a series to 'cater for students as they are, not as we might wish them to be'. He leaves a living legacy of a series that for over 20 years has provided a trusted, stimulating and well-loved accompaniment to post-16 study. Our aim with these new editions is to continue to offer students the best possible support for their studies.

1

Introduction: Poverty and the Poor

POINTS TO CONSIDER
This chapter will introduce you to some of the key concepts used in the study of poverty and welfare. The main themes are:

- Poverty and welfare: some key concepts
- Who were the poor?
- The experience of poverty

Key dates:

1776	Adam Smith's *Wealth of Nations* published. Included definition of 'relative' poverty
1834	Poor Law Amendment Act. Major Act of Parliament that reorganised the Poor Law in England and Wales
1851–2	Henry Mayhew's *London Labour and the London Poor* first published in serial form. The first extensive study to look at poverty in London in this period
1878	'General' William Booth founded the Salvation Army. An attempt to bring Christianity to the poor
1908	Old Age Pensions Act. State pensions introduced for elderly citizens by the Liberal government
1948	National Health Service set up by the post-war Labour government

1 | Poverty and Welfare: Some Key Concepts

Absolute and relative poverty

> **Key question**
> What are the different ways of categorising poverty?

Poverty can be defined in two ways. When we see pictures of people starving to death as a result of famine or disaster we are in no doubt that they are poor. The lack of an adequate income to provide for basic human needs – food, clothing, warmth and shelter – is a clear indication of poverty. Such a condition is often termed *absolute poverty*. People are in absolute poverty because they cannot gain access to basic necessities no matter how they organise their resources. Absolute poverty is still widespread at the start of the twenty-first century, although it is rare in the more industrialised and technologically advanced societies.

However, this does not mean that poverty is absent in these societies.

Another way of defining poverty is to look at it in relation to the general wealth of a society. Already in the first half of the nineteenth century the advances in agricultural production had meant that famine as a result of crop failure in Great Britain (though not in Ireland) had become a thing of the past. But there was general agreement that poverty had not been conquered. Many people, especially those who were forced out of employment by the monumental changes of the **industrial revolution**, were absolutely poor.

Others, however, were still poor even though they had access to the basic necessities of life. There was an assumption that a certain standard of living was normal, and those below this, while they might not be starving or homeless, were certainly poor. Adam Smith, the pioneering economist of the late eighteenth century, agreed that poverty was the absence of the necessities of life, but he defined these as:

> not only the commodities which are indispensably necessary for the support of life, but whatever the custom of the country renders it indecent for creditable people, even of the lowest order, to be without.

In the period 1815–1948 there were people who were absolutely poor, but there were many more who were relatively poor. Both concepts need to be kept in mind in any investigation of poverty and the attempts to respond to it.

The deserving and the undeserving

The link between poverty and morality is very important in understanding the way in which people in the nineteenth and early twentieth centuries looked at the poor. Many observers and investigators of poverty claimed that the poor were often responsible for their own misery. Carelessness, laziness and drunkenness, it was said, were the real causes of poverty. People who were poor as a result of their moral failures were regarded as undeserving; they might be given some help, but this would be of the meanest kind, designed to punish them for their inadequacies and encourage them to mend their ways.

On the other hand, it was acknowledged that some people, although they lived honest and hardworking lives, might find themselves plunged into poverty as a result of circumstances beyond their control. These were the deserving poor, the poor who had a greater moral claim to support in time of need.

Charity workers, welfare authorities, politicians and writers were often obsessed with the need to distinguish the deserving from the undeserving. Their great fear was that too generous a support for the poor would encourage immoral behaviour and reduce the incentive to lead a moral life. The issue of unemployment highlighted this problem. If those without work were given financial help why, it was asked, should anyone bother to work?

Key date

Adam Smith's *Wealth of Nations* published: 1776

Key term

Industrial revolution
The process by which powered machinery was introduced in Britain in the late eighteenth and early nineteenth centuries. Factories were built and the population began to shift from the countryside to the growing towns and cities.

Such a view inevitably led to a search for effective ways to provide support, whilst discouraging immorality. For those responsible for providing welfare to those in need, the Poor Law authorities, this meant (after 1834) subjecting the poor who asked for help to the harshest of regimes (see Chapter 3). This, it was believed, would encourage anyone who could to avoid the Poor Law altogether and lead an independent life.

But what of the deserving poor? Why should those who were unemployed due to a trade depression, for example, be punished as if they had done something wrong? This was the dilemma facing welfare reformers throughout this period, and the problem facing those who found themselves in need of help.

Two images of a family, produced by George Cruikshank in 1847. What has changed between the first picture and the second? What aspects of the second drawing are intended to give you the impression that this family is now poor? Do you think Cruikshank was illustrating the 'deserving' poor or the undeserving? Centre for the Study of Cartoons and Caricature, University of Kent.

Ways of providing welfare

Any society has a number of choices as to the way it provides welfare for its members. Put simply, welfare can be provided either by government, by organisations that are independent of government, or it can be left to individuals. If government itself provides welfare, it can do this either centrally or through local government.

Collectivist solutions

Welfare systems provided by government are known as collectivist solutions. Society collectively, through its government and laws, decides that help must be given to those in need. Collectivist solutions to poverty provided by government have certain features often seen as desirable in welfare systems.

- First, there is a stronger guarantee that they will not break down than is the case with alternative systems. Although it is possible for government welfare systems to collapse when a country enters a periods of crisis, the relatively stable political system in modern Britain has given its citizens a degree of confidence in government welfare provision. However inadequate the system might seem, it is unlikely to break down altogether.
- Secondly, government welfare systems are backed by law, which again gives them an inherent strength.
- Finally, government welfare tends to involve a certain amount of wealth redistribution. Richer sections of the community pay higher taxes, which are then transferred to the poorer sections through welfare benefits. Of course, government welfare systems do not necessarily redistribute wealth from the rich to the poor, but they do tend in that direction.

The relationship between national government and local government is an important feature of welfare in this period. The major collectivist government welfare system in the nineteenth century was the Poor Law (see Chapters 2 and 3). The Poor Law, reorganised by an amending Act in 1834, was a national, state system in that it covered the whole country and the administration was supervised by government officials in London. Nevertheless, the system was financed through local taxes, organised through groups of local parishes known as unions and operated by bodies of locally elected representatives known as guardians. Such a system grew out of the tradition of local government responsibility for the poor, which had existed for hundreds of years. But because different areas had varying levels of poverty and wealth, inequalities inevitably resulted. This led to a demand for nationally administered welfare systems. However, even when the Liberal government brought in national, government-financed old age pensions in 1908 (see Chapter 5), they still relied on local committees to decide who was eligible for the benefits. Only after the Second World War (1939–45) did the

Key question
What are the different ways in which a society can respond to the problem of poverty?

Key dates

Old Age Pensions Act: 1908

National Health Service set up by the post-war Labour government: 1948

Friendly societies
These began when groups of neighbours, friends or workmates decided to form an association to protect themselves in time of need. Each member would contribute a certain amount of money each week and in return they would be entitled to payments from the funds if they found themselves in need due to sickness, unemployment or bereavement.

Trade unions
These were formed by groups of workers to negotiate better wages and conditions with their employers. Like friendly societies, trade unions also provided benefits for members who were in need.

Labour government establish a National Health Service to ensure greater equality of provision across the country.

Voluntary groups

Collectivist responses to poverty can also be provided by voluntary groups. In the nineteenth century, **friendly societies** and **trade unions** were formed when groups of people collectively joined together to provide mutual support for one another in time of need. The members of these organisations chose to pool some of their resources by way of subscriptions so as to provide themselves with help should they need it at a future date. Voluntary organisations like these could be very successful, and in the nineteenth century they provided welfare for millions of working people. However, the cost of subscriptions excluded many of those who were most in need and the organisations were also prone to financial difficulties or even complete collapse. They had neither the financial resources nor the legal power of the state, even though governments did pass laws to regulate the operation of both friendly societies and trade unions.

Individualist solutions

Individualist responses to poverty are those that put personal responsibility at the centre of welfare provision. At one extreme, this could be the attitude that all individuals either sink or swim and should expect no help in time of crisis. It is up to them, according to this view, to save money in the good times to provide for themselves in the bad times. The nineteenth century doctrine of self-help put this type of attitude at the heart of its philosophy. However, self-help also recognised that individualism could work through collective organisations. Private insurance companies provided prudent individuals with a mechanism for protecting themselves against future disaster. Charities, especially those that operated under the guidance of the Charity Organisation Society (see Chapter 4, pages 82–4), gave a little help to those in need primarily in order to help them become self-supporting individuals. Indeed, both the Poor Law and the friendly societies also sought to encourage the poor to stand on their own feet. Thus, in a strange way collectivist systems of welfare might well operate under individualist principles.

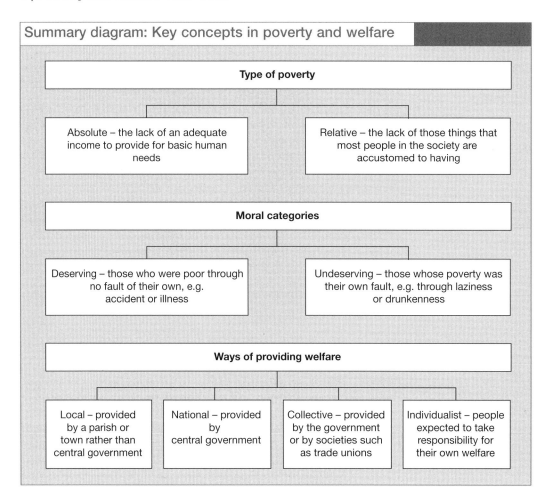

Summary diagram: Key concepts in poverty and welfare

Type of poverty

Absolute – the lack of an adequate income to provide for basic human needs

Relative – the lack of those things that most people in the society are accustomed to having

Moral categories

Deserving – those who were poor through no fault of their own, e.g. accident or illness

Undeserving – those whose poverty was their own fault, e.g. through laziness or drunkenness

Ways of providing welfare

Local – provided by a parish or town rather than central government

National – provided by central government

Collective – provided by the government or by societies such as trade unions

Individualist – people expected to take responsibility for their own welfare

2 | Who Were the Poor?

Key question
What were the different definitions of 'the poor' in the period 1832–1914?

When nineteenth-century commentators wrote about 'the poor' they were referring to any one of a range of different groupings within society. In the widest sense, all those who existed by virtue of their physical or mental efforts alone could be regarded as poor. Sometimes this group were referred to as the 'working class' or 'working classes', sometimes 'the lower orders' or 'the labouring poor', sometimes 'the proletariat' or even 'the people'.

Working class or popular classes?

For many historians, the exact classification is of great significance. In his book *The Making of the English Working Class* (1964), E.P. Thompson argued that the industrial revolution had produced a single working class that was conscious of its own status and identity. This, he believed, was a new and unprecedented development, pregnant with importance for the future progress of society. Other historians have preferred to highlight the distinctions between different groups of workers and have disputed the existence of a united working class. They prefer to use looser terms to describe the mass of the population. For

A photograph of 'slum' children taken around 1895. Are these children living in absolute or relative poverty?

example, the French historian François Bédarida makes the point that a factory worker and a farm labourer have very different lifestyles, even if they are both dependent on their employer. Bedarida prefers the term 'popular classes' because this gives the idea of differences as well as similarities.

Whatever the distinctions or classifications, it is clear that the working class or 'popular classes' were poor relative to those who controlled the nation's wealth and property. One estimate in 1905 suggested that the richest one per cent of the population owned 67 per cent of the nation's wealth, while the bottom 87 per cent of the population shared a mere eight per cent of the wealth. While this does not mean that the majority of the population lived in absolute poverty all of the time, it does help to explain why the majority of the population lived in fear of poverty: they had little surplus wealth to call on in times of need. With few financial resources on which to fall back, any sudden disaster such as illness, death or unemployment could plunge a family into poverty.

Circles of poverty
William Booth and Darkest England

The relationship between poverty, the wider working class and the core of people in permanent poverty was well illustrated by 'General' William Booth, the founder of the **Salvation Army**.

Writing in 1890, Booth was keen to distinguish between the deserving and the undeserving. But Booth understood that poverty was not simply a matter of moral failure:

> Darkest England may be described as consisting broadly of three circles, one within the other. The outer and widest circle is

Key term

Salvation Army
Religious group formed in 1878 with the aim of reviving Christianity in British cities and helping the poor.

Key question
Were 'the poor' a clearly defined or a fluctuating group?

Key date

'General' William Booth founded the Salvation Army: 1878

inhabited by the starving and homeless, but honest Poor. The second by those who live by Vice; and the third and innermost region at the centre is peopled by those who exist by Crime…The borders of this great lost land are not sharply defined. They are continually expanding and contracting…The death of a breadwinner, a long illness, a failure in the city, or any one of a thousand other causes which might be named, will bring within the first circle those who at present imagine themselves free from all danger of actual want.

(William Booth, *In Darkest England and the Way Out*, 1890)

Beyond the outer edge of William Booth's first circle lay the skilled workers in permanent employment. A great deal has been written about the distinction between these relatively prosperous skilled workers – sometimes known as the labour aristocracy – and the mass of unskilled workers. Whilst the skilled and relatively prosperous workers could afford to make some provision for the future, they too were vulnerable to poverty resulting from some crisis in their lives. In the early nineteenth century the clearest example of this was the case of the handloom weavers. Thriving in the early 1800s, the handloom weavers found that they were unable to compete with the new textile factories. These factories used powered machinery to produce cloth much more efficiently. Despite their high level of skill, the handloom weavers were gradually reduced to a state of misery as their earnings collapsed, even though they worked longer and longer hours. Technological change such as this could destroy the prosperity of even the most skilled of the working classes.

The edge of poverty

If even prospering workers could find themselves suddenly facing poverty, then one can imagine how large the spectre of poverty loomed in the lives of those on lower incomes, those at the edge of Booth's first circle. Insecurity and fear were dominant themes in the lives of working people throughout this period. Temporary poverty was likely for the majority of the population, and this could easily lead to permanent poverty. It only took one crisis, one decision by an employer, one accident, and people could find their lives transformed from minimal comfort to wretched misery. When 'the thing', as the American writer Jack London described it, happened, life might never be the same again. The circumstances that could draw an individual into the inner circles of poverty were illustrated by the story of 'Ginger', a man he met in the queue for the casual ward of the Whitechapel workhouse, which was known as 'the spike'. A year earlier, Ginger had fallen while carrying a heavy box of fish for his employer. He suffered a rupture and, despite being patched up in a hospital, was unable to do heavy work again. From that point on, Ginger was a broken man:

His only chance to earn a living was by heavy work. He is now incapable of performing heavy work, and from now until he dies, the spike … and the streets are all he can look forward to in the way of food and shelter. The thing happened – that is all. He put his back under too great a load of fish, and his chance for happiness in life was crossed off the books.

(Jack London, *People of the Abyss*, 1903, p. 43)

The 'inner circles' of poverty

Henry Mayhew's *London Labour and the London Poor* first published in serial form: 1851–2

Key date

Many nineteenth-century observers who ventured into the worst urban slums of industrial England detected a section of the population whose miserable lives were entirely shaped by the poverty in which they existed. Many of these people had sunk to the lowest level of existence as a result of some catastrophe in their lives, whilst others were born into an environment of deprivation, low wages and lack of opportunity. These were the inhabitants of William Booth's inner circles of 'Darkest England'. Writers often referred to this population as if they were a separate race, a people set apart from civilised society.

In his Report on the *Sanitary Condition of the Labouring Population of Great Britain* in 1842, the Poor Law administrator and health reformer Edwin Chadwick was one of the first to describe the poorest areas as an 'unknown country'. Henry Mayhew, a writer who investigated the 'street-folk' of London in the 1850s, wrote of 'unknown regions' that contained 'strange tribes of men.' Throughout the period writers continued to discuss the poorest sections of the population in these terms. They were the outcasts, the 'people of the abyss'.

When social investigators Charles Booth in the late nineteenth century and Seebohm Rowntree at the start of the twentieth century conducted their surveys of poverty, they too recognised a very poor class at the foot of the social ladder. Rowntree defined the really poor in York as those who existed below the 'poverty line', a level beneath which families did not have enough money to maintain 'mere physical efficiency' – they did not have enough to live on.

'Respectable' workers

In one sense there was a justification in distinguishing the plight of the very poor from that of the wider working class. 'Respectable' workers, employed in steady, skilled occupations and living away from the slums and of the inner cities, themselves emphasised their difference from the poorer workers. Writing in 1873, the journeyman engineer Thomas Wright explained that while the craftsman:

… resents the spirit in which the followers of 'genteel occupations' look down on him, he in his turn looks down upon the labourer. The artisan creed with regard to labourers is that the latter are an inferior class, and that they should be made to know and kept in their place.

On the other hand, just like the handloom weavers, even the most respectable and skilled of workers might lose their job, and be plunged into poverty. After the First World War (1914–18) the percentage of the population inhabiting the 'inner circle' reduced, but the mass unemployment of the 1930s drew many back into the depths of poverty.

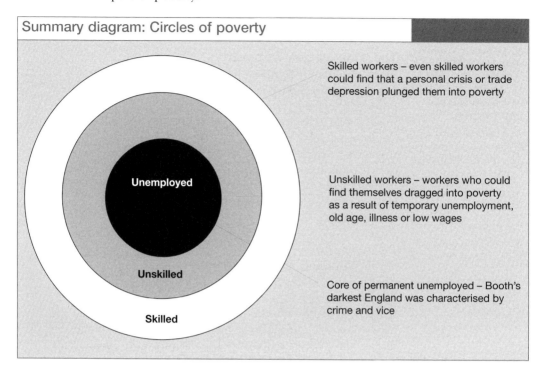

Summary diagram: Circles of poverty

Skilled workers – even skilled workers could find that a personal crisis or trade depression plunged them into poverty

Unskilled workers – workers who could find themselves dragged into poverty as a result of temporary unemployment, old age, illness or low wages

Core of permanent unemployed – Booth's darkest England was characterised by crime and vice

Unemployed
Unskilled
Skilled

3 | The Experience of Poverty

Measuring poverty

The experience of poverty affected all aspects of life for the poor. At various points in the period, writers attempted to measure poverty in financial terms.

Although there was some variation in the level of wages and prices at various points in the period 1815–1914, **inflation** over this period was not significant. It is therefore unsurprising that commentators throughout the period were consistent in the minimum level of income that they believed to be necessary for survival. Roughly speaking, this level, for a small family, was about £1 per week. A single person could live on less. The consequences of not managing to make do with a small income were explained memorably by Charles Dickens' character Mr Micawber:

> 'My other piece of advice, Copperfield,' said Mr Micawber, 'you know. Annual income twenty pounds, annual expenditure nineteen nineteen six [nineteen pounds, nineteen shillings and six pennies], result happiness. Annual income twenty pounds, annual expenditure twenty pounds ought and six, result misery. The blossom is blighted, the leaf is withered, the God of day goes down upon the dreary scene, and – and in short you are forever floored. As I am!'
> (Charles Dickens, *David Copperfield*, 1850)

Key question
What was it like to be poor in nineteenth- and early twentieth-century England?

Inflation
A general rise in the level of prices.

Key term

Currency
The currency of the period consisted of pounds (£), shillings (s) and pence (d). Each pound was subdivided into 20s, and each shilling was made up of 12d. Pennies could themselves be divided up into halfpennies and farthings (a farthing was a quarter of a penny).

In 1901, Seebohm Rowntree set the precise boundary between misery and happiness for a family of five (husband, wife and three children) at 21s 8d (one pound, one shilling and eight pence) per week. The reality of survival on such a tight budget was described by Jack London:

Rent	6s 0d
Bread	4s 0d
Meat	3s 6d
Vegetables	2s 6d
Coals	1s 0d
Tea	9d
Oil	8d
Sugar	9d
Milk	6d
Soap	4d
Butter	10d
Firewood	4d
	21s 2d

… While the table given above will permit no extravagance, no overloading of stomachs, it will be noticed that there is no surplus. The whole guinea is spent for food and rent. There is no pocket money left over. Does the man buy a glass of beer, the family must eat that much less; and in so far as it eats less, just that far will it impair its physical efficiency. The members of this family cannot ride in buses or trams, cannot write letters, take outings, go to a 'tu'penny gaff' for cheap vaudeville, join social or benefit clubs, nor can they buy sweetmeats, tobacco, books or newspapers. And further, should one child (and there are three) require a pair of shoes, the family must strike meat for a week from its bill of fare …

(Jack London, *People of the Abyss*, 1903)

Living in poverty

The diets of those living on such a budget were inevitably limited and it took great ingenuity on the part of the housewife to provide sufficient meals and avoid monotony. Household management skills were also put to the test when attempting to organise living and sleeping arrangements in often cramped and inadequate accommodation. Between 1909 and 1913 the **Fabian Society** women's group conducted a survey of working-class conditions in a 'respectable' district in Lambeth, south London.

The conditions endured are illustrated by one example of a family inhabiting a single 15 feet by 13 feet room:

Key term

Fabian Society
A group of left-wing intellectuals in the late nineteenth century who went on to become founding members of the Labour Party.

Under the window facing the door is the large bed, in which sleep mother, father and two children. A perambulator by the bedside accommodates the baby, and in the further corner is a small cot for the remaining child. The second window can be, and is, left partly open at night. At the foot of the bed which crosses the window is a small square table. Three wooden chairs and a chest of drawers complete the furniture … The small fireplace has no oven, and open shelves go up each side of it. There are two saucepans, both burnt. There is no larder.

The squalid interior of a decrepit London lodging house revealed by torchlight. People lie sleeping on the floor with minimal bedclothes. From *The Illustrated London News*, 1853. What would life have been like living in a cellar dwelling like this?

Some of the poor had slightly better conditions, but many endured a lot worse. As with food and indeed all the other aspects of life, lack of money meant lack of choice, and the Victorian (1837–1901) and Edwardian (1901–10) poor had to do the best they could with their limited resources.

Sometimes, particularly as a result of unemployment, sickness or old age, these resources simply were not enough. It was at these points that the poor were forced to look to friends, charities, institutions such as friendly societies or the state itself for welfare support. The extent to which this support succeeded in alleviating the poverty of the poor is a central question in the history of poverty and welfare in this period.

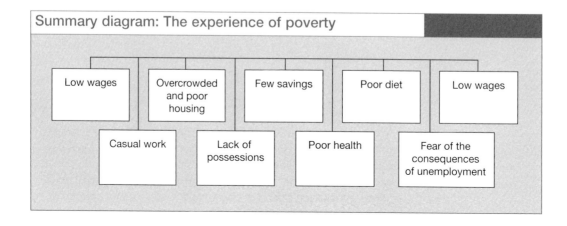

Summary diagram: The experience of poverty

- Low wages
- Overcrowded and poor housing
- Few savings
- Poor diet
- Low wages
- Casual work
- Lack of possessions
- Poor health
- Fear of the consequences of unemployment

2 The Reform of the Poor Law

POINTS TO CONSIDER

This chapter is about the reform of the Poor Law in England and Wales in 1834. During the 1820s and 1830s, there was a growing attack on the way the Poor Law worked. This resulted in an official investigation into the Poor Law, a report and an Act of Parliament that established a new Poor Law. The main themes of this chapter are:

- The operation of the old Poor Law 'system' in the early nineteenth century
- Ways in which the old Poor Law system was being attacked
- The Commission of Inquiry into the Poor Laws and its report
- The 1834 Poor Law Amendment Act
- How historians have interpreted the Act

Key dates

1601	Establishment of the Poor Law
1782	Gilbert's Act. Parishes could combine to share the cost of the Poor Law in their area
1789	Outbreak of the French Revolution
1795	Magistrates in Speenhamland, Berkshire, agreed to subsidise the wages of agricultural labourers from Poor Law funds
1796	Publication of Thomas Malthus' *Essay on the Principle of Population*, calling for abolition of the Poor Law
1798	Publication of Jeremy Bentham's *Pauper Management Improved*, calling for a centralised Poor Law based on 'Houses of Industry'
1817	Publication of David Ricardo's *Principles of Political Economy and Taxation*, calling for abolition of the Poor Law
1819	Sturges–Bourne Act. Allowed the setting up of specialised committees ('select vestries') to supervise the Poor Law
1824	Report of Select Committee on Labourers' Wages.
1832	Establishment of Royal Commission on the Poor Laws
1832	Parliamentary Reform Act
1834	Poor Law Amendment Act. Establishment of the new Poor Law

1 | Introduction

From the end of the sixteenth century the English state had accepted some responsibility for the poorest and most vulnerable members of the population through a series of 'Poor Laws'. By the beginning of the nineteenth century the Poor Law was coming under increasing criticism from **ratepayers**, politicians and academic thinkers alike.

In 1832 the government appointed a Commission to inquire into the workings of the Poor Law, and the report that the commissioners produced resulted in the 1834 Poor Law Amendment Act, a measure that fundamentally altered the way in which state and society treated the poor.

Key question
What was the Poor Law and why was it reformed?

Ratepayers
Property owners who paid rates, a tax on property used to finance local government spending.

Key term

2 | The Operation of the Old Poor Law

The Poor Law originated in the reign of Queen Elizabeth I. The Poor Law Act of 1601 established the main features of Poor Law for the next 233 years. The motivation behind the Act was partly humanitarian, but mainly a concern for social stability. There was a widespread belief among the property-owning classes that the unemployed poor were a potential threat to law and order. Under the Act the state took responsibility for those who were unable to support themselves. Each of the 15,000 **parishes** of England and Wales was made responsible for orphans and those who were sick or elderly. Poorhouses could be built to accommodate these **indigent** poor. The unemployed 'able-bodied' poor were to be provided with suitable work or, if none was available, support (cash or food). Support for the poor, or 'relief' as it was known, was financed through the rates, a local tax based on property values. Each parish appointed overseers who assessed the rates and determined who was in need of assistance. The parish vestry, a committee of ratepayers' representatives, was accountable to the local magistrates for the operation of the Poor Law.

Key question
What were the main features of the Poor Law in England and Wales in the late eighteenth and early nineteenth centuries?

Establishment of the Poor Law: 1601

Key date

Changes in the way the old Poor Law operated before 1834

These essential characteristics of the Poor Law remained unaltered until 1834, but there were some significant modifications:

- The Laws of Settlement
- Gilbert's Act
- The Speenhamland system.

Key question
How was the old Poor Law modified before 1834?

The Laws of Settlement

In the mid-seventeenth century the Laws of Settlement were introduced. These laws were designed to protect an individual parish from being overwhelmed by the poor from other areas. They also aimed to strengthen authority by preventing the poor from moving around and becoming potential troublemakers in

Parish
The smallest unit of local government.

Indigent
Someone who is unable to earn enough to live on through no fault of their own.

Key terms

Gilbert's Act: 1782

Outbreak of the French Revolution: 1789

Magistrates in Speenhamland, Berkshire, agreed to subsidise the wages of agricultural labourers from Poor Law funds: 1795

French Revolution
In 1789 there was a violent revolution in France in which King Louis XVI and his aristocratic supporters were overthrown and subsequently executed.

places where they were not known. The laws established that an individual's place of settlement was the parish in which he had been born, or the parish where he had lived for the previous three years. Overseers could order the removal of a person within 40 days of his arrival in a parish if it was considered likely that he might become an applicant for poor relief.

Gilbert's Act

Gilbert's Act of 1782 was a second modification of the Poor Law. Under this act individual parishes could group together to form larger Poor Law authorities. It was up to each parish to decide whether or not it wished to do this, but the advantage was that some costs could be reduced. For example, the parishes could share a common poorhouse rather than maintain one each. Gilbert's Act also gave legal support to the practice of providing relief to the able-bodied unemployed without forcing them to do some form of work for the parish if nothing suitable was available.

The Speenhamland system

A third set of modifications to the old Poor Laws came in the late eighteenth century.

The **French Revolution** in 1789 produced shockwaves that were keenly felt by the ruling classes across Europe. The subsequent wars between France and Britain contributed to severe disruptions of trade in the 1790s. Faced with increasing poverty and fearing that England might face a revolution of its own, magistrates in some parishes began to look for new ways to reduce the problems of the poor. In the parish of Speenhamland, Berkshire, magistrates decided to subsidise low wages by paying agricultural labourers an allowance that increased according to the number of their children and the price of bread. This practice of subsidising the wages of those in work, rather than just supporting those without work, has subsequently become known as the 'Speenhamland system', but historians now agree that this is a misleading name because it implies that what happened at Speenhamland was new and was the system adopted in all country areas. In fact neither of these things were the case.

Variations from the Speenhamland system

Wage support was not an entirely new feature of the Poor Law and, although many magistrates in counties other than Berkshire now shared the same concerns, the approaches they adopted varied from the Speenhamland system in important ways. Whilst some parishes did pay allowances based on both bread prices and the number of children in a family, others paid just a flat rate allowance to each labourer. Some parishes took each child into consideration, while some paid only families with four or more children. A system known as the labour rate system was used in some places. This meant that landowners who took on unemployed labourers at a wage set by the parish were exempt from paying poor rates. Another variation was the roundsman system, where landowners were free to pay whatever they wanted for unemployed labourers and the parish paid an allowance to make this up to a living wage.

A right to relief?

The old Poor Law was not an early version of the **welfare state**. It did not provide standard, nationwide levels of financial support for those in poverty. Practice varied across the country and in a large number of places care for the sick and elderly was totally inadequate. In many parishes the level of support given to labourers was barely enough to ensure survival. But what all the eighteenth-century modifications to the Poor Law had in common was that they were genuine attempts to deal with the worst effects of poverty in different areas. They reflected a tradition according to which the ruling groups in society accepted some responsibility for the welfare of the poorest. As such, the pre-1834 Poor Law was regarded by the poor themselves as an essential safety net in times of destitution and one from which they had a right to benefit. For example, the 1832 Commission of Inquiry into the operation of the old Poor Law noted that in Yorkshire, 'relief is demanded as a matter of right, and sometimes with insolence'. It was this very notion of a 'right' to relief that came under increasing attack in the years before 1834.

Key term

Welfare state Established by the Labour government after 1945, the aim of the welfare state was to provide support to everyone who needed it from 'the cradle to the grave'. Benefits were to be provided by central government and included a National Health Service.

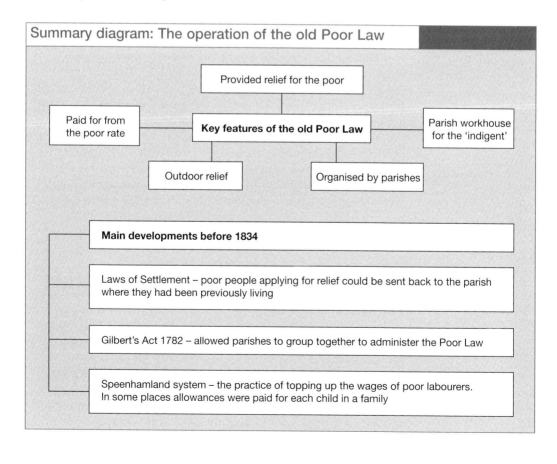

Summary diagram: The operation of the old Poor Law

Provided relief for the poor

Paid for from the poor rate

Key features of the old Poor Law

Parish workhouse for the 'indigent'

Outdoor relief

Organised by parishes

Main developments before 1834

Laws of Settlement – poor people applying for relief could be sent back to the parish where they had been previously living

Gilbert's Act 1782 – allowed parishes to group together to administer the Poor Law

Speenhamland system – the practice of topping up the wages of poor labourers. In some places allowances were paid for each child in a family

3 | The Attack on the Old Poor Law

Key question
What did most late-eighteenth-century writers think was wrong with the Poor Laws? What was most widely suggested as the solution to the problem of the Poor Laws?

In 1832 the Royal Commission of Enquiry into the Poor Law produced its report. This contained a range of serious criticisms of the Poor Law system and recommendations for its reform. But the Commission's report was certainly not the first publication to suggest an alternative method of dealing with the consequences of poverty. From the 1790s onwards some of the most prominent writers and commentators had put forward their own schemes for the relief of the poor. When the commissioners came to look at the Poor Law, there is no doubt that they were considerably influenced by these ideas.

Jeremy Bentham

Jeremy Bentham was a philosopher and writer whose most famous creation was the doctrine of **'utilitarianism'**. Utilitarian ideas were well known in the 1830s and are credited as one of the key influences on the reforms of the Whig government in that decade. Crucially, Bentham's secretary in the later years of his life was Edwin Chadwick, the dominant force behind the 1832 inquiry into the Poor Laws and himself a committed 'Benthamite'.

Key term

Utilitarianism
The idea that all institutions should be tested to see whether they produced 'the greatest happiness for the greatest number' and that institutions should be reformed if they failed to pass this test of utility (usefulness).

Reforms of the Whig government in the 1830s

Date	Reform	Effect
1832	Electoral Reform Act	Reorganised parliamentary constituencies and extended the vote in parliamentary elections to the middle class
1833	£20,000 Education Grant	First time Parliament spent money on school building
1833	Emancipation Act	Abolition of slavery in the British Empire
1833	Factory Act	Limited the number of hours children were allowed to work in factories
1834	Poor Law Amendment Act	Established the new Poor Law
1835	Municipal Corporations Act	Reformed local government and extended the vote in local government elections to middle-class ratepayers

The National Charity Organisation

Key date

Publication of Jeremy Bentham's *Pauper Management Improved*: 1798

Bentham's ideas on poverty and the Poor Law were outlined in his 1798 book *Pauper Management Improved*. His amazing proposal was to give the entire responsibility for the poor to a body to be known as the National Charity Organisation. This was to be a profit-making, private company initially financed by a government subsidy. To begin with, 250 'industry houses' would be established to accommodate about half a million people. Bentham saw this rising to 500 houses, accommodating a million people – around 10 per cent of the total population. Poor relief would only be given to those who entered the house: **outdoor relief** would be abolished. Life within an industry house would be deliberately hard, with strict supervision and discipline, long

Key term

Outdoor relief
Financial support for people living in their own homes rather than the workhouse.

Jeremy Bentham. How far were the ideas of Bentham responsible for the reform of the Poor Law in 1834?

working hours and a meagre diet. Indeed, the conditions were designed to be less desirable than those outside the house so as to deter all but the most desperate from entering it. Those born in the workhouse would be kept there until their early twenties and would be encouraged to marry at an early age: Bentham wanted a young and disciplined permanent population within the house in order to maximise profits. He envisaged that he would be at the head of this centralised operation and had even invented a title for himself – Sub-Regulus of the Poor.

The National Charity Organisation embodied many features that were typical of the Benthamite approach – centralised administration, efficiency and universal minimum standards. Bentham was also keen to emphasise that the poor had a right to relief. However, the scheme was also typical of his thinking in that it showed a complete disregard for the dignity, civil rights or emotional needs of the poor, and indeed treated them as a population of virtual slave prisoners. It also reduced all those who were poor to a state of complete dependence, something that distinguished it from the proposals of many other contemporaries.

Key date

Publication of
Thomas Malthus'
*Essay on the Principle
of Population*: 1796

Thomas Malthus

Thomas Malthus was a parson who also wrote about economic and social issues. His most famous work was his *Essay on Population*, published in 1796.

In this publication he developed his pessimistic theory that the growth of population, so noticeable at the time (see Figure 2.1), would inevitably outstrip the available food supply.

Figure 2.1: UK population growth 1801–51

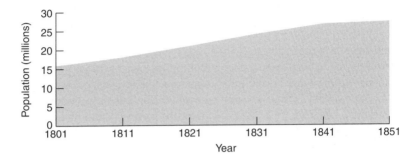

'Population', he wrote, 'increases in a geometrical, food in an arithmetical ratio'. Malthus predicted that while food supply might increase by, for example, 50 per cent, the population was likely to double in the same period. This meant that if population continued to increase at its current rate, famine and disaster were sure to follow. Malthus went on to blame the Poor Laws for the population increase and for the state of the poor generally.

> The labouring poor to use a common expression seem always to live from hand to mouth. Their present wants employ their whole attention, and they seldom think of the future. Even when they have an opportunity for saving they seldom exercise it, but all that is beyond their present necessities goes, generally speaking, to the ale-house. The poor laws of England may therefore be said to diminish both the power and the will to save among the common people, and thus to weaken one of the strongest incentives to sobriety and industry, and consequently to happiness.

Malthus believed that abolishing the Poor Laws would lead to higher wages because, relieved of the burden of high poor rates, landowners would be able to afford to pay more. Abolition would also lead to smaller families because the incentive to have more children in order to get more relief would be removed. Malthus thought that all this would lead to greater prosperity. In later editions of his *Essay on Population* Malthus did concede the need for some family allowances and relief works for the unemployed, but it was his earlier thoughts that continued to influence policy makers in the first half of the nineteenth century.

David Ricardo

David Ricardo was a City stockbroker who had made a fortune during the wars against France. His economic ideas were influenced both by Malthus and by the Scottish economist Adam Smith. In his 1817 *Principles of Political Economy and Taxation*, Ricardo combined Smith's belief in the **free market**, unfettered by any government controls or regulations, and the Malthusian fears about population. His 'iron law of wages' stated that any attempt to raise the pay of labourers through parish doles must necessarily impoverish the population because it would simply encourage dependency, idleness and fecklessness. He wrote that:

> The nature of the evil points out the remedy. By gradually contracting the sphere of the poor laws; by impressing on the poor the value of independence, by teaching them that they must look not to systematic or casual charity but to their own exertions for support, that prudence and forethought are neither unnecessary nor unprofitable virtues, we shall by degrees approach a sounder and more healthful state. No scheme for the amendment of the poor laws merits the least attention, which has not their abolition for its ultimate object.

Like Malthus, Ricardo believed that the Poor Laws would be best abolished altogether.

Robert Owen

Not all suggestions for Poor Law reform sought to reduce the role of the state in the alleviation of poverty. Rather than concentrating on the moral failings of the poor, the pioneer **socialist** Robert Owen blamed the economic system itself for creating poverty. Owen was a factory owner and had established a community in New Lanark, near Glasgow, based on his principles of co-operation. His solution to the problem of unemployment was for the government to settle labourers in new co-operative communities where they would be able to share the full benefits of their work without the exploitation of landowner or factory master. Owen's ideas were influential within the emerging working class but would have entailed a revolutionary overthrow of the existing social and economic order to be implemented. Not surprisingly, his solutions were rejected by property owners and policy makers, both inside and outside Parliament.

Thomas Paine

The radical writer Thomas Paine also had a much more sympathetic attitude to the poor. Paine was an important political thinker, whose works were widely read. He criticised the Poor Laws for their inadequacy but urged that they be reformed so that they provided better support for the poor. In order to finance his suggested reforms, Paine demanded the replacement of the poor rates by a land tax designed to hit the richer landowners. Paine also envisaged a redistribution of land and wealth from the rich to the poor. In the second part of his book *The Rights of Man*, published in 1792, he proposed an elementary social security system that would include family and education allowances for the support of children, and old age pensions. However, despite

Key date Publication of David Ricardo's *Principles of Political Economy and Taxation*: 1817

Key terms

Free market An economic system where businesses and individuals trade without interference from the state. Also known as capitalism.

Socialist A believer in socialism. Socialism is the idea that society should be much more equal and that equality can be achieved through collective control of industry and resources, either through the state or through co-operatives.

the radicalism of these ideas, Paine, like many other commentators of the time, also implied that the able-bodied unemployed would have to go to some form of workhouse if they wanted relief. This idea that some sort of workhouse was the solution to the problems of poverty and poor relief became central to the investigation into the working of the Poor Laws.

The most influential writers and thinkers of the early 1830s had very different views about how society should work. However, they nearly all agreed that the Poor Laws were in need of a radical reform.

Key question
What were the main criticisms of the Poor Laws?

4 | The Commission of Inquiry into the Poor Laws

In 1832 the Whig government decided to set up a Royal Commission to inquire into the working of the Poor Laws. This decision was motivated by both long-term concerns and immediate problems. Three major concerns in the way the Laws were operating had grown since the end of the Napoleonic Wars in 1815:

- the growing cost of poor relief
- the corruption in the system
- the demoralising effect of 'Speenhamland' (see page 15) on agricultural labourers.

The growing cost of poor relief

Ratepayers had become increasingly agitated at the cost of poor relief, which continued to grow even in peacetime. During the wars there was a general acceptance of the need to pay high rates to protect the poor in a time of crisis. Moreover, ratepaying farmers could afford higher rates because of the large profits they were making from high grain prices. After the war these ratepayers had expected poor rates to reduce. As falling wheat prices eroded their profits, they began to demand that the rates should be cut.

In the immediate post-war period the total cost of poor relief rose from £5.7 million in 1815 to a peak of £7.9 million in 1817. After this costs began to fall gradually so that expenditure in 1823 was back to £5.7 million. However, a series of poor harvests produced mounting agricultural distress in the 1820s, resulting in a rise in the cost of poor relief every year from 1823 onwards, reaching £7 million in 1831. Ratepayers began to fill the columns of local newspapers with letters complaining about this burden and demanding that something be done about it.

An illustration of a workhouse around 1810. Those who argued for the reform of the Poor Law were particularly concerned that too much relief was being given outside the workhouse. How do you think they would have regarded conditions within the workhouse like those in the picture?

The corruption in the system

A second criticism concerned the alleged corrupt behaviour of local Poor Law administrators. Contracts for Poor Law work, for example supplying food, were routinely awarded to local tradespeople rather than put out to open tender. Concerned ratepayers suggested that this was just one way in which vested interests were exploiting the system. In 1817, a Select Committee of the House of Commons had echoed these concerns, and the committee's report was followed in 1819 by an Act of Parliament that allowed parishes to set up **select vestries**. These were small committees that could specialise in Poor Law administration and employ salaried assistant overseers to supervise it. By 1827, 2868 parishes (almost 20 per cent of the total) had adopted the Act. However, in many cases the select vestries produced their own forms of corruption. For example, in 1832, 11 of the 20 members of the Morpeth Select Vestry had a vested interest in the sale of beer, and it was widely believed that generous relief payments ended up being spent in the local alehouse or pub. By 1832, the number of select vestries had declined to only 2391, suggesting that they had failed to solve the problem. Ratepayers continued to press for more fundamental reform.

Key date
Report of Select Committee on Labourers' Wages: 1824

The demoralising effect of 'Speenhamland'

The third area of attack on the Poor Law concerned the effect that the so-called Speenhamland system was having on the attitudes and behaviour of the poor. Malthus had argued that the child allowances paid by some parishes encouraged labourers to have more and more children without considering the need to provide for them. The results of the 1821 census, which showed a significant increase in the population, were used to justify these fears. Commentators and ratepayers further claimed that the Speenhamland system was causing a **'demoralisation'** of the workforce. Magistrates told the 1824 Select Committee on Labourers' Wages that under the 'roundsman' system (see page 15), labourers had no incentive to work hard or to respect their employers because they were convinced that the parish would look after their needs. The same committee also noted that another effect of Speenhamland was to reduce wages: farmers had no need to pay proper wage rates when they could get cheap, subsidised labour from the parish. Widespread agricultural disturbances in the early 1830s convinced the government and the ruling élites that the rural population was getting out of control and that this was largely a result of the way the Poor Laws were operating. The demand for reform became increasingly based on social and political concerns as well as economic motives.

Key term
Demoralisation
In the nineteenth century this term was used to describe the condition of workers who allegedly had no incentive to find work because they were being provided for by the Poor Law. They had become dependent on the state.

Key question
How reliable was the information collected by the Royal Commission?

Key date
Establishment of Royal Commission on the Poor Laws: 1832

How did the Commission conduct its inquiry?

The Royal Commission on the Poor Laws consisted of seven members appointed in 1832 and a further two appointed in 1833. The two most influential commissioners were Nassau Senior, the Professor of Political Economy at Oxford University, and Edwin Chadwick, a lawyer who had been Jeremy Bentham's private secretary, until the philosopher's death in 1832.

Under the influence of Senior and Chadwick, the Commission set about the task of gathering a vast body of evidence concerning the operation of the Poor Laws. Twenty-six assistant commissioners were dispatched to carry out this investigation, armed with precise instructions from the commissioners. They were to:

- interview clergy, parish officers and magistrates
- inspect parish documents
- cross-examine witnesses
- attend vestry meetings and
- follow up the replies to questionnaires that had been sent out by the commissioners.

Profile: Edwin Chadwick 1800–90

1800 – Born in Manchester
1832 – Assistant commissioner to Poor Law Inquiry
1834 – Secretary to the Poor Law Commissioners
1837 – Attacked during general election for his position on the abolition of outdoor relief
1842 – Published Report on the Sanitary Conditions of the Labouring Population
1848 – Commissioner on the Board of Health
1854 – Agreed to resign from Board of Health
1890 – Died

Early life

Edwin Chadwick was born in Manchester in January 1800. The son of a successful businessman who had **progressive** political views, he was well educated and qualified as a lawyer. While studying in London Chadwick read the work of radicals like Tom Paine and met thinkers like Jeremy Bentham and John Stuart Mill. Chadwick became Bentham's secretary and was heavily influenced by his work with the philosopher.

The Poor Laws

In 1832 Chadwick was appointed as one of the assistant commissioners investigating the Poor Law. He emerged as one of the most important members of the inquiry and his views were prominent in the final report. When the Poor Law Amendment Act was passed in 1834 Chadwick had hoped to become one of the three commissioners. However he was only offered the position of secretary to the commission – something which continued to irritate him throughout his involvement with the new Poor Law.

In fact, Chadwick was a generally irritable person. Passionately dedicated to the work he did, Chadwick's single-mindedness won him few friends. His determination to uphold the principle that outdoor relief should be abolished resulted in demonstrations against him during the 1837 General Election. The tensions between Chadwick and the commissioners came to a head in 1846 when he used the inquiry into the scandal of the Andover workhouse (see page 55) as an opportunity to criticise his employers. This dispute was partly responsible for the government's decision to abolish the Commission in 1847 and replace it with the Poor Law Board.

Public health

Even while he was working as secretary to the Poor Law Commission, Chadwick had become increasingly interested in another of the great social issues of the day, public health. His Report into the Sanitary Conditions of the Labouring Population was published in 1842. The Report showed how desperate the problem of poor public health had become in the big cities with poor sanitation and inadequate water supplies. Chadwick argued that these conditions were responsible for the terrible outbreaks of

Key term

Typhoid
A bacterial infection often contracted through drinking contaminated water. It was a widespread killer in the nineteenth century.

diseases such as **typhoid**. His work had a big impact on politicians and in 1848 the Public Health Act was passed.

Chadwick became a commissioner on the Board of Health established by the Act and major strides forward were made to improve the conditions in British towns and cities. Unfortunately his difficult personality and uncompromising attitude again made him unpopular and he was pressured to resign from the Board of Health in 1854. Chadwick continued to campaign for reforms in public health and education for the remainder of his long life.

There has been considerable criticism of the way in which the Royal Commission's investigation was conducted. The historian Mark Blaug called the report 'wildly unstatistical', and there is considerable doubt about the accuracy of the picture it painted. Of the 15,000 parishes in England and Wales, only 10 per cent were investigated. Even in those parishes that were visited, the questions asked were often confusing and therefore unlikely to elicit useful replies. For example:

> Have you any, and how many, able bodied labourers in the employment of individuals receiving allowance or regular relief from your parish on their own account or that of their families: and if on account of their families, at what number of children does it begin?

The overseers who filled in the questionnaire replies were often semi-literate and were certainly unaccustomed to dealing with such matters. Nevertheless, criticism of the Commission's methods needs to be tempered by a recognition that such a survey was in itself groundbreaking in an age with very primitive bureaucratic procedures. It would be unrealistic to expect modern standards of accuracy in a survey carried out in the early 1830s. However, what is clear is that Chadwick and Senior had come to their conclusions even before the research was conducted and intended to use its findings merely as a tool to reform the Poor Laws in the fashion they had already chosen.

Key question
What were the Report's most important recommendations?

The 1834 Report

The Report of the Poor Law Commission was widely read. The 400-page 'extract' sold 15,000 copies before the full report, which was a massive document, was published. In the first part of the report, the old Poor Law was attacked using examples from the research of the assistant commissioners. The second part of the report contained the Commission's conclusions and recommendations for reform. The central argument concerned the 'demoralisation' of the labouring class, which the commissioners claimed had resulted from the Poor Laws:

> It appears to the pauper that the government has undertaken to repeal, in his favour, the ordinary laws of nature; to enact that the children shall not suffer for the misconduct of their parents, the wife

for that of the husband, or the husband for that of the wife: that no one shall lose the means of comfortable subsistence, whatever be his indolence, prodigality or vice: in short, that the penalty which, after all must be paid by some one for idleness and improvidence, is to fall, not on the guilty person or on his family, but on the proprietors of the lands and houses encumbered by his settlement. Can we wonder if the uneducated are seduced into approving a system which aims its allurements at all the weakest parts of our nature – which offers marriage to the young, security to the anxious, ease to the lazy, and impunity to the profligate?

It was essential, it was claimed, to make greater distinction between the labourer who was poor, but independent, and the pauper:

Throughout the evidence it is shown, that in proportion as the condition of any pauper class is elevated above the condition of independent labourers, the condition of the independent class is depressed; their industry is impaired, their employment becomes unsteady, and its remuneration in wages is diminished. Such persons, therefore, are under the strongest inducements to quit the less eligible class of labourers and enter the more eligible class of paupers ... Every penny bestowed, that tends to render the condition of the pauper more eligible than that of the independent labourer, is a bounty on indolence and vice. We have found, that as the poor rates are at present administered, they operate as bounties of this description, to the amount of several millions annually.

The distinction between poverty, which the commissioners believed was a natural part of existence, and indigence, which was not, was at the heart of the Commission's analysis. They believed that it was essential to separate the poor from the pauper, physically as well as psychologically. The commissioners had been impressed by the operation in some areas, such as Southwell in Nottinghamshire, of deterrent workhouses – places where the able-bodied poor were forced to live and work if they wanted relief. The Report recommended that all relief to able-bodied persons and their families, other than in such workhouses, should now be outlawed, and that, in order to enforce this workhouse system, a new central authority should be established with powers to compel parishes to co-operate.

Summary diagram: The attack on the old Poor Law

The Poor Law was criticised by:

- Jeremy Bentham who wanted all relief to be given in workhouses administered by a National Charity Organisation that he would direct
- Thomas Malthus who believed that the Poor Law should be abolished, mainly because it encouraged population growth
- David Ricardo who thought that the Poor Law kept wages low and made the poor dependent on the state
- Robert Owen who wanted the Poor Law replaced by co-operative communities for labourers
- Thomas Paine who argued for much higher levels of relief, although he said that relief should only be given in workhouses

The Poor Law was generally criticised because of:

- growing cost
- corruption
- the demoralising effects of the Speenhamland system.

Result:

The Commission of Inquiry into the Poor Laws

The Inquiry

- Led by Nassau Senior and Edwin Chadwick
- 26 assistant commissioners toured the country investigating the Poor Law

The Report

- Condemned the Poor Law for encouraging dependence on the state
- recommended radical change

Key question
What were the main terms of the Poor Law Amendment Act of 1834?

Key date
Poor Law Amendment Act: 1834

5 | The 1834 Poor Law Amendment Act

The government responded to the Royal Commission Report by drawing up a bill that broadly reflected the recommendations in the Report. Some of the powers of the proposed central authority were reduced during the debate, but the key recommendations of the report were implemented. The purpose of the 1834 Poor Law Amendment Act was to bring about a radical reform of the system of poor relief in England and Wales. The Act contained four main mechanisms for achieving this:

- A central authority called the Poor Law Commission would be established to regulate the Poor Law, so that best practice could be enforced all over the country.
- Parishes would be grouped together to form new Poor Law Unions in order to benefit from economies of scale.

- A workhouse would be built in each union in which conditions would be worse than those endured by the most poorly paid independent worker, so that people would be deterred from entering them.
- 'Outdoor relief' for the able-bodied poor would be ended so that those seeking poor relief would have to go to a workhouse.

The Poor Law Commission

The central authority established by the Act was known as the Poor Law Commission, and was made up of three commissioners who were based in London and who were given wide-ranging powers to issue rules and regulations for the management of the Poor Law. Edwin Chadwick was made secretary to the Commission. He had hoped to be a commissioner in his own right and remained bitter that he had been given a subordinate role. The commissioners were initially supported by nine assistant commissioners whose job was to ensure that the decisions of the central authority were executed at a local level. However, their first task was to set up the new Poor Law Unions.

Poor Law Unions

Under the old Poor Law each of the 15,000 parishes in England and Wales was responsible for the relief of poverty in its own area. Now the aim was to amalgamate parishes into groups of about 30, each managed by a board of guardians. The boards of guardians were to be elected by the ratepayers of the whole area, with each parish having at least one representative on the board. Each union was to be responsible for the workhouse in its area.

Workhouses

Under the old Poor Law the local parish workhouse or poorhouse (where it existed – many parishes did not have one) had often been seen as a relatively unthreatening and even friendly institution. The workhouses of the new Poor Law were designed to project a very different image. In order to discourage applicants, conditions in the workhouses were to be less appealing than those enjoyed by the poorest of labourers living outside the workhouse. This became known as the **principle of less eligibility**. If applicants refused to accept workhouse life they were held to have 'failed the workhouse test'.

The abolition of outdoor relief

The pre-1834 practice of providing relief to able-bodied paupers outside the workhouse was intended at first to be restricted and eventually to be abolished, so that those who failed the workhouse test would have no entitlement to poor relief.

Key term

Principle of less eligibility
The idea that the poor would not choose to go to the workhouse if they had any alternative because workhouse conditions were so unattractive.

Summary diagram: The 1834 Poor Law Amendment Act

Main features of the Act

Poor Law Commission – established to regulate the Poor Law, so that best practice could be enforced all over the country

Poor Law Unions – parishes grouped together in order to benefit from economies of scale

Workhouses – built in each union. Workhouse conditions would be worse than those endured by the most poorly paid independent worker, so that people would be deterred from entering them

Outdoor relief – ended for the able-bodied poor so that those seeking relief would have to go to a workhouse

6 | The Key Debate

Key question
How have historians interpreted the Poor Law Amendment Act?

The 1834 Poor Law Amendment Act was one of the most contentious pieces of nineteenth-century legislation, so it is not surprising that historians have engaged in a number of debates concerning its origins. The investigations of the Poor Law commissioners have come under particular scrutiny, with claims that their conclusions were prejudiced and based on incomplete evidence. Whether the Report and the Act were motivated by a specific ideology or were just a pragmatic response to the problems of the time is another area of debate.

Historians have interpreted the 1834 Act in a number of ways:

- a middle-class conspiracy to keep poor rates and wage rates low
- an attempt by the landed élite to retain power over agricultural labourers
- an attempt to impose a new ideology.

A middle-class conspiracy

Key date
Parliamentary Reform Act: 1832

Key term
Enfranchise
The franchise is the right to vote. If you are given the right to vote you become enfranchised.

One interpretation is that the Act was a piece of naked class legislation, inspired by the middle classes, who had been **enfranchised** by the 1832 Parliamentary Reform Act and whose views had therefore to be taken seriously by most MPs. According to this view, Poor Law reform was a simple device to reduce the rate burden on property owners and force the poor to work for lower wages: the alternative was the harsh workhouse. The new Poor Law was part of a process by which the middle-class philosophy of individualism and market forces replaced the older, paternalistic ideas that the rich had some responsibility for the poor.

A variation on this theme has been put forward in Mitchell Dean's book *The Constitution of Poverty* (1991). Dean argues that 'the event of pauperism' (his term for the whole process of the new Poor Law) was crucial in establishing a **capitalist market system** in Britain where the working classes were forced to take responsibility for their own economic situation. Workers had to take employment at any wage rate and find alternative ways of coping with poverty because the state had withdrawn its traditional support. The 1834 Act withdrew the support traditionally provided by the state to those in need. From then on, according to Dean, workers were forced to accept the principles of the free market capitalist economy as the only alternative was the workhouse. This meant accepting lower wages and making some provision for their own provision, for example, through insurance schemes or friendly societies.

The landed élite's attempt to retain power

An alternative interpretation has been suggested by historians such as Anthony Brundage. In his book *The Making of the New Poor Law* (1978) he claimed that the Act was in fact a way of maintaining the traditional social and economic powers of the landed élite. Faced with an increasingly turbulent and disaffected rural peasantry (as demonstrated by widespread rioting and disorder in the early 1830s), landowners decided to restore order and authority by enforcing a new system. Brundage argues that the Royal Commission had, after all, been appointed by the House of Commons before it was reformed in 1832. This House of Commons was elected by the aristocracy, not the middle classes who got the vote as a result of the 1832 Reform Act. Moreover, his view is supported by the evidence that large landowners continued to dominate the administration of the Poor Law through the newly established boards of guardians.

An attempt to impose a new ideology

Some historians have attempted to synthesise the two views by asserting that the new Poor Law served both to strengthen the power of the land-owning élite and to introduce the capitalist market system. According to M.J. Daunton (1995), 'a new ideology had gained **hegemony**, without displacing the landed aristocracy from control of the central state'. By this, Daunton implies that, although the landed aristocracy continued to dominate politics and control institutions like the Poor Law, it did so in the interests of the new capitalist classes. This attempt to reconcile the conflicting views on the significance of the 1834 Act has much to commend it.

Points of agreement

Whatever interpretation they put forward, most historians are in agreement on two things.

- First, the 1834 Act was the most significant development in the history of poverty and welfare in the nineteenth century. The Act set the agenda for the debate on poverty for the next century and determined the nature of proposed alternatives.

Key terms

Capitalist market system
An economy where businesses and individuals trade without interference from the state. Ownership of land and businesses is concentrated in the hands of a relatively small class of people whose control of resources makes them wealthy. Also known as the free market system.

Hegemony
If an idea has gained hegemony it has achieved a position of authority and dominance.

- Secondly, the new Poor Law system was hated by the poor who had to live with the threat of the workhouse hanging over them. During the debate on the Act the MP William Cobbett claimed that the object of the Bill was 'to rob the poor man and enrich the landowner'. This certainly reflected widespread opinion. However, the poor did not accept the new order without a fight. The 1834 Act had been passed by Parliament with little opposition. The Poor Law Commission's implementation of the new act throughout the country was to prove far more difficult.

Some key books in the debate:
Mark Blaug, *The Myth of the Old Poor Law and the Making of the New* (Journal of Economic History, 1963)
Anthony Brundage, *The Making of the New Poor Law 1832–39* (Hutchinson, 1978).
M.J. Daunton, *Progress and Poverty, An Economic and Social History of Britain 1750–1850* (OUP, 1995).
Mitchell Dean, *The Constitution of Poverty* (Routledge, 1991).

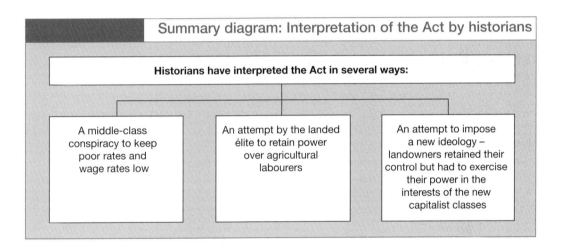

Summary diagram: Interpretation of the Act by historians

Historians have interpreted the Act in several ways:

| A middle-class conspiracy to keep poor rates and wage rates low | An attempt by the landed élite to retain power over agricultural labourers | An attempt to impose a new ideology – landowners retained their control but had to exercise their power in the interests of the new capitalist classes |

Study Guide: AS Questions

In the style of AQA

How important were rising costs in influencing the attitude of Whig politicians towards the reform of the Poor Law in the years 1830 to 1833?

Source: AQA, June 2003 (Alternative Q)

Exam tips

The cross-references are intended to take you straight to the material that will help you to answer the questions.

The important thing with this type of coursework essay question is to maintain a consistent argument throughout, balancing different factors against each other and coming to a clear judgement. In this case, you are required to look at the evidence that concern about rising costs was the reason why Whig politicians wanted to reform the Poor Law and then compare the significance of this with their other concerns (pages 17–23).

In the first section you need to mention how costs were rising and how the Speenhamland and similar systems were contributing to this problem. It is helpful to give evidence showing how Whig politicians talked or wrote about this during the debate on the reform of the Poor Law. The Whigs were particularly keen to keep the rates down, in order to maintain the support of the middle classes who had been given the vote by the 1832 Reform Act.

In the second section you need to outline the other issues of concern to the Whigs:

- the corruption of the old system
- the demoralising effect of 'Speenhamland' including the fears about rising population
- the widespread agricultural disturbances of the 1830s.

You might also mention the way in which politicians were influenced by the Report of the Poor Law Commission.

In the last section of your essay it is vital that you come to a clear judgement about the role played by rising costs in the reform of the Poor Law. Was it the most important influence on Whig politicians or simply one of many concerns? You may wish to place your judgement in the context of the general historical debate about the Poor Law Amendment Act (pages 29–31).

In the style of Edexcel

Read the following source material and answer the questions that follow:

Source 1

From: Thomas Malthus, Essays on the Principle of Population, *published in 1798.*

The labouring poor seem always to live from hand to mouth. Their immediate needs take up their whole attention, and they seldom think of the future. Even when they have an opportunity to save, they seldom exercise it. Everything that is beyond their immediate needs goes, generally speaking, to the ale-house. The Poor Laws of England may therefore be said to diminish both the power and the will to save among the common people. Thus they weaken one of the strongest incentives to good living and industry, and consequently to happiness.

Source 2

From: the Report of the Royal Commission on the Poor Laws, *published in 1834.*

It appears to the pauper that the government has overturned the ordinary laws of nature. It has passed laws to make sure that the children do not suffer for the misconduct of their parents, the wife for that of the husband, or the husband for that of the wife; that no one shall lose the means of providing for a comfortable life, whatever be his laziness, wastefulness and vice. The penalty which must be paid for idleness and wastefulness falls, not on the guilty person or on his family, but on the proprietors of the land and houses in the parish where he lives. Can we wonder if the uneducated are seduced into being part of a system which aims its attractions at all the weakest parts of our nature – which offers marriage to the young, security to the anxious, ease to the lazy, and does not punish the wasteful?

Source 3

Part of the evidence given by Sir James Kay-Shuttleworth to the Royal Commission on the Poor Laws. Here he tells of a visit to a Suffolk workhouse in 1832.

I wandered through lofty and spacious rooms and halls, well-lighted, clean, well-ventilated, but almost untenanted. The yards were surrounded by extensive workshops; large rooms in the main building were filled with machinery but the only busy thing in the establishment was the spider, which had spun its web on the spinning wheels. Eighteen acres of land were attached to the house, on which five cows, eight pigs and a flock of fat poultry were kept. There was a monastic character of quiet and plenty about the establishment. Nevertheless, this house contained only a few aged and decrepit men and women in the corners of some of the spacious rooms, and some able-bodied paupers who lounged on the sunny benches in the yard, watching a group of children at play.

Source 4

A table to show the expenditure on Poor Relief in England and Wales 1815–33. The statistics were collected at the time but the calculation of expenditure per head was calculated by historians in the twentieth century.

Years	Estimated population in thousands	Total poor relief expenditure in thousands of pounds	Expenditure on poor relief per head of population
1815	11,004	5725	9s 10d
1818	11,555	7517	13s 0d
1821	12,106	6359	10s 6d
1824	12,247	5787	9s 0d
1827	13,247	6298	9s 4d
1830	13,805	6799	9s 10d
1833	14,328	6317	8s 10d

Source 5

From: Eric Evans, The Birth of Modern Britain 1780–1914, *published in 1997.*

Political economists, like Malthus and David Ricardo, had a field day attacking what they saw as irrational solutions to the problems of poverty. If labourers knew that the parish would supplement whatever was paid by farmers, then no incentive existed either for labourers to seek work or for farmers to pay more than an absolute minimum. Also if poor relief was given (as in the Speenhamland Sliding Scale) in proportion to the size of the family, would this not encourage the labourer to breed thus making the problem worse?

What lay behind the attacks on the old poor law was the firm belief that a free market would work in the interests of society as a whole. What made the theory attractive to policy-makers was the prospect of reducing the ever-increasing cost of poor relief. Farmers and politicians were convinced of the need for poor law reform not by economic logic but by the prospect of lower poor rates.

(a) **Study Sources 1–3**

How far do Sources 1 and 3 support the argument put forward in Source 2 about the weaknesses of the old Poor Law?

(b) **Study Sources 4 and 5**

Do you agree with the view that the Poor Law was changed in 1834 simply to reduce the poor rates? Explain your answer, using these two sources and your own knowledge.

Source: Edexcel, May 2002

Edexcel Ltd, accepts no responsibility whatsoever for the accuracy or method of working in the answers given.

Exam tips

The cross-references are intended to take you straight to the material that will help you to answer the questions.

(a) This question requires you to make a judgement about how far the evidence in two of the sources supports an argument put forward in a third source. You need to be systematic in the way you construct your answer.

- First, you need to establish exactly what argument is being putting forward in Source 2. There were many arguments made against the old Poor Law but you must only focus on the specific argument in the source. The key point made by the Royal Commission in this source is that the old Poor Law had made people dependent on the state, and removed any incentive for them to make an independent living. There was no penalty for 'laziness, wastefulness or vice'. Try to summarise this argument as succinctly as possible. Don't waste time copying out large parts of the source – you won't get marks for this.
- Next look at Source 1. You need to identify any evidence in this source that supports the argument about dependency, and also any evidence that does not support it. In the last sentence, Malthus concludes his point by claiming that the Poor Laws 'weaken one of the strongest incentives to good living and industry ...'. So this would seem strongly to support the argument in Source 2. However, it is always worth commenting on the origins of the source – who produced it, when and why? Malthus had his own clear point of view on the Poor Laws and the effect they had on population, so his evidence is hardly impartial (see page 19). Although the content of the source supports the argument, its strength as historical evidence is weakened by its authorship.
- You need to repeat the process with Source 3. Kay-Shuttleworth's positive description of workhouse life might be seen as supporting the Commission's argument that the Poor Laws encouraged the poor to become dependent – if workhouse life was so pleasant, why bother finding work outside? On the other hand Kay-Shuttleworth notes that the workhouse was 'almost untenanted'. This suggests that, in this part of Suffolk, people had not become dependent on indoor relief, although Kay-Shuttleworth does not comment on outdoor relief.
- Finally, in your conclusion you need to weigh up the evidence and make a judgement. Does the evidence suggest that Sources 1 and 3 mainly support the argument in Source 2, or mainly refute it? To get in the top band of marks you must come to a clear judgement based on the evidence.

(b) To answer this effectively it is again important to focus on the specific argument put forward in the question – that the Poor Law was changed in 1834 simply to reduce the poor rates. You must look at the evidence in support of this, and the evidence against it, in the specified sources. But you must also develop the argument for and against, using your own knowledge.

Source 4 can be interpreted in a number of ways:

- The growth of poor relief expenditure, between 1824 and 1830, could be seen as providing the pressure for poor law reform, and you know that ratepayers were complaining about these increasing costs (page 21).
- On the other hand, these figures show that the cost of poor relief was much lower than it had been in 1818, and was actually falling in the early eighteen-thirties. This would suggest that the pressure on ratepayers was not quite so acute. You may wish to comment on the reliability of the figures.

Eric Evans in Source 5 supports the argument to the extent that he claims that 'the prospect of lower poor rates' was what convinced farmers and politicians of the need for reform. However, it wasn't 'simply' this argument, because earlier in the extract, Evans shows that political economists attacked the old Poor Law because it took away labourers' incentives and encouraged the poor population to rise. Other arguments against the old Poor Law were:

- the fear that the pauper population was becoming demoralised
- concerns that the old poor law was encouraging population growth
- the belief that the system was often corrupt (page 22).

In your conclusion, try to come to a balanced view on the basis of the sources and your own knowledge. Be clear in your judgement. You may, for example, come to the conclusion that although the reform of the old Poor Law was not *simply* a result of the desire to cut the poor rates, this was the *primary* motivation of those who campaigned for change.

3 The New Poor Law in Operation

POINTS TO CONSIDER

This chapter is about the way the new Poor Law developed in the period 1834–1900. It is about the process of change. You need to develop a sense of why the workhouses became such hated institutions. Finally, try to identify the key ways in which the Poor Law changed in the second half of the nineteenth century. This chapter examines these issues through the following themes:

• The implementation of the new Poor Law 1834–70
• The opposition to the new Poor Law
• The realities of life under the new Poor Law
• The development of the new Poor Law during the nineteenth century

Key dates

1782	Gilbert's Act. Parishes allowed to join together to share the costs of the Poor Law in their area
1834	Poor Law Amendment Act. Recommended a Central Commission, combination of parishes into unions and establishment of the workhouse system
1846	Andover scandal. Parliamentary inquiry revealed mistreatment of paupers at the Andover workhouse
1847	Abolition of the Commission. Replaced by Poor Law Board under parliamentary control
1852	Outdoor Relief Regulation Order. Acceptance that it is not possible to stop outdoor relief for the able-bodied completely
1865	Union Chargeability Act. Made poor rates more equal between rich and poor areas
1869	Poor Law Loans Act
1871	Local Government Board replaces Poor Law Board as the central Poor Law authority
1886	Chamberlain circular. Government encourages local authorities to provide work schemes for the unemployed outside the Poor Law

It is easy to think that the passing of an Act of Parliament automatically leads to its enforcement. This is not always the case. England in the 1830s was still a predominantly rural society where local identity was often stronger than the idea of the nation. The centralisation implicit in the Poor Law Amendment Act was so ambitious that it was bound to provoke fierce resistance. This led to compromises in the implementation of the law. Nevertheless the new system slowly became established as the most important institution for the relief of poverty in Victorian England despite the hatred that it inspired among its enemies.

1 | The Implementation of the New Poor Law 1834–70

Key question
What obstacles faced the commissioners in their attempt to set up the new Poor Law?

The passing of the Poor Law Amendment Act in 1834 did not lead to the immediate establishment of a new system. On the contrary, the process by which Poor Law Unions and workhouses were established was slow and varied considerably across the country. Despite their powerful constitutional position – they were not directly accountable to Parliament and they held both **legislative** and **executive powers** – the commissioners to a great extent had to rely on persuasion to enforce their will because there was no effective mechanism by which to make reluctant localities do what they were told. This meant that the assistant commissioners faced a number of problems when they attempted to implement the Act:

Poor Law Amendment Act: 1834 *(Key date)*

Legislative powers
The power to make laws.

Executive powers
The authority to enforce laws.

(Key terms)

- They had to overcome local objections to their plans.
- They had to deal with surviving old Poor Law administrations that were outside the new law.
- They had to persuade the new authorities to build new workhouses.
- When these initial tasks had been achieved they still had to impose their will regarding the operation of the new system.

Local objections
The first job of the assistant commissioners was to set up the new unions of parishes. To achieve this, consultation with the local community was required and public meetings were called. The original model for the organisation of the new Poor Law had proposed unions of equal size based on a market town and serving local parishes with a combined population of about 10,000. This meant, on average, getting the agreement of 30 parishes per union. This was a troublesome task: the local interest groups represented at the public meetings frequently refused to be slotted into such a neat pattern.

The assistant commissioners were under additional pressure to get quick results because the unions were also intended to be the administrative units for the registration of births, deaths and marriages which was due to be introduced in 1837. For both these reasons compromises regarding the geography of the new unions

were inevitable, and the shape of many reflected the interests of
local landowners rather than the principles of the Act.

Gilbert Unions and select vestries

Key date

Gilbert's Act: 1782

The Commission also had to contend with the unions that had
already been set up under previous acts.

- 'Gilbert Unions' were areas that had already amalgamated their
  parishes for poor relief purposes under an Act of 1782 (see
  page 15) and now often refused to be brought into the new
  system.
- The same was true for those parishes that had established local
  poor relief committees known as select vestries under the
  Sturges Bourne Act of 1819 (see page 22).

Both the Gilbert Unions and the select vestries remained outside
the control of the Commission and the assistant commissioners
were forced to work around these areas when planning the new
unions.

Building new workhouses

Even after they had established a new union, the commissioners
faced a further difficulty. Although they could demand the
alteration of an existing workhouse, they had no power to order
the building of a new one. This could only be undertaken if a
majority of members of the local board of guardians voted for it.
As a result, it was possible for Poor Law unions to delay
implementation of the new workhouse system. Many assistant
commissioners showed immense political skill in persuading
boards of guardians to erect new workhouses, but where they were
less persuasive the building of the new workhouse could be
considerably delayed.

Imposing the Commission's authority

The Commission's greatest and longest lasting problem was that
of enforcing its will even after the workhouses had been built and
the unions established. The setting up of the new Poor Law
appeared to be a bureaucratic revolution with the establishment
of a powerful central department with a team of inspectors
dispatched to monitor local performance. But the reality was less
dramatic. In 1836 the number of assistant commissioners was
increased from nine to 21, but even with this expansion it was
hard for them to make a sustained impact. With responsibility for
large areas, close supervision was very difficult.

In 1834 one of the assistant commissioners, Colonel A'Court,
complained that he had 'worked like a slave' to complete his
inspection of Hampshire. He had been 'really shocked to reflect
on the length of time it requires to inspect even one very
insignificant district'. Six months later he added that he 'never
had such hard work in my life. One more such district and I really
think it would quite kill me'. In 1844 assistant commissioner
William Day revealed that in a period of 20 weeks he had

SCALE OF FEET.

1 Work Room.	15 Store.	29 Piggery.
2 Store.	16 Potatoes.	30 Slaughter House.
3 Receiving Wards, 3 beds.	17 Coals.	31 Work Room.
4 Bath.	18 Work Room	32 Refractory Ward.
5 Washing Room.	19 Washing Room.	33 Dead House.
6 Receiving Ward, 3 beds.	20 Receiving Ward, 3 beds.	34 Women's Stairs to Dining
7 Washing Room.	21 Washing Room.	Hall.
8 Work Room.	22 Bath.	35 Men's Stairs to ditto.
9 Flour and Mill Room.	23 Receiving Ward, 3 beds.	36 Boys' and Girls' School
10 Coals.	24 Laundry.	and Dining Room.
11 Bakehouse.	25 Wash-house.	37 Delivery.
12 Bread Room.	26 Dead House.	38 Passage.
13 Searching Room.	27 Refractory Ward.	39 Well.
14 Porter's Room.	28 Work Room.	40 Cellar under ground.

PERSPECTIVE VIEW OF A WORKHOUSE FOR 300 PAUPERS. (F.)

SAMPSON KEMPTHORNE, Architect,

CARLTON CHAMBERS, 12, REGENT STREET.

The 'square plan' workhouse designed by the architect Sampson Kempthorne in 1835. This workhouse could accommodate between 300 and 500 inmates. Kempthorne also designed smaller '200-pauper' workhouses for rural areas. What aspects of this workhouse do you think might be intimidating for poor people applying for relief?

'travelled a distance of 2596 miles, two-thirds of it with my own horses'. It became impossible to comply with the requirement that assistant commissioners visit each union in their area twice a year. This situation never improved and by 1900 there was often only one annual visit.

The difficulties faced by assistant commissioners in the regions were mirrored by the Commission itself at the centre. Although they accumulated an impressive archive of reports and statistical returns and generated a mountain of instructions, it was impossible for the underpaid and understaffed **Somerset House** office clerks to cope efficiently with the deluge of information in which they found themselves drowning. The Commission's desire to play down failures and publicise success meant that administrative problems tended to be ignored rather than dealt with. Thus the Poor Law Commission exercised a much lower degree of effective centralisation than had been expected.

Key term

Somerset House
The London headquarters of the Poor Law Commission.

Did the Commission succeed?

Despite the problems they faced, the assistant commissioners were generally successful in establishing the new unions:

Key question
How successful was the Commission in establishing the new system?

- By 1840, 14,000 English parishes with a total population of 12 million had been incorporated into Poor Law Unions. Only 800 parishes, containing two million people, remained outside the system.
- The rural southern counties of England were held up by the Commission as an early and overwhelming success. Most of the 350 new workhouses that had been built by 1839 were in this region.

However:

- in Cornwall local resistance meant that few new workhouses were built
- in those parts of the north where resistance was strongest the implementation of the Poor Law Amendment Act was much delayed. Very few workhouses were built in the West Riding of Yorkshire or in Lancashire until the 1850s and 1860s. In Todmorden, Yorkshire, the guardians demolished their old workhouse and refused to build a replacement until 1877.

The attack on outdoor relief

The authors of the 1834 Act intended that all outdoor relief to the able-bodied would end quite quickly. Building a new workhouse was intended to pave the way for this to happen. But in this key area of policy the commissioners could only achieve their aims to a limited extent. In the south, the Commission began issuing orders prohibiting outdoor relief to the able-bodied poor from the late 1830s and the rural north came under similar regulations in 1842.

In 1844 the Commission felt able to apply a general Outdoor Relief Prohibitory Order to all these unions, with the result that probably three-quarters of the country was banned from giving outdoor relief to able-bodied men. However, even in these areas, the rules could be interpreted in a flexible way, particularly as the Order allowed the guardians to make exceptions in the case of accident or emergency. If paupers were certified unfit by a doctor they could continue to receive outdoor relief and some assistant commissioners complained to the Commission that paupers were using medical certificates to frustrate the law. These complaints reveal how difficult it was for the central authority to impose its will.

In the rest of the country, particularly in the urban areas, guardians continued to give outdoor relief to the able-bodied. Even the biggest workhouses could not accommodate all those in need of relief in times of heavy unemployment and in any case it was cheaper for the guardians to maintain an outdoor pauper than one in the workhouse. The Commission made some attempt to bring these unions into line by issuing them with Labour Test Orders in 1842. These orders stated that if outdoor relief were to be given to able-bodied men, it could only be in return for some form of parish work such as stone breaking. The Commission also ruled that such relief should be paid at least partly in the form of food or fuel rather than totally in cash. However, many unions continued to ignore the orders.

Outdoor Relief Regulation Order

In August 1852, the Poor Law Board (see page 58) attempted to impose uniformity on the system by imposing stricter regulations. Opposition from the boards of guardians resulted in a revised order in December. This 1852 Outdoor Relief Regulation Order relaxed both the compulsory labour rule and the instructions to pay some relief in kind in the event of a trade depression. Following this the majority of unions across the country were allowed to replace the workhouse with outdoor labour as the condition of relief. By 1871 only one in six unions was operating under the 1844 Order which banned outdoor relief to able-bodied men. One of the central policies of the New Poor Law had proved impossible to implement.

Outdoor Relief Regulation Order: 1852

Key date

Situation by 1870

Certainly in the first three decades after it was introduced, the Poor Law Amendment Act was implemented in different ways and at different times in different parts of the country. The extent to which the Commission was able to enforce its will depended on a number of factors:

- The strength of local resistance by those who might come under the Act.
- The particular interests of those who held power in the region.
- The specific circumstances of the locality.
- The degree of skill shown by the assistant commissioners in persuading the guardians to follow the central Commission's policies.

Initiatives on outdoor relief 1842–52

Date	Order	What the order demanded	Effect
1842	Labour Test Orders	If outdoor relief were to be given, it could only be in return for some form of parish work such as stone breaking. Such relief should be paid at least partly in the form of food or fuel rather than totally in cash.	Applied to about a quarter of all unions, mainly in urban areas, but many continued to ignore the orders.
1844	Outdoor Relief Prohibitory Order	Unions established under the 1834 Act banned from giving any outdoor relief to able-bodied men unless agreed by the Commission.	Probably three-quarters of the country was banned from giving outdoor relief, but orders were often ignored and the order was not applied in much of the north.
1852	Outdoor Relief Regulation Order	This relaxed both the compulsory labour rule in times of trade depression and the instructions to pay some relief in kind. Following this the majority of unions in England and Wales were allowed to replace the workhouse with outdoor labour as the condition of relief, but could provide outdoor relief without compulsory labour if there was a trade depression.	Majority of paupers remained outside the workhouse. In 1855 there were 776,286 'outdoor' paupers compared to 121,400 'indoor' paupers.

However, despite all these obstacles, by the late 1860s the overwhelming majority of parishes had been incorporated into Poor Law Unions. Even though most paupers continued to receive outdoor relief, across the nation workhouses had sprung up as symbols of the new system and they held over 150,000 inmates by 1870.

Summary diagram: The implementation of the new Poor Law 1834–70

Obstacles facing the Commission:

- Local objections to their plans for new Poor Law Unions
- Surviving old Poor Law administrations that were outside the new law
- Some new authorities were reluctant to build workhouses
- Boards of guardians did not always accept the orders given by the Commission

Did the Commission succeed?

To this extent it did succeed:

- By 1840 the system was well established – 14,000 English parishes with a total population of 12 million had been incorporated into Poor Law Unions. Only 800 parishes, containing two million people, remained outside the system.
- The rural southern counties of England were an early success – most of the 350 new workhouses which had been built by 1839 were in this region.
- By the late 1860s the overwhelming majority of parishes had been incorporated into Poor Law Unions.
- Around 350 new workhouses were built and by 1870 they contained 150,000 inmates.

To this extent it did not succeed:

- In those parts of the north where resistance was strongest the implementation of the Poor Law Amendment Act was much delayed – very few workhouses were built in the West Riding of Yorkshire or in Lancashire until the 1850s and 1860s. In Todmorden, Yorkshire, the guardians demolished their old workhouse and refused to build a replacement until 1877.
- In Cornwall, local resistance meant that few new workhouses were built.
- Outdoor relief was not abolished – by 1871 only one in six unions was operating under the 1844 Order which banned outdoor relief to able-bodied men.

2 | The Opposition to the New Poor Law

The reasons for opposition

The poorest sections of English society had many reasons to oppose the new Poor Law:

- Hatred of the new workhouses and fear of workhouse life.
- Fear that the result of the new system would be wage cuts for workers.
- Centralisation which took control away from local people.

The new system threatened to remove the traditional right of the poor to a basic level of support from their parish when they fell on hard times. The building of the new workhouses, or **Bastilles** as they quickly came to be called, symbolised a harsh new form of authority under which the poor were to be punished for their poverty. The proposal that relief would be given only to those

Key question
Why did people oppose the 1834 Act?

Bastilles
Named after the infamous prison fortress in Paris that was seen as a symbol of injustice and tyranny. At the start of the French Revolution in 1789 the prison was stormed and the prisoners released.

Key term

An anti-workhouse poster from the late 1830s. Look particularly at the punishments, the work being done, the attitude of the workhouse master (in the doorway to the left of the picture) and the contents of the truck being pulled on the right of the picture. How do the details in the poster illustrate popular fears about workhouse life?

who entered the prison-like workhouses suggested that poverty itself had become a crime. Within the workhouses the strict regime was deliberately designed to be repellent. The new buildings were usually situated at some distance from the applicant's home, which made them seem more impersonal and threatening than the familiar, local parish institutions. This distance also fuelled the rumours that spread about the new Poor Law.

The terror of the workhouse

The worst rumours were based on the fear that the workhouses had been built as extermination centres for the poor. After all, the Poor Law Amendment Act had been partly inspired by the writings of the Reverend Thomas Malthus, who believed that the nation's problems were caused by overpopulation. Assistant commissioner W.J. Gilbert reported that in Devon in 1836:

> There was not anything too horrible or absurd to be circulated, and nothing too incredible for their belief … Amongst other ridiculous statements circulated, the peasantry fully believed that all the bread was poisoned, and that the only cause for giving it instead of money was the facility it afforded of destroying the paupers; that all the children beyond three in a family were to be killed …

The most extreme example of such anti-Poor Law propaganda was 'The Book of Murder!'. This was based on two anonymous pamphlets that discussed the possibility of gassing pauper children to reduce the population. Though the origins of these works are still unclear, it was easy for the terrified poor of the 1830s to believe claims that they had in fact been produced by the Poor Law commissioners themselves.

Some fears were based on reality. The growth of medical research in this period resulted in an increased demand for human bodies. The 1832 Anatomy Act allowed workhouse masters to deliver the bodies of deceased paupers to medical schools for dissection. For many poor people this was an appalling prospect – even in death they would not be free of the Poor Law.

Under the old system parish officials had made a distinction between the deserving poor, who were in trouble through no fault of their own, and those whose poverty was self-inflicted. Hard-working people were worried that they would now be thrown together with the roughest elements of society in the new workhouses. Bradford's radical anti-Poor Law leader Peter Bussey asked:

> Did the new law draw a line of demarcation between the good and the evil? No. In the Bastille they found the most virtuous people crowded with the most vicious people on earth, and the treatment of one the same as the treatment of the other, and both worse than the common felon.

Driving down wages

Anti-Poor Law campaigners also claimed that the purpose of the workhouse was to drive down wages by forcing labourers to take any alternative form of employment, no matter how badly paid. When the Commission proposed a plan to move unemployed agricultural labourers north to the factory towns between 1835 and 1837, this seemed to confirm these claims. Mill owners had asked for the scheme specifically to limit rising wage rates in the north of England.

The concerns of the guardians

Many of those who had operated the old Poor Law opposed the new system in order to protect their existing powers. In particular, those vestrymen or guardians who believed that they were already running a good system resisted change. As Joseph Ellison, a member of the Dewsbury board of guardians, told the 1837 Parliamentary Select Committee on the Poor Law Amendment Act:

> … under no system of management could things be carried on more satisfactorily, both to the rate payers and to the paupers; and this is the opinion of nineteen-twentieths of that township where I reside. The general feeling is this, 'What a pity that a system that has worked so well, and has produced so much good, should now be broken up!' That is the universal exclamation …'

Ellison, and men like him, feared that the cost of building the new workhouses and maintaining the poor inside them would be excessive. Local authorities in urban areas were concerned that the new workhouses would be too small to deal with the flood of paupers expected in times of depression. On the other hand, it was argued that workhouses would stand empty and be a waste of resources in more prosperous times when work was plentiful. Rural ratepayers in many areas realised that outdoor relief cost only half the amount of indoor relief. Others feared that the abolition of traditional forms of poor relief would snap some of the **paternalist** bonds between rich and poor which operated as a form of social control. The evangelical reformer Richard Oastler said that the new law, 'lays the axe to the root of the social compact; it must break up society and make England a wilderness'.

Centralisation

One of the strongest arguments against the new Poor Law came from those who attacked the centralisation implicit in the new regime. The three commissioners were depicted as London-based tyrants seeking to impose their will on the entire kingdom. One of the most powerful opponents of centralisation was the proprietor of *The Times* newspaper, John Walter – a Berkshire magistrate whose generous operation of outdoor relief under the old system had been singled out for criticism by the Royal Commission. During the debates on the Poor Law Amendment Bill in 1834, Walter's newspaper had denounced the proposed new law, claiming that it undermined the principle 'that the

Key term

Paternalist
Where an institution rules in what it regards as the best interests of the people but without consulting them about this – kindly but oppressive rule.

people should be made to govern themselves as much as possible, at least in their domestic concerns and relations'.

The Commission's powers were indeed considerable and influential landowners were shocked at the degree of authority that the new body was given to intervene in the affairs of their locality. To these landowners, the independence of the local parish and county was a cornerstone of English liberty and they never came to terms with the bureaucratic centralisation of the 1834 Act.

The extent of the opposition
Rural England

Key question
How widespread was the opposition to the Act?

In rural England resistance to the Act often took the form of riot and disorder. The case of the Amersham Union in Buckinghamshire is often quoted as a typical example of rural opposition. In May 1835 a mob took to the streets to prevent a small group of paupers being moved from Chesham to the new workhouse in Amersham. The local inhabitants seem to have seen this move as the beginning of the end for their old, familiar local workhouse and its replacement by a grim and distant 'bastille'. Despite at first preventing the transfer of the paupers, the demonstrators were eventually forced to give way after the local magistrates read the **Riot Act**, swore in special constables and called up reinforcements of both Metropolitan Police and armed **yeomanry**. Similar incidents occurred across the south of the country. Disturbances were reported in Kent in the spring of 1835 and in East Anglia as late as 1844. However, on no occasion did these protests succeed in blocking the new law.

The northern factory towns

In the urban north of England resistance was more fierce. The campaign for extended legislation to protect factory workers known as the **Ten Hour Movement** was already well established and both leaders and supporters quickly mobilised to block what they saw as a new attack on working people. The hard edge of the northern anti-Poor Law agitation was felt in 1837 and 1838 when the Commission first attempted to set up new Poor Law unions in the industrial areas of Lancashire and the West Riding of Yorkshire.

Chadwick had urged the commissioners to establish the new Poor Law immediately in the north while there was relative prosperity, but his advice was ignored. By 1837, the shadow of unemployment was starting to spread as a trade depression began and the threat of the workhouse became a real one for many workers. Huddersfield guardian George Tinker wrote to the Commission in June 1837 to advise them of 'the perfect state of organisation into which the district has been put and the violent and unprincipled measures which are in operation to defeat your intentions'. He warned that 'in the present alarming state of the district it will be dangerous to put the Law into operation' and

Key terms

Riot Act
The 1715 Riot Act made local magistrates responsible for the control of unruly citizens. If a crowd of more than 12 people did not disperse after the Riot Act was read to them the magistrate could order their arrest.

Yeomanry
A reserve volunteer force that could be used to suppress public disorder and to assist the regular army in the event of invasion or insurrection.

Ten Hour Movement
A campaign in the 1830s whose aim was to see legislation passed imposing a maximum 10-hour working day in factories.

'Attack on the workhouse at Stockport' from the *Illustrated London News*, 1842. Protests against the new Poor Law were sometimes violent and the fear of disorder often forced the authorities to moderate the way that they enforced the law.

went on to describe a recent meeting of the local board where a mob of 6000–8000 people, led by Richard Oastler, disrupted the proceedings by smashing down the gates of the workhouse and threatening to pull down the building and attack the guardians.

Bradford and Dewsbury

Violent protests also occurred in nearby Bradford in October 1837 and in Dewsbury in 1838. The Bradford riot was quelled only with the aid of troops who opened fire, though there were no fatalities. The South Lancashire Anti-Poor Law Association had established 38 local committees by 1838 and an office in Manchester with full-time staff. The West Riding Central Anti-Poor Law Committee organised a massive demonstration at Peep Green, Leeds, on 16 May 1837, which was attended by possibly 200,000 people.

Todmorden

The most determined resistance came in the town of Todmorden. The campaign there was led by the Radical MP and enlightened factory owner John Fielden, whose tactics included closing down his own factory in protest at the election of guardians and refusing to pay his poor-rates. Fielden's workers rallied to his defence when the board attempted to enforce payment and they proceeded to attack the homes of the local guardians. Once more troops were required to restore order.

The north-east, London and the Midlands

In contrast to the scenes in the factory towns of Lancashire and Yorkshire there were few major disturbances elsewhere. In the north-east the new Poor Law was established with relative ease and in London the Metropolitan Anti-Poor Law Association formed by Earl Stanhope in February 1838 made little impact. A major pottery strike in Stoke-on-Trent in 1836 and a recession in the Nottingham stocking trade in the same year pushed many into poverty but despite this the workers of the Midlands took little direct action to frustrate the commissioners. However, the absence of violent protest did not mean that the Act had been fully accepted. The new boards of guardians represented local interests and were determined to interpret the law in the way that best suited their particular situation. Although the poor themselves were not represented on the boards, the guardians had to include the degree of local resistance in their calculations. The decision to build a workhouse and the extent to which outdoor relief was to be curtailed were both related to the amount of protest and the anticipated reaction in each area.

A successful protest movement?

There has been some historical debate on the nature of the opposition to the new Poor Law. The most common view has been that much of the opposition was a spontaneous reaction by people who wanted to maintain their traditional rights but had no coherent organisation or strategy. The only anti-Poor Law movement, according to these historians, was that which grew up in the factory towns of Lancashire and the West Riding of Yorkshire. In contrast, some historians have detected a more coherent set of beliefs among anti-Poor Law campaigners throughout the country. What is clear is that the movement was short lived. There are two possible reasons for this:

- First, it was based on too broad an alliance: **evangelical Tories** and **working-class radicals** had different interests and were bound to disagree eventually.
- Secondly, in the late 1830s many anti-Poor Law campaigners turned to **Chartism** as a means of reforming the Poor Law. The failure of the existing MPs to oppose the new Poor Law convinced them that only a parliament elected by working men would repeal the Act.

Key terms

Evangelical Tories
The Tories were one of the major political groups in Parliament in the 1830s. Evangelical Tories were those who were influenced by their Christian principles to take action against the evils of society.

Working-class radicals
Workers who believed that the government should be more democratic and do much more to support their class.

Key question
Was the opposition effective?

Key term

Chartism
A mass campaign for political reform in the 1830s and 1840s. The six points of the 'Charter' included the right to vote for all men and payment of MPs so that working men could stand for Parliament. Despite huge support, the movement was unsuccessful and faded away in the 1850s.

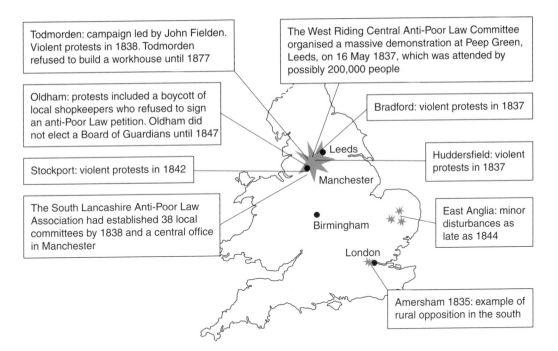

Opposition to the new Poor Law.

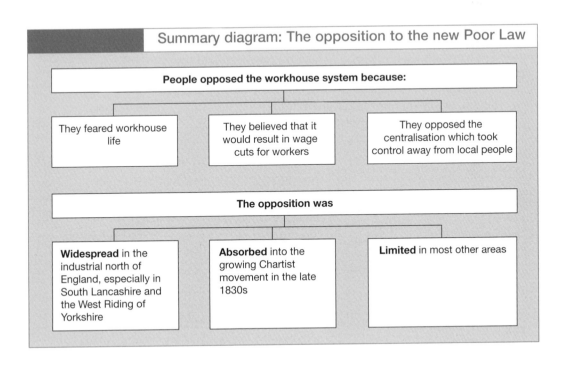

3 | The Realities of Life Under the New Poor Law

The principle of less eligibility was a key aspect of the new Poor Law. The notion that conditions in the workhouse had to be less attractive than the conditions that the poorest independent labourer would experience inevitably meant that the new system had to be harsh. However, the commissioners were very keen to make clear that their intention was not to introduce a system of deliberate cruelty. In fact, they claimed that their centralised and regulated system actually protected paupers by outlawing the abuses that existed under the old Poor Law. Some historians have agreed with this view and have explained many of the worst scandals as representing the continuation of the old Poor Law despite the efforts of the Commission. Other historians view the workhouse system as an example of institutionalised cruelty. It is possible to form some judgement regarding this debate by looking at life under the new Poor Law both for those excluded from relief and for those who entered the workhouse.

Key question
Was the new Poor Law deliberately cruel?

Poverty outside the workhouse

The poor who remained outside the workhouse because of their fear and hatred of it certainly experienced hardship. In his book on the workhouse Norman Longmate describes how in the mid-winter of late 1836, 209 men applied for relief at Cuckfield in Sussex. When faced with the choice of the workhouse or nothing, only 11 accepted the offer of the workhouse, and three of these decided to leave after a few hours. The commissioners held the view that such people were obviously not really in need because they managed to survive outside the workhouse. However, without the possibility of any outdoor relief, life must have been grim indeed for those who refused indoor relief. Statistics for the period after 1834 suggested a decline in the number of people claiming relief, but in places like Cuckfield this did not necessarily mean a decline in poverty.

Key question
Why did some people choose to stay outside the workhouse system?

Life in the workhouse

Inside the workhouse every aspect of life was governed by detailed regulations laid down by the commissioners. The regime was designed to be unpleasant. Some of the most disliked aspects of workhouse life included:

Key question
What was life like in the new workhouses?

- compulsory uniforms
- segregation of men and women
- long, boring days
- hard, repetitive work
- dull food
- petty rules.

On entering the workhouse paupers were forced to give up their own clothing and put on an ill-fitting uniform. Guardians were allowed to add variety to the clothing but they rarely did so. Men and women were strictly segregated within the institution and no concessions were made for married couples. This aspect of the workhouse system was particularly resented and seemed to contradict Victorian ideas about the importance of the family. Nevertheless, depriving paupers of normal marital relations was a deliberate aspect of the regime, designed to increase the deterrent effect. It also discouraged pauper families from staying in the workhouse too long – an aspect of the old Poor Law that had been much criticised.

The workhouse timetable

The workhouse routine was designed to be both monotonous and arduous. The timetable was modified later in the century, but the changes from the original version were slight. In summer months this was a typical day:

5.00am	Wake-up call. Compulsory prayers
6.00–7.00	Breakfast
7.00–12.00	Work
12.00–1.00	Dinner
1.00–6.00	Work
6.00–7.00	Supper
8.00pm	Compulsory prayers and bed

The winter day began at 7.00am but was otherwise similar to the summer timetable.

Discipline

Discipline in the workhouse was strict, but the commissioners saw this as progressive. Under the old Poor Law workhouse inmates had been subject to the arbitrary authority of overseers who were not constrained by any set of clear rules and who were often able to abuse their charges without fear of the consequences.

Under the new law an elaborate set of instructions specified exactly what workhouse masters could and could not do. Adults and girls could not be beaten and, although rations could be reduced, they could not fall below a certain minimum. Most workhouses had punishment cells and the regulations allowed paupers to be confined in them for a range of minor offences. Being in the wrong part of the building, failing to work hard enough, making too much noise or disobeying the authorities were all punishable acts. Paupers also needed permission to leave the workhouse or to be visited by friends or relatives. So, although the regulations were partly designed to control workhouse officers, they also represented a petty form of tyranny that dominated all aspects of an inmate's life.

Work

Work was deliberately hard and unpleasant. Oakum picking was a common task for both men and women: a number of old ropes, often knotted and tarred, had to be untwisted and unravelled inch by inch so that the fibres could be reused. Women were also set tasks such as washing, cleaning and cooking. Stone pounding and stone breaking were common tasks for men. This was hard, tedious, back-breaking work. The most infamous work given to both sexes in the 1830s and 1840s was bone crushing, although this was prohibited in the second half of the century. Crushed animal bones were used as agricultural fertiliser and could be sold to local farmers. The dust and fragments produced from bone crushing were a health hazard and it was said that visitors could locate the bonehouse by its vile smell, especially in hot weather.

Picking oakum: a London workhouse in 1905.

Food

Anti-Poor Law campaigners frequently suggested that the poor were being starved in the workhouse, but the amount of food recommended by the commissioners was in fact greater than the average consumed by independent labourers (although much less than that provided for prisoners). However, in order to uphold the principle of less eligibility the meals were made to be as dull and boring as possible. Food had to be eaten at set times in large dining rooms and talking was not allowed at mealtimes. Guardians could choose between six official 'dietaries' that specified exactly how much paupers were allowed for each meal.

The monotonous diet provided basic nutritional requirements but the quality was variable and the food was often poorly prepared. In the 1830s many boards of guardians increased the humiliation of the workhouse inmates by refusing to provide cutlery and paupers had to eat with their hands or drink gruel or soup from the bowl.

	Breakfast	Dinner	Supper	
Monday	Bread and cheese	Bread and cheese	Bread and cheese	Water was the only drink allowed for adults. Elderly paupers were allowed a few extras such as tea, and the local medical officer could prescribe additional nourishment for the sick. Other dietaries replaced cheese with gruel for breakfast.
Tuesday	Bread and cheese	Suet pudding and vegetables	Bread and cheese	
Wednesday	Bread and cheese	Bread and cheese	Bread and cheese	
Thursday	Bread and cheese	Bread and cheese	Bread and cheese	
Friday	Bread and cheese	Suet pudding and vegetables	Bread and cheese	
Saturday	Bread and cheese	Bread and cheese	Bread and cheese	
Sunday	Bread and cheese	Meat and vegetables	Bread and cheese	

Figure 3.1: Workhouse dietary No. 2.

Dinner time at St Pancras workhouse in London, around 1900. Separation of the sexes is evident here, and you can also get a sense of the uniformity imposed on workhouse inmates by the new Poor Law.

Key date

The Andover scandal: 1846

Key term

Select Committee
A group of MPs who investigate a particular issue.

The Andover scandal

Despite the Commission's rules, well-publicised incidents of abuse occurred on a number of occasions. For example, in March 1846 a **Select Committee** of the House of Commons was appointed to investigate allegations of wrongdoing at the Andover workhouse in Hampshire. This revealed an appalling state of affairs. The inmates had been systematically underfed: even the children's milk was watered down. The situation had first come to light when one of the guardians expressed concern over what was happening in the bonehouse and the inquiry confirmed that these concerns were justified. Paupers had been so undernourished that they had taken to eating the marrow and rotting meat on the bones they had been set to crush. Children had been so starved that they had eaten the raw potatoes thrown out for the workhouse pigs. The workhouse master, Mr M'Dougal, was shown to be a drunk and a bully who inflicted cruel punishments on those under his rule. Beatings were inflicted on children and confinement in the cells followed the slightest infringement of the rules. Some inmates were forced to spend the night in the workhouse mortuary as a punishment. Burials were conducted as cheaply as possible, with infant corpses receiving the minimum of ceremony. Witnesses also reported numerous instances of sexual abuse of female inmates by both M'Dougal and his 17-year-old son.

The Report of the Select Committee found that the workhouse master and matron were unfit persons to hold such positions and also condemned both the Andover board of guardians and the Poor Law commissioners for allowing such a situation to go unchecked. Although M'Dougal was forced to resign, he received no further punishment. Nevertheless the revelations of the inquiry were widely reported and had a powerful effect on public opinion.

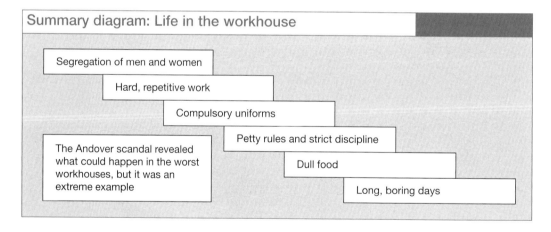

Summary diagram: Life in the workhouse

- Segregation of men and women
- Hard, repetitive work
- Compulsory uniforms
- Petty rules and strict discipline
- Dull food
- Long, boring days
- The Andover scandal revealed what could happen in the worst workhouses, but it was an extreme example

The key debate

How cruel was the workhouse?

The evidence about workhouse life has led to a number of different interpretations:

- The workhouse system was hard but more fair than the old system.
- The workhouse system was inevitably physically cruel.
- The workhouse system was one of psychological cruelty.

The Andover scandal was an extreme example of how the workhouse system could produce horrific results. Most historians accept that while the Andover case was unforgivable it was also untypical. Many of the other alleged atrocities produced by opponents of the new Poor Law have been shown to be either gross exaggerations or complete inventions. This has led some historians to state that the new Poor Law was no more cruel than the old Poor Law and to agree with the commissioners' claims that their centralised control did indeed reduce the opportunities for brutal workhouse masters or penny-pinching guardians to misuse their power. Other historians have remained critical. They point out that a system that was designed to be harsh inevitably encouraged some of those in authority to overstep the mark in their enthusiasm to deter the poor from applying for relief.

A third interpretation emphasises the way in which the institutional arrangements of the workhouse system inflicted a form of psychological, as opposed to physical, cruelty. Silent mealtimes, monotonous work and the absence of even the smallest of extra comforts were all matters of deliberate policy, not accident. The petty rules, strict discipline and prison-like uniforms all combined to deny the identity and dignity of the pauper and take away his or her individuality. Moreover, in the interests of deterrence the commissioners fostered the idea of the workhouse as a grim place from which the poor would do well to stay away. The commissioners were thus responsible for creating a climate of fear that pervaded working-class life for over a century. Ironically, the propaganda of the anti-Poor Law campaigners helped to strengthen this image and terrify people into avoiding the workhouse. The cartoon on page 45, which appeared as an anti-Poor Law wall poster, is a good example of the way in which aspects of workhouse life could be exaggerated.

Some key books and articles in the debate:
M.A. Crowther, *The Workhouse System 1834–1929* (Methuen, 1981).
Ursula Henriques, *How Cruel was the Victorian Poor Law?* (Historical Journal XI, 1968).
David Roberts, *How Cruel was the Victorian Poor Law?* (Historical Journal VI, 1963).

4 | The Development of the New Poor Law During the Nineteenth Century

By the 1860s the new Poor Law was well established even though it was being implemented in different ways in different parts of the country. However, the setting up of the new administration and the building of new workhouses did not mean that the system stopped developing. Some aspects of the new Poor Law did remain consistent throughout its history, but many others changed in response to outside pressures and new ideas. These developments occurred in four main areas:

• central administration
• finance

- outdoor relief
- provision of services for children, the sick and the elderly.

The central administration of the Poor Law

The three London-based commissioners established by the 1834 Act had a remarkable degree of authority. This had been thought necessary in order to set up and enforce the new Poor Law as quickly and as efficiently as possible. It had been envisaged that the Commission's extraordinary powers would be of a temporary nature and the 1834 Act had limited its life to an initial period of five years. During this period, particularly in the late 1830s, the central administration was subjected to heavy criticism from the opponents of the poor law, with *The Times* referring to them as 'The Three **Bashaws** of Somerset House'. As a result of this pressure Parliament renewed the Commission's powers only on a year-to-year basis after 1839. By 1842 the direct resistance to the new Poor Law had passed its peak and Parliament was prepared to give the Commission another five years in office. However, they also reduced the effective power of the Commission by cutting back the number of assistant commissioners to nine, the establishment originally proposed in the 1834 Act.

The end of the Commission

In 1847 Parliament decided that it was time to replace the Somerset House administration. The main cause of the Commission's demise turned out to be the Andover scandal (see page 55). The Select Committee's report had condemned the central authority as well as the local administration. In particular, the MPs had described as a 'cruel injustice' the Commission's treatment of Henry Parker, the assistant commissioner responsible for Andover. Parker had been made the scapegoat for the wrongdoing at the workhouse and had been dismissed after his initial report on the affair. The dismissal of another assistant commissioner was also attacked as 'irregular and arbitrary'. The Select Committee's investigations had also exposed the tensions within Somerset House, especially the animosity between Edwin Chadwick and the commissioners. Chadwick had never reconciled himself to his subordinate position as secretary to the Commission and used the opportunity provided by the Andover enquiry to criticise his employers. The picture revealed by the Select Committee convinced Parliament that they needed to exert a tighter authority over the administration of the Poor Law.

The Poor Law Board

The Poor Law Commission was replaced in 1847 by a new body, the Poor Law Board. This consisted of a president, two secretaries and a number of cabinet ministers who also sat on the board. Although the cabinet ministers actually had little direct involvement in the administration of the law, both the president and one of the two secretaries were usually MPs. The intention was to provide more direct political control over the Poor Law administration so as to make it more responsive to public opinion.

Key question
How did the central administration of the Poor Law change during the nineteenth century?

Key term

Bashaws
A Bashaw was an authoritarian military governor in the Turkish Empire and a popular symbol of tyrannical rule.

Key date

Abolition of the Commission: 1847

Changes to the central administration of the Poor Law		
Date	How the central administration worked	Reason for the change
1834	Poor Law Commission established with three commissioners and 21 assistant commissioners	Need to establish the new Poor Law
1842	Assistant commissioners reduced from 21 to nine	New Poor Law Unions had been set up in many areas
1847	Poor Law Board replaced the Commission. The Board consisted of a president, two secretaries and a number of cabinet ministers who also sat on the Board	Need to exert political control over the Poor Law; concerns about tensions within the Commission
1871	Poor Law Board replaced by the local government board with local government minister as the president of the Board	Need to integrate Poor Law with other local government welfare services

The Local Government Board

By the 1870s there had been a significant extension of government interest in the areas of health and welfare. This was partly due to the political pressures exerted by working-class men who had won the right to vote in 1867. As new social legislation was usually enforced through local authorities, it seemed logical to combine the responsibility for the Poor Law with responsibility for the rest of local government. Therefore in 1871 the Poor Law Board was replaced by the Local Government Board. Because the Poor Law Board had been successful in avoiding new scandals like Andover, and because health and welfare issues now had a higher profile, the government retained direct control over the new authority. From 1871 onwards the president of the Local Government Board was normally a cabinet minister.

Poor Law finances

The Union Chargeability Act

Key question
How did the financing of the Poor Law change?

Key dates
Union Chargeability Act: 1865

Poor Law Loans Act: 1869

Key term
Rateable value
How much a property was worth for the purpose of assessing the rates that should be paid on it.

Until the 1860s each parish had to pay for its own paupers. This meant that some rich landowners with large estates paid very low poor rates because their parish had only a few paupers. In contrast, the parishes with the largest numbers of paupers paid the largest amounts of money and therefore charged the highest rates, despite the fact that they were often the poorest parishes in the union. In some areas this system had resulted in financial crisis with heavily pauperised parishes unable to raise the necessary sums.

The 1865 Union Chargeability Act attempted to remedy this problem. The cost of poor relief payments was transferred from the individual parish to the union as a whole. Each parish contributed to the common union fund on the basis of its **rateable value**, not on the number of paupers it had. This spread the burden over the entire union and meant that the poorer parishes were subsidised by the wealthier. Ratepayers were charged according to the value of their property and the reform meant that within each union the rich now paid more than poorer inhabitants. These changes resulted in a more equitable system of Poor Law finances.

The Poor Law Loans Act

Many boards of guardians had refused to upgrade the facilities in their workhouses to provide for children, the sick and the elderly because of the cost involved. Most boards were dominated by middle-class guardians who had pledged to keep the poor rates as low as possible. The 1869 Poor Law Loans Act helped to improve this situation. From 1863 guardians had been authorised to raise loans for building works from the **Public Works Commissioners**. The 1869 Act extended the repayment period on these loans from 20 to 30 years. This meant that the amount that had to be repaid each year was reduced and so, therefore, were the rates. This Act, along with the other financial changes of the 1860s, made it possible for guardians to consider higher expenditure on the Poor Law without raising the poor rates to unacceptable levels.

The persistence of outdoor relief

The authors of the 1834 Act had aimed to abolish outdoor relief completely. Opposition to the workhouse had led to a relaxation of the ban on outdoor relief in the 1850s. But by the late 1860s the results of this policy were becoming a cause for concern. The 1860s had witnessed an increase in spending on outdoor relief of over 25 per cent and the ratio of outdoor paupers to the total population had increased from one in 27 to one in 25. This was partly due to the need to relieve the textile operatives who had been thrown out of work in the **Lancashire 'cotton famine'**.

Guardians in other areas continued to see outdoor relief as the cheap option: in the 1860s the cost of maintaining a pauper in the workhouse was around six shillings a week whereas outdoor relief was about two shillings. These small outdoor payments were given on the assumption that recipients would supplement them by earnings from low-paid work or charity, since it was clear that the payments alone were not enough to live on. When the Poor Law Board was replaced by the Local Government Board in 1871 the new body was quick to issue a circular attacking outdoor relief. This restated the principles of the 1834 Act and warned that outdoor relief was demoralising the able-bodied poor and removing their incentives to find work.

The drive to reduce outdoor relief in the late nineteenth century was aided by the growing number of charity organisations that were being established in the period (see page 76). Charity payments seemed to be targeted at the 'deserving' poor and allowed the Poor Law authorities to take a tougher line with paupers whom they could classify as indigent and 'undeserving'. Deterrent workhouses of an especially hard nature were opened in places such as Poplar in East London. Only able-bodied paupers were invited to the Poplar workhouse (separate arrangements were made for the sick and the elderly) and the work set there was much heavier than in other workhouses. The

Public Works Commissioners
A government-appointed body that had the power to grant loans for building projects.
Key term

Key question
Were the Poor Law authorities successful in abolishing outdoor relief to the able-bodied?

Local Government Board replaced Poor Law Board as the central Poor Law authority: 1871
Key date

Lancashire 'cotton famine'
The US civil war (1861–5) resulted in a disruption of the supply of raw cotton. Lancashire textile mills were forced to lay off their workers when they ran out of supplies.
Key term

Figure 3.2: Poor relief in England and Wales 1840–1900

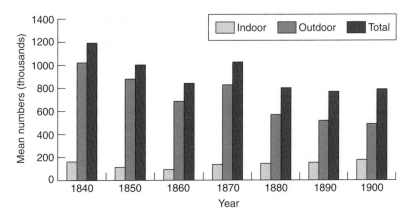

Figure 3.3: Number of paupers per 1000 of population 1840–1900

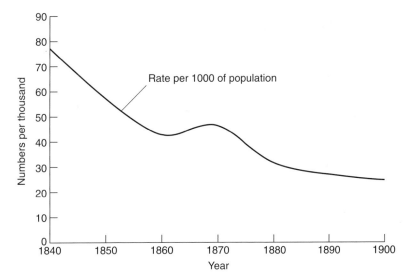

combination of a more aggressive insistence on workhouse relief and the benevolence of the charities brought the desired effect: the number receiving outdoor relief had reduced significantly by 1900. Although the workhouse population had risen by the turn of the century, the proportion of paupers in the total population had declined from 4.7 per cent in the 1860s to around 2.5 per cent in 1900.

Additional work schemes

A final development also helped to keep the level of pauperism down. Following a trade depression and the onset of mass unemployment in the 1880s, Joseph Chamberlain, president of the Local Government Board, issued a famous circular to boards of guardians in 1886. This recommended that they provide additional work schemes such as street cleaning and paving, to 'persons whom, owing to precarious condition and circumstances, it is undesirable to send to the workhouse, or to treat as subjects for pauper relief.' Though limited in its effect, this initiative clearly echoed some of the practices of the old Poor Law and represented a further retreat from the principles of 1834.

Key date

Chamberlain circular: 1886

The development of specialist services for the poor

Chadwick's original plans for the Poor Law had proposed separate institutions for different categories of pauper:

- the able-bodied
- the elderly
- the sick
- children.

Because of the costs involved, this plan was never carried out and, although there was segregation in the new workhouses, all the different categories of pauper were housed within the same institution. Even in the early days of the Commission this caused problems. Guardians did not want to separate children from their mothers, but neither did they want these children 'contaminated' by the rougher elements to be found in the female wards. The usual compromise was to allow infants under two to stay with their mothers but to remove children over two years old to separate quarters.

The emphasis on maintaining the deterrent aspects of workhouse life had, in the first half century of the new Poor Law, frustrated attempts at improving facilities for children, the sick and the elderly. When the Local Government Board began its crackdown on outdoor relief in the 1870s it faced a problem. For, although the logic of the Poor Law supported a toughening of conditions for the able-bodied poor, it was hard to justify any imposition of such conditions on those who were poor through no fault of their own. By the late nineteenth century there was an increasing awareness that the elderly, children and those who were sick had to be treated in new ways.

The elderly

In fact, elderly paupers had always been regarded in a somewhat different light to the 'able-bodied' by those who managed the Poor Law. The Royal Commission had hoped that 'the old might enjoy their indulgences' even though the 1834 Act itself made little direct reference to the elderly. Workhouse dietaries suggested that the elderly should get a little extra but this was not intended as a right. Dietary No. 2 (see page 55) recommended an ounce of tea and some milk and sugar for those over 60, but an additional meat pudding dinner on Thursdays was given only to those 'for whose age and infirmities it may be deemed requisite'. Similarly, dietary No. 3 provided only for the old to receive extra food 'if deemed expedient to make this change'.

Deterrent workhouse conditions for the elderly were to an extent consistent with the general thinking behind the new Poor Law. Without some incentive to do otherwise, it was feared that the elderly would automatically throw themselves onto the parish. Labouring people, according to this way of thinking, should put something aside for their old age or ensure that they had families to support them. If they failed to be prudent that was their own fault. Consequently, in the early years of the new system the

Key question
In what ways did the Poor Law develop specialist services during the nineteenth century?

Key question
How did Poor Law provision for the elderly change?

elderly were given deterrent work and endured similar conditions to the younger workhouse inmates.

By the middle of the century the attitude towards older people was beginning to change. The compulsory separation of elderly couples was relaxed in 1847 when the Poor Law Board ruled that separate bedrooms had to be provided on request for couples over 60. However, little was done to implement this ruling and in 1895 only 200 married couples had their own workhouse rooms.

Inquiries into the condition of the aged poor led the Local Government Board to issue specific advice on the treatment of the elderly in 1900. The Board recommended that adequate outdoor relief should be given to the 'aged deserving poor' and that where indoor relief was necessary old people should be 'granted certain privileges which could not be accorded to every inmate of the workhouse'. These privileges were to include extra day rooms, flexible eating and sleeping times, greater visiting rights, and the compulsory provision of tobacco, dry tea (so that they could make a cup whenever they wanted) and sugar. In these ways conditions for aged paupers in the early twentieth century were better than they had been in the mid-nineteenth. Nevertheless, despite these improvements, the possibility that they would end their days in the workhouse remained a dreadful worry for many old people.

Key question
How did Poor Law provision for children change?

Children

Children under the age of 16 made up approximately one-third of the pauper population throughout the nineteenth century. Workhouse schools had been established from the 1830s and were the earliest forms of state education. They aimed to give pauper children the opportunity to escape from the poverty of their parents though a sound basic education. However, there has been some debate about how effective these schools actually were. Lack of money frequently resulted in the employment of inadequate teachers, and the stigmatising of all paupers encouraged some guardians to neglect their schools.

Nevertheless, Poor Law schools in some areas provided higher standards of basic education than comparable **voluntary schools**, although their curriculum was narrower. After 1846 a government grant was available to pay the salaries of Poor Law teachers. Some ambitious industrial schools had been built by urban unions in Leeds, Manchester, London and other cities in the middle decades of the century. These schools were separate from the workhouses, served the pauper children of a whole district, and concentrated on what Commissioner George Nicholls described as 'honest and useful industrial courses' that would equip pauper children to become 'good servants or good workmen'. The best of these institutions were heavily influenced by the ideas of Dr James Kay (later Sir James Kay-Shuttleworth), an assistant commissioner who went on to become the first secretary to the Privy Council's Committee on Education. However, they received increasing criticism as the desirability of segregating pauper children began to be questioned. The creation of state-run schools after

Key terms

Voluntary schools
Schools that were set up and run by religious societies.

1870 Education Act
This Act set up local education boards to build schools in areas where there were not enough voluntary schools. The Act established the principle that every child had the right to an elementary education.

the **1870 Education Act** allowed most pauper children to be integrated into mainstream education.

The sick

Medical relief

Illness was one of the chief causes of poverty yet the authorities paid relatively little attention to it in the early phase of the new Poor Law. The 1834 Act had made only a brief mention of the possibility of providing medical relief. Medical officers were appointed by the boards of guardians in each union but it was the workhouse masters and Poor Law relieving officers who decided whether or not a pauper was entitled to medical relief. The result of this arrangement was that medical relief was kept to a minimum as the authorities tried to keep costs down: in 1840 only £150,000 out of a total Poor Law expenditure of £4.5 million went on medical services.

Workhouse infirmaries

Basic infirmaries had been attached to workhouses under the old Poor Law and this practice continued after 1834. However, the infirmaries were intended only for the short-term use of the workhouse inmates and most were unable to meet the demands of the long-term sick who needed care. Conditions were poor and the infirmaries were inadequately staffed. The unclean conditions in the workhouse hospital in Huddersfield came to light following an outbreak of typhus. The two nurses in the hospital were themselves pauper inmates and one of them was frequently ill. This state of affairs was typical of many workhouse infirmaries, and in the first 30 years of the new Poor Law little was done to raise standards.

Changing attitudes

Real improvements in Poor Law medicine date from the late 1860s when public opinion was alerted by an inquiry conducted

> **Key question**
> How did Poor Law provision for those who were ill change?

The Holborn Union Poor Law Infirmary, built in 1887. This building is still in use as part of an NHS hospital in the early twenty-first century. Do the scale and design of the building suggest any changes in attitudes in the later nineteenth century?

for the medical journal *The Lancet*. This had revealed some scandalous conditions in London workhouse infirmaries and forced the government to take action. Gathorne Hardy, President of the Poor Law Board, signalled a major change in attitude when he blamed the failures of medical care on the deterrent nature of the workhouse system. 'The sick', he declared, 'are not proper objects for such a system'.

Towards a national health service?

The way to take the sick out of the deterrent system was to establish hospitals which were separate from the workhouses. In London, this was made possible by the 1867 Metropolitan Poor Act. This amalgamated the medical services of the different London Poor Law unions and created the new Metropolitan Asylums Board, which became the hospital authority for the whole of the capital. As with the other financial reforms of the 1860s, spreading the cost of Poor Law expenses over a larger area enabled improvements to be made. By 1882, six fever hospitals, four asylums and 20 infirmaries were in operation in London. Across the country Poor Law authorities began to follow this lead and between 1861 and 1891, 1000 beds per annum were being added to public provision. These were promising signs, although the quality of medical care remained variable. By 1900, the Poor Law was providing a national, state-funded system of basic medical care. Some historians have seen in this process the origins of the National Health Service and Poor Law buildings have continued to be used as the basis of major hospitals into the early twenty-first century.

Summary diagram: The development of the new Poor Law in the nineteenth century

Main developments

Central administration

- The Commission 1834–47
- The Poor Law Board 1847–71
- The Local Government Board 1871–1929

Poor Law finances

- The 1865 Union Chargeability Act resulted in a more equitable system of Poor Law finances
- The 1869 Poor Law Loans Act made it possible for guardians to consider higher expenditure on the Poor Law without raising the poor rates to unacceptable levels

The persistence of outdoor relief

- Increase in outdoor relief in mid-century
- Drive to reduce outdoor relief after 1871
- Chamberlain circular 1886 allowed work schemes for the unemployed outside the workhouse

Specialist services for the poor

- The elderly – a more relaxed workhouse regime
- Children – better educational provision
- Medical services – improvements in the quality of workhouse infirmaries

Study Guide: AS Questions

In the style of Edexcel

Read the following source material and answer the questions that follow.

Source 1
Extracts from the Report of the Royal Commission into the Poor Laws, *published in 1834.*

> The great source of abuse is the out-door relief given to the able-bodied for themselves or for their families. This is given in goods or in money.

> We recommend that all relief whatever to able-bodied persons or to their families, otherwise than in well-regulated workhouses, shall be declared unlawful and shall cease. All relief given to children under the age of sixteen shall be considered as if it was given to their parents.

> With regard to the able-bodied poor, the remedy is to make the lazy become industrious.

Source 2
From: Third Annual Report of the Poor Law Commissioners, *published in 1837.*

> The administration of relief by the Nottingham Board of Guardians had hardly begun before the interruption in the American [cotton] trade led to massive unemployment. It became evident that a need would soon arise for relieving more persons than could be provided for within the walls of the union workhouses. We felt it to be our duty to authorise the Guardians that the rule which prohibited them from giving relief to able-bodied male persons except in the workhouse should be suspended whenever they found it necessary to do so.

Source 3
Part of an order from the Guardians of the Lymington Union to the master of the workhouse dated March 1844, and the agreement of the Poor Law Commissioners, dated April 1844.

> The master must make every adult pauper who is fit for work, in return for food and lodgings in the workhouse, to do the following tasks: the pounding of 28lbs of bones or picking 2lbs of oakum. No pauper shall be kept against his or her will for more than four hours while doing this work. Also work shall not be required from any pauper whose age, strength and capacity it is not suited.

> We, the Poor Law Commissioners, do consent to, and approve of, the above order of the Board of Guardians of the Lymington Union.

Source 4
From: Alan Kidd, State, Society and the Poor in Nineteenth-Century England, *published in 1999.*

> The Poor Law Commission began its work in the mid-1830s, steadily at first, establishing the union structures and issuing orders and regulations. But the administrative history of the New Poor Law in its first twenty years is one of conflict and compromise. There was compromise between local and central control. Equally, there was a mismatch between the intentions of the central authority and the interests of many localities, especially in the industrial North.

Source 5
From: a speech by the Methodist preacher and anti-poor law campaigner Joseph Rayner Stephens in Newcastle, January 1838.

> ... Sooner than wife and husband, father and son, should be sundered and dungeoned, and fed on 'skillee', sooner than wife and daughter should wear prison dress... Newcastle ought to be and should be one blaze of fire, with only one way to put it out, and that with the blood of all who supported this abominable measure...

(a) **Study Sources 1, 2 and 3**
    How far does the evidence of Sources 2 and 3 show that the recommendations made by the Royal Commission into the Poor Laws (Source 1) had been implemented?
(b) **Study Sources 2, 4 and 5 and use your own knowledge**
    Do you agree with the view that the implementation of the new Poor Law in the years until 1850 involved more conflict than compromise? Explain your answer, using these three sources and your own knowledge.

Source: adapted from Edexcel, June 2005

Exam tips
The cross-references are intended to take you straight to the material that will help you to answer the questions.

(a) This question requires you to make a judgement about how far the evidence in two of the sources supports an argument put forward in a third source. You need to be systematic in the way you construct your answer.

   • First, you need to establish exactly what argument is being put forward in Source 1. There were many recommendations made by the Royal Commission into the Poor Laws, but you must only focus on the specific point in the source. The key recommendation made by the Royal Commission in this source is that outdoor relief for the able-bodied poor was to be ended. Don't waste time copying out large parts of the source – you won't get marks for this.

- Next look at Sources 2 and 3. You need to identify any evidence in the sources that shows that outdoor relief had been abolished, and also any evidence that shows that it continued. Clearly the decision to suspend the rule denying outdoor relief to the able-bodied unemployed in Nottingham shows that, in this case, the recommendation of the Royal Commission was not being implemented. On the other hand, the source suggests that the suspension of the rule was only to be temporary, during periods of mass unemployment. Source 3 shows that in Lymington workhouse inmates were being forced to do hard labour with the Commission's approval. You could infer from this that the Lymington guardians were unlikely to be giving outdoor relief, although this is not explicitly stated.
- Finally, in your conclusion, you need to weigh up the evidence and make a judgement. Does the evidence in Sources 2 and 3 mainly support the view that outdoor relief to the able-bodied had been ended, or mainly refute it? To get in the top band of marks, you must come to a clear judgement based on the evidence.

(b) To answer this effectively it is again important to focus on the specific argument put forward in the question – that the implementation of the new Poor Law up to 1850 involved more conflict than compromise. You must look at the evidence in support of this, and the evidence against it, in the specified sources. But you must also develop the argument for and against, using your own knowledge.

- Source 2 shows that the Poor Law authorities were prepared to suspend their rules in certain circumstances. This could be interpreted as a sign of compromise, but the source does not reveal the possible conflict that may have preceded this decision.
- Source 5 is an example of the violence with which some people were prepared to oppose the implementation of the new Poor Law. Your own knowledge of the opposition movement in Lancashire and Yorkshire can be used here to support the argument for conflict (pages 48–50). However, you should also point out that this kind of violent conflict was limited in scale. For example, in Newcastle, there is no evidence to show that serious conflict resulted from Stephens' words. In most areas there was only limited violent protest.
- Source 4 refers to both compromise and conflict and you need to develop this, using your own knowledge of the way the Poor Law Amendment Act was implemented between 1834 and 1850 (pages 41–3).
- In your conclusion, try to come to a balanced view on the basis of the sources and your own knowledge. Be clear in your judgement. You may for example come to the conclusion that conflict was more important than compromise in the implementation of the new Poor Law, or you may be convinced that the opposite is true.

In the style of OCR

1. Study the four sources on the new Poor Law, and then answer both of the sub-questions.

(a) **Study Sources A and B.**
Compare these sources as evidence of reasons for opposition to the new Poor Law in the south.

(b) **Study all the sources.**
Using all these sources and your own knowledge, assess the view that the new Poor Law was resisted far more successfully in the north than the south from 1834 to 1847.

Source A
From: the Poor Law Commissioners' 1836 report on the implementation of the new Poor Law in southern rural counties.

The new Poor Law of 1834 could not possibly be carried into effect without difficulty and resistance. Pauper labourers quickly understood the Act and in many districts set themselves to seek a livelihood by their own efforts. In other places, where a reliance on the poor rate was habitual, every method has been used to obstruct the law. Partial riots have occurred but, with the aid of the Metropolitan Police, occasionally aided by military force, these have been put down.

Source B
From: the Second Annual Report of the Poor Law Commission, 1836. W.J. Gilbert, one of the nine new Assistant Commissioners and active throughout the south, gives evidence to the Poor Law Commissioners of resistance to the new Poor Law in Devon, a rural south-western county.

The leaders of the opposition who benefited from former abuses are old overseers, small shopkeepers, beer-shop keepers and the small farmers who received half of their labour costs from parish funds.

In North Devon we found that the poor were deceived. Few really understood the intentions of the Guardians. When understood, the most riotous submitted and received the changes gladly. They had believed all bread was poisoned to kill paupers. A story to stir up the small rate-payers was that £20,000 was to be immediately imposed on them for a workhouse.

Source C
From: George Tinker, The State of the Huddersfield Union, June 1837. A Poor Law guardian and supporter of the new Poor Law complains of the actions taken by some magistrates in a northern industrial town.

The mob, led by the notorious agitator Richard Oastler, broke open the gates of the workhouse and threatened to pull it down if we the Guardians did not stop our meeting. It was with difficulty that our meeting was moved to another place.

On the way to our second meeting, we pro-Poor Law
Guardians were surrounded by the mob, and our lives
threatened. The magistrate present, despite the broken
windows and injured constables, placed us under the merciful
protection of Oastler, and refused to take further action. Only
eleven out of thirty-nine Guardians present voted to proceed.
They were singled out and the mob told their names.

Source D
From: Fourth Annual Report of the Poor Law Commission, 1838.
The Poor Law Commission describes resistance to the new Poor
Law in the northern mill town of Todmorden, where the Fielden
brothers had their mills and were leading members of the Anti-
Poor Law League. They were the largest employers in the area.

In Todmorden Poor Law Union an attempt was made by the
Fieldens to prevent the new law by throwing all their workforce
out of employment. This attempt to intimidate the Guardians
having been defeated by the magistrates, they reopened their
works.

On the Guardians demanding the sums needed for relief, the
Todmorden overseers adopted a course of passive resistance.
They have been convicted and fines imposed. Two constables
enforcing these fines were violently assaulted by persons
assembling by ringing a bell in one of Fieldens' factories, from
which a large number of workers emerged and took part in a
riot. The magistrates then decided to station troops at
Todmorden for the present.

Source: OCR, June 2004

Exam tips
The cross-references are intended to take you straight to the material
that will help you to answer the questions.

(a) The question asks you to compare the sources as evidence for
opposition to the new Poor Law in the south, so you must focus
on this issue.

- Source A is from the Commissioners themselves. They claim
  that many labourers found work as an alternative to the
  workhouse. By this, they justify the new Poor Law, by
  showing that such people had become dependent on the
  state. However, some paupers were so reliant on the Poor
  Law that they used 'every method' to obstruct it. The
  implication is that such resistance was without justification.
- Source B also claims that many labourers accepted the new
  system, 'gladly' in the view of assistant commissioner Gilbert.
  However, Gilbert claims that opposition was led, not by the
  poor, but by those tradesmen and farmers who had benefited
  from the corruption of the old Poor Law. Through false stories

they were the ones who stirred up both the poor and the ratepayers against the new system.

(b) Good answers to this type of question need to achieve a balance between using the evidence in the sources and employing your own knowledge.

- It is important to see the sources as a set, and so worth pointing out that all the sources are from those attempting to implement the new Poor Law.
- You also need to point out that all the sources represent snapshots of particular places, at specific times. You must view the sources in the context of your own knowledge about resistance to the implementation of the new Poor Law.
- Sources A and B deal with opposition in the south of England. Although both show a degree of resistance to the new Poor Law, the commissioners in Source A claim that the riots have been 'put down', and Gilbert in Source B implies that opposition ended when people understood the reality of the Poor Law, rather than the propaganda against it.
- You need to use your own knowledge of the implementation of the new Poor Law in the south (page 48) to make a judgement as to how representative these sources are regarding the level of resistance in this part of the country. For example, you know that none of the protests in the south actually succeeded in blocking the implementation of the new law.
- Sources C and D describe opposition in the north of England, but in contrast to Sources A and B, they give no indication that the anti-Poor Law protests have been crushed – in fact, the resistance seems to have been successful.
- Again, you need to use your own knowledge of the implementation of the new Poor Law in the north (pages 48–50) to make a judgement as to how representative these sources are regarding resistance in the north.
- Finally, you must come to a clear judgement as to whether or not resistance was more successful in the north than in the south.

Study Guide: Advanced Level Questions

In the style of AQA

1. 'The Poor Law Amendment Act of 1834 was an effective response to the problems of rural society but not to the problems of urban areas.'

   Assess the validity of this statement about the provision of poor relief in the years between 1830 and 1870.

Source: AQA, June 2004

Exam tips
The cross-references are intended to take you straight to the material that will help you to answer the question.

The question is about the effect of the Poor Law Amendment Act in the period 1830–70. To achieve the highest marks for your answer to this question it is important that you come to a clear judgement as to the validity of the quote, based on a detailed analysis. One approach to this is to plan an answer in four sections.

- To begin you need to write something about the aims of the Act itself and the Royal Commission that informed it (pages 25–9). Do not spend too much time on this. The point is to clarify what the Act was intended to do so that you can eventually make a judgement as to how effective it was. Don't go through all the features of the Act and the establishment of the system – that isn't really the point of this question. Instead explain the main aims of the Act: (a) to reduce the poor rates, (b) to re-establish social control in rural areas, (c) to deal with immoral behaviour, and (d) to cut unemployment.
- Next, examine the effect of the Act in rural areas. You can use the aims outlined in your first section to organise your material and provide a basis for judgement. It will be difficult to quote the statistics given in Figures 3.2 and 3.3 (see page 61) as they do not distinguish between urban and rural areas. However, you do know that the workhouse system was established reasonably quickly in the southern rural counties and with relatively little resistance. The figures also show that, up until 1860, the percentage of paupers in the population was reducing, as was the cost. This would suggest that it was quite effective in rural areas.
- In contrast there was resistance to the new Poor Law in urban areas and it took longer to establish the workhouses in the northern factory towns. The increase in the number of paupers in the 1860s was due to the Lancashire cotton famine and mass unemployment. Outdoor relief was the only way to deal with such a crisis and you could argue that this showed how ineffective the new Poor Law was in dealing with urban industrial problems.
- Finally, you need to come to a judgement. There is some evidence to support the claim in the question. On the other hand it is difficult to determine with precision the effect of the Poor Law on issues such as moral behaviour. It is certainly possible that the fear of the workhouse did act as a means of controlling both the rural and urban populations.

4 Changing Attitudes to Poverty 1850–1900

POINTS TO CONSIDER

This chapter examines the ways in which the problem of poverty was seen in the second half of the nineteenth century. It concerns the way attitudes can change. This chapter examines these issues through the following themes:

- Mid-nineteenth-century ideas on poverty and welfare
- The portrayal of the poor
- The changing background to the debate
- The growing awareness of poverty

This chapter also shows how these new writings suggested a more active role for the state in the provision of welfare.

Key dates

1843	Metropolitan Visiting and Relief Association established. Mid-Victorian example of a local welfare charity
1844	First retail co-operative set up in Rochdale
1850–2	Henry Mayhew published *London Labour and the London Poor* in a series of pamphlets
1851	Great Exhibition. Celebration of British industrial wealth and supremacy
1852	Publication of Charles Dickens' *Bleak House*
1859	Publication of Samuel Smiles' *Self-Help.* Outlined the philosophy underlining many Victorian attitudes to poverty and welfare
1869	Foundation of the Charity Organisation Society. Attempted to control the distribution of charity so that it encouraged independence and self-help
1870	Local Government Board took responsibility for the Poor Law. New drive to restrict availability of outdoor relief
1870	Education Act. Beginning of state-controlled education system
1875	Friendly Societies Act. Attempt to make friendly societies more reliable
1875	Public Health Act. Local authorities forced to improve sanitary conditions

1886	Unemployment crisis. Mansion House fund set up to aid the destitute
1889	Publication of first volume of Charles Booth's *Life and Labour of the People in London*
1901	Publication of Seebohm Rowntree's *Poverty: A Study of Town Life*

1 | Introduction

Attitudes to poverty in the first half of the nineteenth century were dominated by three ideas:

- First, it was believed that poverty was caused by the personal failure of the individual concerned. Laziness, drunkenness and extravagance were seen to be the causes of hardship.
- Secondly, it was assumed that people could help themselves out of poverty by adopting the values of self-help (see page 75). It was argued that hard work, thrift and sobriety would lead to prosperity and respectability for anyone who followed this ethic.
- Thirdly, the idea that the government should help to solve poverty by giving the poor more money was seen as disastrous. It was said that government handouts would simply encourage dependency and the poor would have no incentive to help themselves. This was the idea behind the harshness of the new Poor Law. It was also the idea behind the attack on indiscriminate **philanthropy** by some charity organisations.

In the second half of the century three new perceptions began to challenge the old certainties:

- the extent of poverty
- the responsibility for poverty
- the role of the state.

Each of these will be considered in turn.

The extent of poverty

Writers of many types, including government officials, journalists, novelists and social investigators, began to paint an increasingly distressing picture of the extent of poverty, particularly in the big cities. The poor, it seemed, represented a large percentage of the population – maybe up to a third. Moreover, despite indications that society as a whole was becoming increasingly prosperous, there was little sign that the percentage of people in poverty was decreasing. Worse still, the horrible depths of poverty and the nightmarish vision of life in the city slums came as a shock to comfortable middle-class opinion. It seemed as though their society was somehow failing.

Key question
What were the three dominant ideas about poverty in the mid-nineteenth century and how were they challenged after 1850?

Philanthropy
Philanthropists were relatively wealthy people who used their money to provide for poor people, for example through setting up housing schemes.

Key term

Key date

Foundation of the
Charity Organisation
Society: 1869

The responsibility for poverty

The second idea exposed by these revelations was that the poor
were not necessarily responsible for their own situation. This is
not to say that writers stopped commenting on the social and
moral failings of the poor. On the contrary, nearly all of the most
important writers in this period continued in their accounts to
find drunkenness, cruelty and criminality amongst the poor. And
they continued to condemn these things and highlight them as
causes of poverty.

However, investigators began to find that some of the poor,
perhaps the majority, were not the authors of their own
misfortune. Time and again it was revealed that poor people tried
to work hard and lead decent lives, but found themselves trapped
in circumstances over which they had no control. Unemployment,
irregularity of work, low wages, sickness or death were forces
largely beyond the control of the individual. This was a challenge
to the whole idea that people could always rescue themselves
from poverty.

The role of the state

This notion led to a further proposition. If individuals were
indeed victims of social and economic circumstances beyond their
control, should not a larger power intervene on their behalf to
protect them from the consequences? Despite the attempts of
philanthropists and friendly societies, it became clear to many that
only the state itself was powerful enough to undertake this role.

Conclusion

It would be misleading to suggest that these changes in attitude
came about in a smooth and linear fashion. Indeed the high
point of 'individualist' thinking was probably around 1869–70,
when the Charity Organisation Society (see page 82 below) was
founded and the Poor Law authorities began their 'crusade'
against outdoor relief. Social investigators such as Charles Booth
remained attached to individualist solutions, even after they had
revealed that poverty had causes bigger than the individual.
Nevertheless, it is fair to say that as the century drew to its close,
a new consensus was beginning to emerge. Individual action was
not enough by itself to tackle poverty. Collective solutions were
also required.

2 | Mid-nineteenth Century Ideas on Poverty and Welfare

Key question
What was 'self-help'?

Self-help

The idea that people should help themselves rather than rely on
the state for welfare was the basis of the 1834 Poor Law
Amendment Act. People were forced to make other arrangements
for dealing with poverty if they wanted to avoid the threat of the
workhouse. In 1859 Samuel Smiles' book *Self-Help* was published.
The book was a best seller. This suggests that the idea of self-help
had become widely accepted.

Key date

Publication of Samuel
Smiles' *Self-Help*:
1859

In some ways the idea of helping one's self could be seen as a justification of the capitalist system, which had allowed individuals to accumulate wealth with little regard for their more unfortunate neighbours. For the prosperous Victorian middle classes the idea of self-help was convenient. It suggested that their own position was morally justified because anyone, no matter how humble, could help himself to rise up to a position of prosperity. It also absolved the middle classes from the duty of funding the poor through higher taxes because it implied that poverty was the fault of the individual and only the individual could relieve their own condition. In *Self-Help*, Samuel Smiles wrote that

> 'Heaven helps those who help themselves' is a well-tried maxim, embodying in a small compass the results of vast human experience. The spirit of self-help is the root of all genuine growth in the individual; and, exhibited in the lives of many, it constitutes the true course of national vigour and strength. Help from without is often enfeebling in its effects, but help from within invariably invigorates. Whatever is done for men or classes, to a certain extent takes away the stimulus and necessity of doing for themselves; and where men are subjected to over-guidance and over-government, the inevitable tendency is to render them comparatively helpless.'

But there was also a sense in which self-help encouraged collective action rather than just individual ambition. In the 1866 edition of *Self-Help*, Smiles made the point that, 'the duty of helping one's self in the highest sense involves the helping of one's neighbours' and he praised the work of friendly societies and mutual aid associations. So far as working-class people were concerned, self-help could be a hymn of praise to individual effort or an encouragement to co-operative support and solidarity. The latter interpretation provided a foundation for the growth of friendly societies, trade unions and co-operatives in the second half of the nineteenth century.

Charity

While the philosophy of self-help in its Victorian form was relatively new, ideas of philanthropy and charity were much older. Most societies have a tradition of giving, and the practice of the rich giving to the poor had deep roots in English society. Before the industrial revolution, charitable giving had been one way of building a connection between the classes and keeping the poor to some extent grateful and deferential to the rich.

In the nineteenth century charitable giving was still a way in which the wealthy could gain prestige and status. But charity increasingly took on another function. Groups like the Charity Organisation Society began to insist that charity had a moral purpose. Charity was to be given to the poor only on the condition that they accept the values of thrift and self-help. People often resented the attempt to impose 'respectable' middle-class forms of behaviour that might be difficult to observe in

Key question
What was new about charity in the nineteenth century?

Friendly societies, trade unions and co-operatives

- *Friendly societies*

Friendly Societies Act: 1875

These began when groups of neighbours, friends or workmates decided to form an association to protect themselves in time of need. Each member would contribute a certain amount of money each week and in return they would be entitled to payments from the funds if they found themselves in need due to sickness, unemployment or bereavement. As real wages rose in the middle of the nineteenth century, so the friendly societies continued to expand. By 1872 there were 34 affiliated societies with over 1000 members each.

Burial societies were a cheaper alternative which provided support in the event of a family death. The scale of these working-class self-help institutions in the late nineteenth century is impressive: it is probable that a majority of working-class people had some form of friendly society protection by 1900. However, the poorest were effectively denied this option and even those who could afford the higher levels of contribution necessary for sick benefit could still find themselves in need in old age.

- *Trade unions*

Like the friendly societies, the trade union movement expanded in the mid to late nineteenth century. Insofar as the purpose of trade unions was to negotiate for higher pay for their members, these working-class institutions made an important contribution to raising the standard of living of their members. However, as with friendly societies, membership of trade unions in the mid-nineteenth century tended to be concentrated among skilled and relatively prosperous workers, such as the engineers and the carpenters. Some of these 'new model' unions could provide good levels of welfare for their members. The big unions of unskilled workers, which were formed in the 1880s and 1890s, were simply unable to provide the kind of benefits offered by the new model unions because their low-paid members could not afford to pay such high subscriptions. Instead, they concentrated on using their funds to improve pay and conditions by financing strikes, rather than providing welfare schemes.

- *Co-operatives*

First retail co-operative set up in Rochdale: 1844

The co-operative movement was yet another impressive example of working-class self-help. Co-operative shops were owned by their members and returned all their surplus profits to the membership by way of dividends. By 1891 there were a million co-op shareholders. However, retail co-operatives had a strict rule about not providing credit and for the poorest sections of the population buying now and paying later was an essential survival strategy.

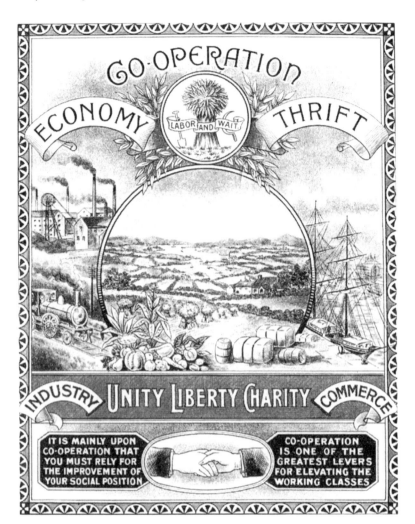

A Co-operative Society poster, c1898. Along with friendly societies and trade unions, co-ops were a way for working people to collaborate so that they could improve their condition without relying on the middle classes. What messages is the poster trying to convey?

impoverished circumstances. Some, who accepted the values of self-help, also began to feel that accepting charity was a sign of failure. Working-class accounts of life in this period frequently report individuals who were 'too proud' to accept charity.

Other poor people were prepared to go along with the expectations of philanthropists and charity visitors in order to boost their meagre finances. Those in desperate need had little choice but to accept charity if they wanted to survive. However, many were also well aware that the aim of the donors was to change their behaviour. Groups like the Charity Organisation Society, which linked charity to moral improvement, could be unpopular in working-class communities even if the resources they had to offer were desperately needed.

A Church of England charity poster, 1892. The Church was a major provider of charity in the late nineteenth century. What is the message of the poster? How do you think this relates to the ideas of the Charity Organisation Society?

Key question
How much charity was being raised for the poor in Victorian England?

The extent of charity

It is difficult to quantify precisely the volume of charitable giving in nineteenth century Britain. Much giving, such as a casual act of generosity to a beggar on the street, went unrecorded, and the accounting records of charities were often poorly kept. However, the statistical evidence that does exist, along with the weight of contemporary opinion, suggests that a massive and growing volume of charity developed in the second half of the century.

Across the country thousands of endowed charities and trusts distributed small amounts of money in their local communities.

The Report of the Royal Commission into the Poor Laws of 1909 estimated that the gross income of the **endowed charities** was just under £1 million, of which two-thirds went to groups of people specified in the particular charity's rules (e.g. local elderly people) and one-third to the poor generally. Sir Henry Longley, the chief charity commissioner, had estimated similar figures in 1895.

London-based charities were particularly impressive. William F. Howe in his 'Classified Directory' produced regular surveys of 700–800 London charities out of the 1000 or so of which he was aware. Excluding Missionary and Bible societies, Howe estimated the income of the London charities in his survey to have been £2,250,000 in 1874–5, rising to £3,150,000 in 1893–4. By way of comparison, the national expenditure of the Poor Law in 1893 was £9,218,000.

Many historians of charity such as F.K. Prochaska have repeated the claim that charitable expenditure on the poor far exceeded state expenditure on poor relief in the late nineteenth and early twentieth centuries. However, only a fraction of charitable donations ended up in the pockets of the poor, for they included an array of diverse good causes. Nonetheless the biggest beneficiaries of this generosity were medical charities, and poor people relied on these in times of illness. The frequency with which charity is referred to in contemporary accounts leaves little doubt that it was a significant feature of Victorian society. *The Times* in 1885 claimed that the receipts of philanthropic charities in London were greater than the budgets of several European governments.

Middle-class philanthropy

Those who had become wealthy through the expansion of trade and commerce held the major resources that charities required. Giving to charity became a symbol of Victorian respectability and middle-class families were expected to contribute. Indeed, one study of middle-class households in 1896 revealed that on average these families spent a larger share of their income on charity than on any other item in their budget except food.

General charities

General charities for the aid of the poor could be national or local, sometimes established to deal with a temporary crisis or sometimes set up as permanent institutions.

For example, the Metropolitan Visiting and Relief Association was founded in 1843 to deal with destitution in the capital and raised £20,000 in its first year. Between 1860 and 1886 the middle-classes responded to distress amongst the London poor by establishing three Mansion House Funds under the patronage of the Lord Mayor of London. In total, these funds raised £135,000. On a national scale, Queen Alexandra's appeal for the relief of distress raised £750,000 in 1905.

Philanthropic employers

Philanthropic employers were sometimes prepared to divert a proportion of their profits to the welfare of their workers. Some of the most famous examples include the mill owner Sir Titus Salt in Bradford, the chocolate manufacturer Cadbury in Birmingham and the soap magnate William Lever on Merseyside. Each of these employers built houses for their workers with good facilities and provided a range of welfare services. Welfare provision for the employees at Colman's Mustard factory in Norwich were supervised by Caroline Colman, the proprietor's wife, and included a sickness benefit society, a clothing club, medical facilities and blanket and parcel distributions for the needy.

Beneficial though these improvements were, they could also be seen as a way of keeping workers productive and tied to their job. Many workers found living in a 'company town' oppressive. The owners often interfered in the life of their employees outside the hours of work, often in day-to-day affairs. For instance, Titus Salt apparently objected to washing lines, which he found unsightly. He banned the inhabitants of his manufacturing community, Saltaire, from using them. Salt apparently rode his horse around this Bradford neighbourhood cutting down the washing of those employees who defied him on this issue. At a more serious level, the penalty for a worker who lost their job could include the loss of home and benefits.

Five Per Cent Philanthropists

Employer philanthropists usually limited their welfare provision to members of their own workforce. The so-called Five Per Cent Philanthropists who engaged in the provision of housing for the working classes cast their net wider. George Peabody's Housing Trust and Sir Sidney Waterlow's Improved Industrial Dwellings Company both limited their shareholders' profits to five per cent in order to keep down rents to affordable levels. The housing philanthropists did help to improve the lives of their tenants at a time when the idea of state-provided council housing was in its infancy. Yet by 1900 seven of the largest trusts and companies still housed fewer than 80,000 people in London, where the greatest need and the greatest effort were concentrated. 'Casual' workers, without regular incomes, were also excluded from philanthropic housing, as regularity of rent paying was deemed essential.

Octavia Hill

Rent was not the only condition of tenancy. The housing philanthropist Octavia Hill took on the management of run-down east end properties on behalf of the landlord. Hill was explicit about the social changes she expected from those under her control. She was convinced that it was the habits of the poor that drove them into destitution and she provided accommodation only on the strict condition that her tenants behaved in the way she prescribed:

On what principles was I to rule these people? On the same that I had already tried … with success in other places … firstly, to demand a strict fulfilment of their duties to me – one of the chief of which would be the punctual payment of rent; and secondly, to endeavour to be so unfailingly just and patient, that they should learn to trust the rule that was over them … I would make a few improvements at once … but, for the most part, improvements should be made by degrees, as the people became more capable of valuing and not abusing them.

Octavia Hill was a pioneer in the techniques of housing management and social case work. She was convinced that she could help the destitute to escape from poverty by working with them to modify their lifestyles. In her view poverty was the result of individual failings rather than the consequence of social and economic circumstances. Hill was also a prominent member of another organisation that explicitly made improved behaviour a condition for the receipt of philanthropy: the Charity Organisation Society.

The aims of the Charity Organisation Society

Key question
How did the Charity Organisation Society attempt to regulate charity?

The Charity Organisation Society (COS) was founded in 1869. Its aim was to regulate and organise existing charities so that support given to the poor would be distributed on strict lines. The core of COS philosophy was the belief that indiscriminate charity would inevitably demoralise the poor in just the same way as the old Poor Law was said to have done. Just as its critics believed that the Speenhamland system (see page 15) of supplementing wages undermined hard work and independence, so, in the eyes of the COS, unregulated charity would encourage the poor to become idlers and beggars rather than 'respectable' and independent citizens. Conversely, the COS predicted that charitable support given in a specific way to deserving cases would help them to become independent once more.

Social science

This was an age when many organisations and individuals sought to base their actions on 'scientific' lines. The COS believed that their principles were based on the science of society, or 'social science'. As part of this scientific approach, they also adopted a research procedure in order to inform their work. The method adopted was that of investigation: a COS volunteer would conduct a close examination of the lifestyles of those applying for help in order to determine whether or not their case was a worthy one.

The establishment of the COS coincided with the new efforts of central government to reduce spending on outdoor relief after 1870. Both the Local Government Board (which from 1870 was responsible for the Poor Law) and the COS shared the view that the 'undeserving' poor (i.e. those who were believed to have brought about their own poverty through their moral failings) should be given only the option of the workhouse. The 'deserving' poor on the other hand, who had fallen on hard times

Key date

Local Government Board took responsibility for the Poor Law: 1870 through no fault of their own, could be offered limited charity to help them to get back on their feet.

The COS wanted charities in each area to adopt procedures like the Birmingham ticket system. Here charity providers gave applicants a ticket that they would then take along to the local COS office. Following a rigorous inquiry into their circumstances, the applicant then took the ticket containing the result of the investigation back to the originating charity. Depending on the outcome they would be given help or sent away. The basis on which COS visitors made such decisions is indicated by the guidelines of the Southampton COS. These recommended,

> the rejection of undeserving drunkards and incorrigible idlers; those who were careless and improvident … and those who were in an absolute state of destitution fit only for the workhouse.

Charitable aid was to be given only to those who would benefit, morally as well as materially, from the help they were given. Relief was always to be temporary, personal and designed to reform the habits of the individual concerned. It was to be part of a plan for the moral improvement of the recipient.

The impact of the COS

The COS was a powerful institution in the 1870s and 1880s and was supported by key figures from the ruling élite. The 54-strong inaugural council which met in London in 1869 included people from Parliament, the aristocracy, the established church, banking, the professions and the armed forces. In the 1870s the COS had 24 vice-presidents including dukes, earls, viscounts and leading public figures. The organisation's propaganda emphasised its success in working with the new strict Poor Law and in weeding out 'scroungers' and its ability to target relief at those who deserved it. Yet the success of the COS in imposing its hard-line approach to charity is questionable. Outside London, provincial COS branches often failed to recruit enough volunteers or raise adequate funds. This meant that they were unable to regulate charitable relief. Relationships with local Poor Law boards of guardians were frequently strained as COS branches trespassed into Poor Law territory or criticised local unions for their relief policies. Old and new charities alike were reluctant to give up their right to decide how to spend their money to the COS 'charity police'. Many charities, especially those run by evangelical Christians, opposed the lack of compassion inherent in the COS's 'scientific principles'.

One historian of the COS, Robert Humphreys, has noted that, 'Most outsiders saw their technique as an obsession with probing and prying into poor people's personal affairs'. There was a strong smack of **social authoritarianism** in the COS approach to poverty and welfare. Even in the late nineteenth century not everyone was prepared to go along with this. Much charity continued to be given in an indiscriminate way, despite the objections of the COS and its supporters.

Key question
Was the Charity Organisation Society successful?

Key date
Unemployment crisis. Mansion House Fund set up to aid the destitute: 1886

Key term
Social authoritarianism
The imposition of values and ways of living on people regardless of what those people wanted.

Soup kitchen, from the *Illustrated London News*, 1867. The Spitalfields soup kitchen in London's east end provided food for a vast number of poor people, as the picture shows. Similar soup kitchens existed in other towns and cities. How do you think the COS would have regarded this type of charity?

The 1886 Mansion House Fund, which was set up to relieve distress in London, drew stinging criticism from the COS, which alleged that the fund was being distributed without proper regard to the circumstances of the recipients. Despite these objections, the fund still raised £80,000. However, even though it failed to live up to its own publicity, there is little doubt that the COS did have a major influence on the way charities operated. Those seeking help were more often than not forced to package their requests in terms that emphasised that their case was deserving in the eyes of the philanthropists.

3 | The Portrayal of the Poor

Henry Mayhew

Henry Mayhew was one of the earliest writers to document the depths of poverty that existed in Victorian London. Mayhew was born in 1812, one of 17 children. Like five of his six brothers, Henry joined his father's law practice, only to abandon this for a career in journalism. He was one of the founders of the satirical magazine *Punch* in July 1841. He co-edited the publication for a few months and continued to contribute to it until 1845.

> **Key question**
> How did the portrayal of the poor by Mayhew challenge the view that poverty was the result of individual moral failure?

View of a dust-yard from Henry Mayhew's *London Labour and the London Poor*. Mayhew described how dust-yard workers, mainly women, sifted through the rubbish brought back by dust collectors in search of anything that could be sold. Often these women were forced into this work because of the poor wages of their husbands. Mayhew describes the pigs and chickens that also rooted around for food in the rubbish. What aspects of this picture would have upset Mayhew's middle-class readers?

Key date

Henry Mayhew published *London Labour and the London Poor* in a series of pamphlets:1850–2

Mayhew and the *Morning Chronicle*

In the late 1840s Mayhew was recruited to the *Morning Chronicle* to act as London correspondent for their national investigation into labour and the poor. Starting in October 1849, he wrote 83 letters for the *Chronicle*, describing the working and living conditions of the London poor. But in October 1850 he fell out with the management of the newspaper and started to publish his investigations independently as a series of weekly parts. From late December 1850 until February 1852, Mayhew published 63 two-penny pamphlets under the title *London Labour and the London Poor*. This work, along with some new material, was eventually reproduced as a four-volume book in 1861–2, also under the title *London Labour and the London Poor*.

London Labour and the London Poor

The full title of Mayhew's four volume work was *London Labour and the London Poor; A Cyclopaedia of the Condition and Earnings of Those That Will Work, Those That Cannot Work and Those That Will Not Work*. It seems that his original aim was to survey a sample of the whole working population of London, arranged under the sub-headings of the title. However, the first three volumes of *London Labour* in fact dealt only with one particular category of Londoner, 'The London Street-Folk; comprising Street Sellers, Street Buyers, Street Finders, Street Performers, Street Artisans,

Street Labourers.' Volume four dealt with 'Those That Will Not Work, comprising Prostitutes, Thieves, Swindlers and Beggars.'

The result is that Mayhew's survey concentrated on some of the most precarious and bizarre occupations in the capital, at the expense of those in more regular work. The lives of rat-catchers, pure-finders (collectors of dog excrement which was used to 'purify' leather), sewer-hunters, glass-eye sellers, street sellers of literature (at least 28 different types), costermongers (hundreds of different types), dredgermen, mud-larks, crossing-sweepers, snake-swallowers and an infinite variety of other ways of scraping a living are painstakingly described by Mayhew. He calculated that there were about 50,000 'street folk', the majority of whom led lives of pitiful wretchedness. What most had in common, despite the variety of their callings, was the marginal and unpredictable nature of their work.

Mayhew's conclusions

Mayhew's investigations centred on face-to-face interviews with the subjects of his study. He claimed that he recounted the stories of the people he interviewed exactly as they had told them. He used the literal language and pronunciation of his interviewees and promised his readers that he had added nothing to what they said. The result was a series of extremely powerful accounts conjuring up a world previously unknown to Mayhew's middle-class readers, an 'undiscovered country of the poor' as he described it. As a result of his research Mayhew came to a number of conclusions:

- The level of poverty experienced by the street-folk of London was desperate and unacceptable.
- The condition of the street-folk was not necessarily of their own making. Some people might be responsible for their own situation, and Mayhew was willing to condemn the idle. But circumstances were the primary cause of poverty. 'The deserving poor', he wrote, 'are really those who cannot live by their labour, whether from under-payment, want of employment, or physical or mental incapacity'. His description of the daily scramble for work of casual labourers at the London docks emphasised how reliant people were on forces beyond their control. If the wind blew in the wrong direction, the ships would be delayed and the dockers would starve. 'That the sustenance of thousands of families should be as fickle as the very breeze itself' he wrote, 'that the weathercock should be the index of daily want or daily ease to a vast number of men, women and children, was a climax of misery that I could not have imagined to exist'.
- Finally, Mayhew challenged the complacency of his middle-class readers with this reality and threatened an alarming future if nothing was done. Having reminded his readers of the 'truth' that they too could have been in the same predicament but for good fortune and the help of others, Mayhew continued:

It is the continued forgetfulness of this truth – a truth which our
wretched self-conceit is constantly driving from our minds – that
prevents our stirring to improve the condition of these poor people;
though, if we knew but the whole of the facts concerning them,
and their sufferings and feelings, our very fears alone for the safety
of the state would be sufficient to make us do something on their
behalf. I am quite satisfied, from all I have seen, that there are
thousands in this great metropolis ready to rush forth, on the least
evidence of a rising of the people, to commit the most savage and
revolting excesses.

The threat of social revolution by the desperate and dispossessed
of London was a powerful way of focusing middle-class attention
on the problem of poverty.

Was Mayhew's work reliable?

Mayhew's work has been attacked by a number of historians. His
investigation was erratic and the original plan to survey the whole
labouring population collapsed. His concentration on the most
marginal workers and his failure to deal with the numerous
groups of workers in more regular occupations (e.g. 168,000
domestic servants) is said to have produced an exaggerated
picture of the extent of poverty. Mayhew was a popular journalist
who needed to sell his publications to earn a living, and this may
have motivated him to present the most dramatic and colourful
scene. Some of his characters, such as Jack Black the rat-catcher,
were certainly larger than life. The accuracy of Mayhew's work
has also been questioned. Some of his interviews may have been
staged: there is evidence that particularly interesting 'specimens'
of the London poor were brought to his office, where their stories
were embellished by Mayhew and his assistants. Many of
Mayhew's statistics have also been shown to be unreliable.

Whatever the reliability of his work, Mayhew's writing certainly
had a major impact on the understanding of poverty. The weekly
pamphlets had a circulation of some 13,000 and inspired at least
eight imitators and two popular stage plays in the 1850s.
Reviewers in newspapers and magazines praised Mayhew's efforts
and expressed their shock and horror at his revelations. Mayhew
revealed a previously hidden world and in describing that world
he raised questions about accepted views on poverty and
challenged those in authority to respond.

Charles Dickens

Charles Dickens was the best-selling novelist of the Victorian
period. His major works, published in weekly parts, each sold
tens and even hundreds of thousands of copies. In the 12 years
after his death in 1870 Dickens' books sold four million copies in
England alone. They were read by all classes and his characters
were more familiar and famous than most living celebrities of the
age. His portrayal of poverty and the poor was therefore an
important influence on public opinion and on the consciousness
of policy makers.

Key question
How did the portrayal
of the poor by
Dickens challenge the
view that poverty was
the result of individual
moral failure?

Charles Dickens. Dickens' novels brought the plight of the poor to the attention of a wide audience. His stories put a human face to poverty. In *Oliver Twist* Dickens highlighted some of the worst features of the workhouse.

Though he was a social campaigner as well as a novelist, Dickens' primary intention was to write a good story, and his tales held no consistent view on the problem of poverty or its solution. Nevertheless, Dickens' work did consistently emphasise two points. First, it portrayed the poor as real people who suffered like everyone else. This might not seem like a great achievement but, at a time when the poor were often portrayed as idlers or criminals, if they were portrayed at all, this did help to bring a human dimension to a social problem. In *Bleak House* (1852) Dickens described the 'outcast' life of Jo, the poor crossing sweeper:

> It must be very puzzling to see the good company going to the churches on Sundays, with their books in their hands, and to think (for perhaps Jo *does* think, at odd times) what does it all mean, and if it means anything to anybody, how comes it that it means nothing to me? To be hustled, and jostled, and moved on; and really to feel that it would appear to be perfectly true that I have no business here, or there, or anywhere; and yet to be perplexed by the consideration that I *am* here somehow, too … It must be a strange state, not merely to be told that I am scarcely human (as in the case of offering myself as a witness), but to feel it of my own knowledge all my life! To see the horses, dogs, and cattle, go by me, and to know that in ignorance I belong to them, and not to the superior beings in my shape, whose delicacy I offend!

Key date

Publication of Charles Dickens' *Bleak House*: 1852

Secondly, Dickens was a fierce critic of the new Poor Law and the workhouse system. Oliver Twist was serialised in the late 1830s and contained vivid descriptions of the horrors of workhouse life. Throughout his career his invective against the effects of the new poor law continued. In the last novel he completed, *Our Mutual Friend*, the character Betty Higden was asked why she reacted so strongly to the mention of the poor house:

> 'Dislike the mention of it?' answered the old woman. 'Kill me sooner than take me there. Throw this child under cart-horses' feet and a loaded wagon, sooner than take him there. Come to us and find us all a-dying, and set a light to us all where we lie, and let us all blaze away with the house into a heap of cinders, sooner than move a corpse of us there!'

Though Dickens' hostility to the Poor Law failed to bring about its repeal in his own lifetime, it did contribute to a growing unease at the way the poor were treated by authority.

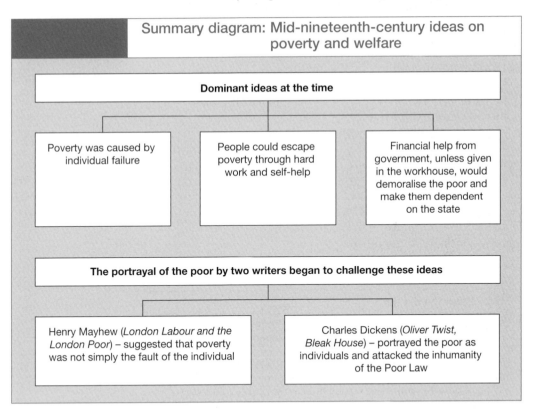

Summary diagram: Mid-nineteenth-century ideas on poverty and welfare

Dominant ideas at the time

Poverty was caused by individual failure

People could escape poverty through hard work and self-help

Financial help from government, unless given in the workhouse, would demoralise the poor and make them dependent on the state

The portrayal of the poor by two writers began to challenge these ideas

Henry Mayhew (*London Labour and the London Poor*) – suggested that poverty was not simply the fault of the individual

Charles Dickens (*Oliver Twist, Bleak House*) – portrayed the poor as individuals and attacked the inhumanity of the Poor Law

4 | The Changing Background to the Debate

Three developments in the second half of the nineteenth century underpinned the changing debate on the treatment of poverty:

- the growth of the electorate
- the spread of state intervention
- the relative decline of the British economy.

Key question
Why did attitudes towards poverty begin to change in the second half of the nineteenth century?

The growth of the electorate

The Great Reform Act of 1832 had extended the right to vote to most middle-class men. However, in the first half of the century the working classes were excluded from direct participation in national electoral politics. Leading figures were opposed to any extension of the franchise, which they believed would result in disaster. 'Power in the hands of the masses', according to Lord Palmerston (Prime Minister, 1855–8 and 1859–65), 'throws the scum of the community to the surface'. Yet, in the final third of the century, this stance began to change as the ruling classes felt it necessary to enfranchise increasing numbers of working-class men. The 1867 Reform Act gave the right to vote to an extra one million men, including skilled artisans. A further act of 1884 resulted in six out of ten men having the vote. The major political parties now faced a situation where they had to appeal to working men if they wanted their votes, and social welfare legislation was perceived as a way to do this.

More importantly, the spectre of socialism and social revolution in Europe and the appearance of revolutionary parties like the **Social Democratic Federation** in Britain, convinced some politicians that welfare reform was essential in order to tempt the working class away from more radical politics. In an 1895 speech, A.J. Balfour, soon to be the Conservative Prime Minister, argued that collective action through social legislation was the 'most effective antidote' to **socialism**.

Social Democratic Federation
A political party whose policies were influenced by the revolutionary ideas of Karl Marx.

Socialism
The belief that state control of essential services and resources can be used to redistribute wealth from the rich to the poor to create a fairer society.

Key terms

Nineteenth-century electoral reform acts	
Date	What the act did
1832	Great Reform Act gave the vote to middle-class men and removed some of the most corrupt aspects of the old electoral system
1867	Second Reform Act gave the vote to skilled working men
1872	Introduced the secret ballot
1883	Corrupt practices in elections, such as bribery and vote-buying, made illegal and election expenses were limited
1884	Third Reform Act – increased the British electorate from 3.2 million to 5.7 million
1885	Redistributed parliamentary seats from areas with small populations to the growing cities. This increased the influence of working-class voters

Key dates

Education Act: 1870

Public Health Act: 1875

Great Exhibition: 1851

Key terms

Laissez-faire
Literally means 'let it be'. The idea that the state should not be involved in economic or social issues but leave them for individuals and businesses to sort out.

Great Exhibition of 1851
Held at the Crystal Palace in London, this was a showcase for the achievements of British industry and empire.

Great Depression
Used to describe the British economy from 1873 to 1896. It was characterised by a fall in prices and profits and a rise in unemployment.

Charles Darwin
A naturalist most famous for developing the theory of evolution in his 1859 book *The Origin of Species by Means of Natural Selection*.

National efficiency
Used by politicians around 1900 to describe the population's ability to compete in the world, both economically and militarily.

The growth of state intervention

The spread of state intervention pre-dated the late nineteenth century concerns about the dangers of socialism. Despite claiming to support the idea of *laissez-faire*, governments from the 1860s onwards were increasingly prepared to take action to deal with social problems. Factory and workshop legislation limited the rights of industrialists to over-work their employees and forced them to provide basic minimum standards of safety. Public Health Acts, most famously that of 1875, forced Local Authorities to overcome the objections of property owners and provide water and sanitation in their areas. The 1870 Education Act established state education and was followed in 1880 by legislation that made elementary school attendance compulsory. A consensus had developed that it was not tolerable for workers to be mangled by unguarded machines, for sewage to run down the streets or for children to grow up without a minimum education. As the state accepted responsibility for these elements of social life so, it was argued, it should take some responsibility for the problem of poverty.

Problems with the British economy

The 1880s and 1890s also witnessed a growing concern about Britain's position in the world. The **Great Exhibition of 1851** allowed most Victorians to celebrate the high point of British industrial supremacy. But the confidence of the mid-Victorian period was shaken by the realisation that other nations, such as Germany and the USA, were challenging British economic power. Historians disagree as to the severity of the **Great Depression** of 1873–96, but at the time people certainly believed that something had gone wrong. The very terms 'unemployed' and 'unemployment' entered the currency of debate in the 1880s. Unemployment figures for this period are not precise, but as many as 10 per cent of workers were out of work in 1886. In 1895, a House of Commons Select Committee on Distress from Want of Employment was established, the first enquiry of its kind and an indication of the concern of the authorities.

Charles Darwin's ideas about evolution and the survival of the fittest were also under intense discussion at this time and some commentators argued that the impoverished condition of the British race was the reason for Britain's apparent failure in the battle for economic survival. Politicians began to suggest that economic decline was a consequence of a decline in the efficiency of the population. This **national efficiency** debate gathered momentum at the turn of the century and encouraged some politicians to believe that state-sponsored social welfare was essential in order to protect Britain's position in the world. The dramatic revelations about the extent of poverty that were published at the time added considerable fuel to the fire of this debate.

5 | The Growing Awareness of Poverty

The changing economic and political situation in Britain meant that attitudes towards poverty were likely to change. The work of the social investigators Charles Booth and Seebohm Rowntree made it impossible for governments to ignore their findings.

Charles Booth
Booth's background

Charles Booth was born in 1840 into a wealthy Liverpool trading family. He inherited £20,000 on the death of his father and, with his brother, Alfred, set up a business that expanded into a large and prosperous steamship company. Though plagued by poor health, Booth was a prodigiously hard worker. He was an earnest man, anxious to do good in the world as well as make money. In the mid-1870s, after a spell in Switzerland recovering from serious ill-health, Booth, his wife Mary and their two children settled in London. Here they quickly became involved with the debates regarding poverty and philanthropy, particularly as Mary Booth's uncle was a leading light in the Charity Organisation Society and her cousins worked with Octavia Hill (see page 81).

Booth's beliefs

Booth did not agree with the COS notion that the poor were largely responsible for their own condition. But he also rejected the socialist argument that the capitalist system itself was the cause of poverty. In 1885 Booth became involved with the Mansion House Inquiry into Unemployment, and the following year he decided to investigate the realities of poverty for himself. Working with a small team, he estimated that the project would last for three years. Seventeen years and 17 volumes later, *Life and Labour of the People in London* was finally completed.

Life and Labour of the People in London

Booth and his team attempted to classify the population according to the nature of their work, earnings and style of life. He acknowledged that the classes he identified shaded into one another and overlapped at the fringes, but he believed that the distinctions between these classes were fundamental to the understanding of poverty and prosperity.

- *Class A.* At the bottom of the social scale were class A, described as the lowest class of occasional labourers, loafers and semi-criminals. Booth believed this to be a largely 'hereditary' class: people were born into class A and were rarely able to escape from it. The lives of those in class A were characterised by disorder. Booth wrote that, 'they degrade whatever they touch', and he variously described them as 'savages' and 'barbarians'. Fortunately, Booth found that only 0.9 per cent of the population were in class A.
- *Class B.* Above the lowest group were class B, characterised by casual earnings. Because their work was low paid and sporadic,

Key question
What new ideas about the causes of and solutions to the problem of poverty were suggested by the investigations of Charles Booth?

Key date
Publication of first volume of Charles Booth's *Life and Labour of the People in London:* 1889

the 7.5 per cent of the population in this class were 'very poor'. Casual dock workers were the largest occupation within class B. Booth believed that these people were, for 'mental, moral or physical reasons', incapable of better work.

- *Class C.* Class C had better earnings than B but their work was irregular and their income intermittent. They might earn 15–20s a week when they were employed, but they were involved in a constant struggle to make ends meet.
- *Class D.* Class D also had low incomes (not more than 21s per week) but at least they had regular work. They tended to be more prudent than those in class C but, like them, were 'poor'. C and D together made up 22.3 per cent of the population.
- *Classes E, F, G and H.* Classes E and F were in 'comfort' rather than poverty. Together, they comprised 51.5 per cent of the population. Class E were workers in regular employment earning 22–30s per week. Class F were the best paid artisans and workmen. Classes G and H were the lower and upper middle classes and constituted 17.8 per cent of the population.

Key findings

With such an enormous survey (to which must be added various other texts and the investigators' surviving research notes), it is little wonder that historians have disagreed as to Booth's message. Nevertheless, two key findings regarding poverty seem to have emerged from this gigantic study. First, Booth's calculations demonstrated that 30.7 per cent of the London population were living in poverty. This was a shocking statistic and one which was taken up by social reformers as an indication of the scale of the problem. Secondly, Booth showed that poverty was a consequence of circumstance as much as individual folly. In a sample of 4000 'poor' (classes C and D) and 'very poor' (classes A and B) households, Booth attempted to quantify the causes of poverty (see Figure 4.1).

These figures indicated that most poverty was caused by problems relating to employment. In particular, Booth drew attention to the problem of irregularity of work. Many of the poor

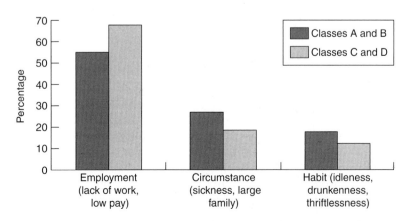

Figure 4.1: Reasons for poverty.

people in classes B and C found that work was only available for a few days in the week or at certain times of the year. This meant that it was impossible for them to organise their lives with any certainty because they did not know what their income would be, in some cases from one day to the next.

Booth did not abandon the idea of individual responsibility: he used subjective terms such as 'shiftless' to describe some groups. However, he emphasised that poverty was still poverty whatever the cause. He pointed out that it was easy for the comfortable middle classes to criticise the poor for their behaviour but that it was not so easy for anyone to lead a regular life when faced with such irregularity of income. Unlike many contemporary social commentators, Booth did not condemn the working classes for drinking, and saw drink as a consequence of poverty as much as a cause of it.

Criticisms of Booth

Despite the monumental achievements of Booth's study, *Life and Labour of the People in London* was criticised at the time. Helen Bosanquet of the COS attacked the statistical basis of the investigation, which she claimed underestimated the sources of income available to poor families. This criticism suggested that Booth overestimated the extent of poverty. Bosanquet maintained that only the individual case-work of the COS could reveal the true circumstances of the poor. Although Booth's investigators had spent some time living in poor neighbourhoods, most of their work was based on the evidence of school-board visitors and other middle-class groups who came into contact with the poor. It has also been pointed out that his definition of 'the line of poverty' was imprecise and varied throughout the study.

Historians have also questioned the accuracy of Booth's work, though not necessarily from the same perspective. The historian Karel Williams noted that, as part of the investigation, Booth surveyed school teachers as to their opinion of how many children were in poverty. This survey suggested that 45 per cent of the population was in poverty – a much higher figure than the 30.7 per cent indicated by the school-board visitors. Williams and others have also criticised Booth's failure to come up with convincing solutions to the problems he discovered: he never abandoned his individualist views despite his discovery of the extent of the problem.

'State slavery'

In one area Booth did suggest a radical form of action by the state. He believed that the group identified as class B were 'The crux of the problem'. Class A, though the most degraded, were small in number and could be dealt with through a mixture of charity and tough policing.

Class B were both more numerous and more problematic. This group dragged classes C and D into poverty by their inadequacy and their inability to maintain themselves at a decent standard. Class B's lack of ability, added to the hazards of **casualised work**,

Casualised work
Irregular work, often with no guarantee of employment from day to day.

Key term

meant that it was impossible for its members to help themselves. The only solution was to remove them from the labour market altogether by placing them in state-run labour colonies: a form of 'state slavery' as Booth himself admitted. The removal of class B from the labour market would provide more employment opportunities for classes C and D and allow them to rise out of poverty. Such a proposal demonstrated both a ruthless determination to deal with poverty and a ruthless disregard for the individual rights of some of the poor. But the fact that even a confirmed individualist like Charles Booth could come up with such a collectivist solution, even if it was a harsh one, is an indication that attitudes towards poverty were shifting.

Booth and the elderly

Booth also believed in a collectivist solution to the issue of poverty among the elderly. In 1894 he published a survey entitled *The Aged Poor in England and Wales* in which he claimed that 40–45 per cent of the elderly were living in poverty. In 1893 he had been recruited onto the Royal Commission on the Aged Poor. Here he was an advocate of old age pensions, which he believed should be provided by the state, without the need for the elderly themselves to have paid into any pension scheme. The proposal was rejected on the grounds that it would cost too much, but Booth had forced a radical solution onto the agenda.

The impact of Booth's work

By revealing that 30.7 per cent of the population of London were in poverty, by indicating that poverty was caused by economic circumstance more than by individual failure, and by suggesting that the state had to take a bigger role in dealing with this problem, Charles Booth had a profound impact on the debate about poverty and welfare.

Seebohm Rowntree
Rowntree's background

Seebohm Rowntree was a member of the famous York chocolate and cocoa-producing family. As devout Quakers, the Rowntrees had shown a philanthropic concern for the welfare of their workers and Seebohm was, like Booth, interested in gaining more precise information on the lives and conditions of labouring people. One of the criticisms of Booth's *Life and Labour of the People in London* was that its findings were unrepresentative. The metropolis inevitably attracted the poor from elsewhere, drawn by the bright lights and the chance of work. A total of 30.7 per cent of Londoners might live in poverty, but was this really typical of the rest of the country? Rowntree hoped to build on Booth's work by conducting a similar investigation into his own city, York. He also hoped to give more precision to Booth's idea of a line of income below which poverty could be said to exist.

Key question
What new ideas about the causes of and solutions to the problem of poverty were suggested by the investigations of Seebohm Rowntree?

Key date
Publication of Seebohm Rowntree's *Poverty: A Study of Town Life:* 1901

Poverty: A Study of Town Life

Rowntree published *Poverty: A Study of Town Life* in 1901. The investigation consisted of three distinct elements:

- Rowntree's investigator visited the homes of the wage earners of York. About two-thirds of the population were visited and the information gained was supplemented by reports from other sources such as the local clergy. Based on this information, a decision was made as to whether or not households appeared to be 'in obvious want or squalor'. This total turned out to be some 28 per cent of the population.
- Next, Rowntree obtained information on the incomes of wage earners from local employers.
- Finally, he calculated the minimum income necessary for a family to exist at **mere physical efficiency**. This sum was 21s 8d for a family of five. Rowntree stressed that this 'poverty line' was the absolute minimum. If families at this level spent their money on anything other than the basic necessities they would go hungry.

Mere physical efficiency
The bare minimum necessary for survival.

Key term

On this basis, matching incomes to minimum expenditure, Rowntree demonstrated that just under 10 per cent of the population of York were living, somehow, beneath the poverty line. Their incomes were insufficient to meet the minimum outgoings needed to survive. This type of distress Rowntree called 'primary poverty'. He also investigated the reasons for this primary poverty and concluded that in most cases low wages were the cause (see Figure 4.2).

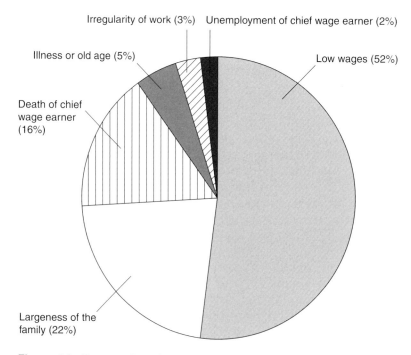

Figure 4.2: Reasons for primary poverty in York 1899.

The poverty line

Rowntree concentrated on the 10 per cent of the population living below the line of 'merely physical efficiency'. But despite the way in which he defined this as the **poverty line**, these were not the only poor in York. His investigator had found 28 per cent of those visited were in poverty. By subtracting the 10 per cent in primary poverty from the initial 28 per cent found to be 'in obvious want or squalor', Rowntree calculated that the remaining 18 per cent were in 'secondary poverty'. He defined this group as families who would have had just enough income to survive if they had not spent some of their money inefficiently – in other words on things that were not absolutely essential, like food and heating. Though Rowntree did blame alcohol for some of this 'other expenditure', he accepted that people had legitimate social and recreational needs that they were entitled to satisfy. It was unreasonable to expect people always to spend their money only on the absolute essentials.

Life-cycle poverty

Rowntree went on to develop the idea of life-cycle poverty. This showed that the degree of poverty experienced by families changed over time. Typically, a young couple might be relatively prosperous when first married, especially if they were both earning. As they had children, their prosperity would decline with the possible loss of the mother's income and the cost of feeding and clothing the children. At this point, many families might slip below the poverty line. As the children reached working age the family income would again rise for a period. But when the children left home and old age deprived the parents of their earning power, poverty might return once more. At any of these stages, illness, the death of a wage earner or the loss of regular work could also plunge the family deeper below the poverty line.

Key term
Poverty line The amount of income necessary to live at a basic level.

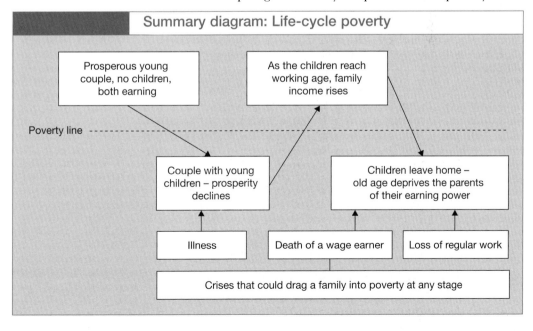

Summary diagram: Life-cycle poverty

Just as she had attacked the work of Charles Booth, so Helen Bosanquet of the COS also criticised Rowntree. Again, she claimed that he had overestimated the proportion of those in poverty by setting the poverty line at too high a level. This was somewhat ironic as Rowntree had set the line at a deliberately low level precisely to counter this type of criticism. Indeed, later in his life he made the point that the level of austerity represented by 21 shillings and 8 pence allowed basic physical survival but was not adequate to meet people's essential social and psychological needs. 'Working people' he wrote, 'are just as human as those with more money. They cannot live on a "fodder" basis. They crave for relaxation and recreation just as the rest of us do.'

Rowntree's poverty line only measured those who were in primary poverty. The two-thirds of the poor who were above the line were still poor, even if they had a little bit more than the bare necessities essential for physical survival.

The impact of Rowntree's work

Rowntree's work, as with that of Booth, had a major impact on the understanding of poverty at the turn of the century. His finding that 28 per cent of the population of York were living in poverty was close to Booth's conclusion that 31 per cent of the London population were poor. This suggested that poverty on this scale was a national rather than just a London problem. Rowntree's precise identification of the primary poverty line made an important contribution to the debate about the causes of poverty. At a time when the belief that poverty was caused by wasteful and extravagant spending was still very strong, Rowntree showed that, no matter how thrifty they were, the 10 per cent of the population in primary poverty simply had insufficient to live on. He also demonstrated that the causes of this poverty were circumstances, such as low wages, that were beyond the control of the individual.

Rowntree drew on his scientific background as a research chemist and his use of statistics gave his work an apparent scientific precision that lent authority to his views. Finally, Rowntree's enumeration of the causes of primary poverty and his development of the idea of life-cycle poverty gave direction to the search for welfare solutions to the problem of poverty. If unemployment, children, illness and old age were key causes, the state could target its support for the poor into these areas. Rowntree was a political activist as well as a social researcher, and these conclusions were to prove influential in the formation of Liberal Party welfare policy at the beginning of the twentieth century (see Chapter 5).

Summary diagram: The changing background to the debate and the growing awareness of poverty

Developments that began to change the debate on poverty and welfare

The growth of the electorate – meant that working-class voters had more influence over political decisions about welfare

The spread of state intervention – meant that there was a growing acceptance that the state did have an important role in dealing with social problems

The relative decline of the British economy – resulted in periodic trade depressions with which the Poor Law was unable to cope. The decline also raised questions about Britain's 'national efficiency'

Pressure to change welfare policy also increased because of the writings of two social investigators

Charles Booth (*Life and Labour of the People in London*) – a statistical survey of the causes of poverty which suggested that poverty was usually not the fault of the individual

Seebohm Rowntree (*Poverty: A Study of Town Life*) – an investigation into poverty in York, which supported Booth's conclusions and popularised the concept of the 'poverty line'

Study Guide: Advanced Level Questions

In the style of Edexcel

How far do you agree that prevailing ideas about the proper role of the state were the key factor determining what provision was made for the poor in the period 1830–1939?

Source: Edexcel, June 2004

> ### Exam tips
>
> *The cross-references are intended to take you straight to the material that will help you to answer the question.*
>
> This type of question requires an understanding of the changing perception of poverty in the late nineteenth century. However, to answer the question effectively you need to include material from a longer time period than that covered in this chapter. See pages 178–80 for extended exam tips on answering this type of question.

5 The Liberal Social Reforms 1906–14

POINTS TO CONSIDER

This chapter examines the important welfare measures passed by the Liberal government immediately before the First World War. The main themes are:

- The reasons for the Liberal social reforms
- The impact of the Royal Commission on the Poor Laws 1905–9
- The social reforms, which dealt with the welfare of children, the elderly, the low paid, the unemployed and the sick
- Whether the reforms represented the origins of the welfare state

Key dates

1900	Formation of the Labour Representation Committee. Beginning of Labour Party
1903	Joseph Chamberlain announced support for protectionism. Conservative Party split on this issue
1904	Report of the Inter-Departmental Committee on Physical Deterioration. Revealed poor condition of many schoolchildren
1905	Unemployed Workmen Act
1905–9	Royal Commission on the Poor Laws
1906	Liberals won General Election with landslide majority
1906	Education Act. Free school meals for poor children
1907	Education Act. Medical inspections for school-children
1908	Children Act. Reformed the law relating to children
1908	Old Age Pensions Act
1909	Trade Boards Act. Minimum wages established in certain low-paid industries
1909	Labour Exchanges Act. Offices set up to advise the unemployed of vacancies
1911	National Insurance Act. Compulsory health and unemployment insurance

1 | Reasons for the Liberal Social Reforms

Key question
Were the Liberal reforms motivated by genuine concerns about poverty, or were they a result of other political and economic pressures?

Apart from a short-lived administration in the 1890s, the Liberals had been out of office for 20 years before they won the 1906 election with a landslide majority. Welfare reform was not the main issue on which they had fought the election, yet within a decade the Liberals had passed a set of measures that radically changed the way government dealt with the issue of poverty. There is no simple explanation as to why the Liberals embarked on this period of social reform, but at least five factors need to be examined in order to understand their motivation:

- the 1906 Liberal election victory
- the rise of socialism
- New Liberalism
- unemployment
- the national efficiency debate.

What the Liberals hoped to achieve clearly had a major influence on the nature of the legislation. Were they consciously attempting to make a radical break with the past, or were they just responding to pressing problems in a pragmatic fashion?

The 1906 Liberal election victory

Key dates
Joseph Chamberlain announced support for protectionism: 1903

Unemployed Workmen Act: 1905

Liberals won General Election with landslide majority: 1906

If the Liberals had failed to win the 1906 election they would not have been in a position to introduce any social reforms. The Conservatives had dominated politics in the late nineteenth century and won the 1900 election with a big majority, so Liberal success was far from inevitable. A continuation of Conservative government would have been unlikely to produce such a burst of reform. They had passed the 1905 Unemployed Workmen Act, which established distress committees in all major towns and cities; these had the authority to provide temporary relief works for the unemployed. However, this was a short-term response to an immediate crisis, and the Conservatives had shown little inclination to deal with other aspects of poverty.

Historians are in general agreement that the Liberals did not win the 1906 election because they promised social reform. Their leader, Henry Campbell-Bannerman, was reluctant to commit his party to action on old age pensions or unemployment, and nearly a third of Liberal candidates failed to mention Poor Law reform or pensions in their election addresses. The dominant themes of the campaign were in fact free trade and 'Chinese slavery'.

Free trade

Key term
Protectionism
The policy of imposing taxes on imports to make them expensive relative to home-produced goods.

Free trade had become an issue because of leading Conservative Joseph Chamberlain's decision to support a policy of **protectionism** in 1903. Protectionism meant the establishment of customs duties and tariffs to protect British goods from cheap foreign imports. As the price of foreign goods rose because of these tariffs, it was believed that people would buy the relatively cheap home-produced items. This would lead to a drop in unemployment as the increase in demand forced employers to take on more labour.

Chamberlain, who had implemented a major programme of housing and health reforms as Mayor of Birmingham in the 1880s, also believed that the revenue generated by tariff reform could be used to finance welfare reforms like old age pensions. However, free trade was the policy associated with Britain's industrial prosperity and had been elevated to a moral principle by Liberals in the mid-Victorian era. Chamberlain's initiative divided the Conservatives between protectionists, free-traders and moderates who wanted a compromise. On the other hand, it united the hitherto divided Liberals: 98 per cent of their candidates mentioned the defence of free trade in their election addresses. Crucially, the Liberals successfully portrayed the threatened introduction of tariffs on imported grain as a 'bread tax' which would force up the price of food. This was electorally disastrous for the Conservatives.

Chinese slavery

'Chinese slavery' was the title given to the practice of shipping Chinese labourers into Britain's South African territories as cheap labour. The appalling conditions and lack of freedom to which these workers were subjected became a scandal, and the Conservative government's failure to take action cost them votes. Liberal, and particularly Labour, candidates were quick to link this with the Conservatives' failure to overturn the **Taff Vale judgement** of 1901. This legal case had, in effect, prevented trade unions from going on strike, and trade unionists claimed that it was part of a process designed to drive down workers' conditions in Britain as well as in the Empire.

Other electoral factors

The issues of free trade and Chinese workers did great damage to the Conservatives. Other factors also contributed to their defeat:

- Improved Liberal organisation meant that a much higher proportion of seats were contested and the higher turnout in 1906 compared to 1900 helped the Liberal and Labour votes.
- The newly formed **Labour Party** entered into an electoral pact with the Liberals: the parties agreed not to not stand against each other and this prevented the anti-Conservative vote from being split.

The election result

The final result, which saw the Conservatives reduced to 157 seats and the Liberals increased to 400, was the product of a wide range of policies and circumstances. Social reform was but one element in the explanation.

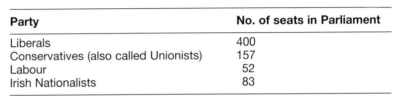

Party	No. of seats in Parliament
Liberals	400
Conservatives (also called Unionists)	157
Labour	52
Irish Nationalists	83

Figure 5.1: The House of Commons after the 1906 election.

The rise of socialism

The Liberal social reforms can be seen as a response to the growth of socialism at the start of the twentieth century. The Labour Party had been created by the **Trades Union Congress** (TUC) in 1900 to give organised labour a political voice. The immediate goal of Labour representatives was to secure the legal position of the trade unions, but both the TUC and the Labour Party were also committed to a programme of social reforms,

A cartoon from the magazine *Punch*, 1909. What is the clue that the 'suspicious looking party' is meant to represent Labour? What explanation of the reasons for the Liberal social reforms is suggested by the cartoonist?

including the abolition of the Poor Laws and the introduction of benefits such as old age pensions. Twenty-nine Labour MPs were elected in 1906 and although they supported the new government, many Liberals felt that Labour had the potential to replace them as the main alternative to the Conservatives. By introducing their own programme of social reform some Liberals believed that they could trump Labour and stop working-class voters defecting to them.

At a deeper level, politicians in both the Liberal and Conservative parties were worried about the threat of socialism. The Labour Party had committed itself to a moderate and non-revolutionary programme, but there was a concern that a much more radical brand of socialism, committed to the destruction of the capitalist system, might arise if action were not taken to improve conditions for the working classes. Germany was seen as a good example of a state where the government, especially under Chancellor Bismarck, had limited the growth of socialism by the introduction of social reforms. David Lloyd George, the Liberal Chancellor of the Exchequer, went on a visit to Germany in 1908 to investigate their welfare system. Winston Churchill, the President of the Board of Trade, wrote to Prime Minister Herbert Asquith in the same year recommending that the government,

> thrust a big slice of Bismarckianism over the whole underside of our industrial system, and await the consequences whatever they may be with a good conscience.

Churchill and Lloyd George both represented a more radical strand of Liberalism which was a key influence on the shape of the Liberal reforms.

New Liberalism

'New Liberalism' emerged in the 1890s as a radical tendency within the Liberal Party. Whereas traditional **'Gladstonian' Liberalism** had believed in low taxation and a minimal, *laissez-faire* role for the state, New Liberalism stood for increased taxes on the rich in order to finance state intervention on behalf of the poor. Intellectually underpinned by the writings of the Oxford philosopher T.H. Green, and popularised by newspapers such as the *Manchester Guardian*, *Daily Chronicle* and *Daily News*, New Liberalism was given a powerful impetus by the revelations of Booth and Rowntree (see pages 92–8).

Many New Liberals were involved with the settlement movement. This was a scheme whereby university graduates would spend some time living in poor areas, working on education and other projects. The most famous of these, Toynbee Hall in East London, was also a base for Booth's researchers. Confronted with the realities of poverty, New Liberals realised that old Liberal beliefs had to be amended in the light of persistent poverty. Liberal MP J.M. Robertson explained that,

'Gladstonian' Liberalism
Policies associated with the late-nineteenth-century Liberal leader William Gladstone who, though a reformer in many areas, believed in low taxation and a minimal, *laissez-faire* role for the state.

Key term

Profile: David Lloyd George 1863–1945

1863 – Born in Manchester
1890 – Elected Liberal MP for Caernarfon
1905 – President of the Board of Trade
1908 – Chancellor of the Exchequer
1908 – Introduced Old Age Pensions Act
1909 – Proposed 'People's Budget'
1911 – Introduced National Insurance Act
1915 – Minister of Munitions
1916 – Prime Minister
1922 – Resigned as Prime Minister
1945 – Died

Early life and career

David Lloyd George was born in Manchester. His father died when David was an infant and his mother took him to Wales to live with her brother. 'Uncle Lloyd' effectively became David's adopted father and encouraged his education. After leaving school David was able to study law and became a solicitor. He became involved in Liberal politics and in 1890 at the age of 26 he was elected MP for Caernarfon. When the Liberal Party won power in 1905 Lloyd George was appointed President of the Board of Trade. His success in this post led to his promotion to Chancellor when Asquith became Prime Minister in 1908.

Chancellor of the Exchequer

As Chancellor Lloyd George was the central figure in the Liberal social reforms. He piloted the Old Age Pensions Act through the Commons in 1908 and was responsible for the 1909 budget which raised the money to pay for many of the reforms. This budget, which involved increasing taxes on the rich, was fiercely opposed by Conservatives in Parliament. The House of Lords, where the Conservatives had a majority, blocked the budget, provoking a **constitutional crisis**. Lloyd George led the Liberals' attack on the lords in the '**Peers versus people**' elections that followed in 1910. The Liberals clung on to power by a small majority and the budget was passed.

Lloyd George argued passionately for a welfare system that would support people who found themselves in poverty through a crisis that was beyond their control. As he explained to an audience in Kennington in 1911:

> So long as the head of the family is in good health, on the whole with a fierce struggle he can keep the wolves of hunger in the vast majority of cases from the door; but when he breaks down in health, his children are at the mercy of these fierce ravaging beasts, and there is no one to stand at the door to fight for the young. What happens in these cases? In hundreds of thousands there is penury, privation, everything going from the household, nothing left unpawned, except its pride.

Key terms

Constitutional crisis
A political confrontation relating to the rules under which the country is governed.

'Peers versus people'
Used to describe the electoral conflicts of 1910 between the Conservatives, who had a majority in the House of Lords, and the Liberals, who had a majority in the House of Commons.

His solution was the National Insurance Act, a piece of legislation that he introduced in 1911.

Prime Minister
After war broke out the Liberals soon formed a coalition government with the other political parties in Parliament. In 1915 Lloyd George became Minister of Munitions and then Secretary of State for War. By 1916 criticisms of Prime Minister Herbert Asquith's leadership were growing and the crisis came to a head in December when Asquith resigned and was replaced by Lloyd George. Under Lloyd George's leadership the war was brought to a victorious conclusion. He then led a Conservative-dominated coalition to success in the 1918 general election and he was Prime Minister of the coalition government until 1922. However, the split between Lloyd George and Asquith did massive damage to the Liberal Party and they fell behind the emerging Labour Party as the alternative to the Conservatives.

Later career
Although Lloyd George remained as an MP throughout the interwar period, he was never again to hold ministerial office. He continued to be an advocate of social reform. David Lloyd George died after a long illness just before the end of the Second World War.

Laissez-faire is not done with as a principle of rational limitation of state interference, but it is quite done with as a pretext for leaving uncured deadly social evils which admit of curative treatment by state action.

New Liberalism gradually became the dominant force in Liberal politics at the beginning of the twentieth century. Its key supporters, J.A. Hobson, L.T. Hobhouse and Herbert Samuel, were all talented writers as well as politicians and by 1906 many in the party had come to accept New Liberal ideas. In the Liberal government, Churchill and Lloyd George were the most prominent New Liberals but H.H. Asquith, who was chancellor from 1906 to 1908 and then prime minister, also accepted the need for redistributive taxation and welfare reforms.

Unemployment
While the investigations of Booth and Rowntree had shown that the poorest sections of the population were in a more or less permanent state of distress, the late nineteenth and early twentieth centuries also saw a growing awareness of a different cause of poverty. Unemployment could be a problem not just for the 'residuum' of casual and marginal workers, but could also plunge even skilled and 'respectable' workers into poverty.

In the mid-Victorian period there had been an assumption that economic growth would lead to an increasing demand for labour,

A work scheme for the unemployed in Poplar, London, 1905. What criticisms might have been made of such schemes?

but the 'Great Depression' of 1873–96 and the growth of foreign competition forced a reassessment. It became clear that periodic spells of mass unemployment were possibly inevitable as the pattern of trade went from boom to slump. The Poor Law was not designed to deal with this type of crisis: the forces causing distress had nothing to do with the failure of the individual and workhouses simply could not accommodate the numbers involved.

In 1886 a meeting of 20,000 unemployed workers in Trafalgar Square in London had developed into a riot. Following this, the government had encouraged Poor Law guardians to establish temporary work schemes to alleviate distress (see Chapter 3, page 61). The 1905 Unemployed Workmen Act was also passed following an increase in unemployment and demonstrations. Again, this Act allowed local Distress Committees to establish relief work for the unemployed.

The Liberals in opposition had to demonstrate that they were also concerned about unemployment. Their leader, Henry Campbell Bannerman, was reluctant to be too specific, but it was clear that once in government the Liberals would be forced to take action. Though their promises lacked detail, the Liberals committed themselves to some degree of intervention on behalf of the unemployed.

National efficiency

Towards the end of the nineteenth century, concerns were increasingly expressed regarding the 'efficiency' of the British population. The success of foreign economies suggested that the British workforce was inferior to that of their foreign rivals. The work of Booth and Rowntree, by revealing the depths of poverty in English cities, reinforced this concern.

What really alarmed some people was the prospect of this 'national deterioration' weakening Britain's military capability. The 1899–1902 **Boer War** seemed to confirm the worst of these fears. Not only had British forces struggled to overcome an inferior enemy, but the details that emerged from army recruiting centres suggested that a high proportion of volunteers had been rejected on the grounds of physical incapacity. In his 1901 book *Efficiency and Empire*, Arnold White reported that, 'two out of three men willing to bear arms in the Manchester district are virtually invalids', and in 1903 Major-General Sir Frederick Maurice claimed that only two out of five enlisted men remained fit for service after two years. This, he stressed, was not a reflection on the hardships of army life but on the level of unfitness within the population.

The result of these concerns was the appointment, in 1903, of a government Inter-Departmental Committee on Physical Deterioration to inquire into the extent of the problem. The committee found that there was no evidence that the British 'race' was deteriorating in the way that some had claimed, but it did confirm that the physical condition of the poorest parts of the population was a cause for concern. It drew particular attention to the unhealthy state of children in these areas and criticised their parents for inadequate care. If parents were failing to exercise proper care over the welfare of their children, then the state would have to undertake the responsibility for providing the welfare necessary. Such a conclusion clearly provided at least part of an agenda for a future government interested in social reform.

Key date

Report of the Inter-Departmental Committee on Physical Deterioration: 1904

Key term

Boer War
Fought in South Africa from 1899 to 1902, after a dispute between settlers of Dutch origin ('Boers') and the British Empire.

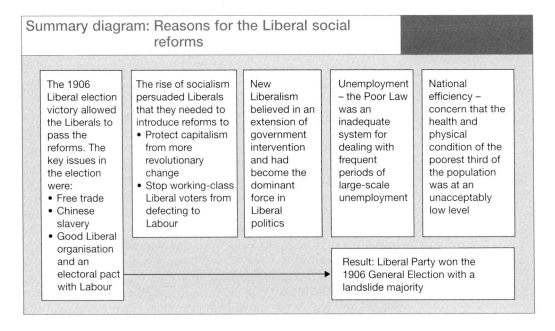

Summary diagram: Reasons for the Liberal social reforms

| The 1906 Liberal election victory allowed the Liberals to pass the reforms. The key issues in the election were: • Free trade • Chinese slavery • Good Liberal organisation and an electoral pact with Labour | The rise of socialism persuaded Liberals that they needed to introduce reforms to • Protect capitalism from more revolutionary change • Stop working-class Liberal voters from defecting to Labour | New Liberalism believed in an extension of government intervention and had become the dominant force in Liberal politics | Unemployment – the Poor Law was an inadequate system for dealing with frequent periods of large-scale unemployment | National efficiency – concern that the health and physical condition of the poorest third of the population was at an unacceptably low level |

Result: Liberal Party won the 1906 General Election with a landslide majority

Key question
What did the two reports of the 1905–9 Royal Commission on the Poor Laws recommend?

Key date

Royal Commission on the Poor Laws: 1905–9

2 | The Royal Commission on the Poor Laws 1905–9

The commission

In 1904 the Conservative government decided to establish a Royal Commission to inquire into the working of the Poor Laws and the relief of distress. The immediate cause was the growing problem of unemployment, but there were also increasing concerns about the suitability of the Poor Law as a means of dealing with poverty in the new century. The Commission, which met the following year, was chaired by Lord George Hamilton, and its 20 members shared a wide range of expertise on the subject. They included:

- Poor Law guardians
- civil servants from the Local Government Board
- leading members of the Charity Organisation Society (COS) (see page 82)
- religious leaders
- trade unionists
- social investigators Charles Booth and Beatrice Webb.

The inquiry

The detailed inquiry conducted by the Commission ran to 47 volumes and was the product of hundreds of interviews and visits. Though much of the evidence did point to the inadequacies of the workhouse system, the Local Government Board seemed determined to return to the principles of 1834. When questioned by the Commission, J.S. Davy, the civil servant in charge of the Poor Law division, confirmed that the loss of personal reputation, personal freedom (through detention in the workhouse) and political rights (paupers lost the right to vote) should continue to form the main elements of ineligibility.

The majority report

The commissioners themselves were divided as to what should be done to reform the system and two reports were produced. The majority report, inspired by Helen Bosanquet and the COS members, accepted the need for a reform of the system. It criticised the working of the boards of guardians and the indiscriminate and excessive use of outdoor relief, but it also acknowledged 'The unsuitability of the general workhouse as a test or deterrent for the able-bodied'. COS influence was especially clear in the comment that 'The causes of distress are not only economic and industrial; in their origin and character they are largely moral', and in the complaints about the lack of co-operation between the Poor Law and charities.

The majority report recommended the replacement of the boards of guardians by public assistance committees. These would be made up of elected local councillors and local philanthropists. Individual casework was encouraged as the key strategy for dealing with poverty and voluntary aid committees, representing local charities, would be established to facilitate this.

The minority report

The majority report accepted that the Poor Law should continue to be the main institution dealing with poverty. This was unacceptable to some of the commissioners, who believed that much more fundamental reform was required. They produced a minority report inspired by commissioner Beatrice Webb and her husband Sydney. This was signed by Mrs Webb herself, the socialist and Poor Law guardian George Lansbury, the trade unionist, Francis Chandler, and the Dean of Norwich, Russell Wakefield. The minority report emphasised the economic cause of poverty and the need for the state to take action to deal with unemployment. It recommended that:

- the Poor Law should be broken up
- specialist committees should be set up by local councils to deal with specific types of poverty:
  - education committees to deal with issues of child poverty
  - health committees to deal with the sick and disabled
  - pensions committees to deal with the elderly poor
- the problem of unemployment was beyond the capacity of local authorities
- a Ministry of Labour should be established to deal with this issue. It would supervise:
  - massive public work schemes
  - a national system of Labour Exchanges to help the unemployed to find work
  - training schemes and maintenance payments for those who remained out of work.

The split within the Commission was an important reason why neither report resulted in direct government action. The recommendations of the majority seemed inadequate to the New Liberals, while the enthusiastic campaigning of the Webbs for the minority report alienated the government. Nevertheless, the work of the Commission kept the issues of poverty, unemployment and welfare at the forefront of public debate. This in itself forced the Liberals to come up with solutions to these problems. Indeed the government had already begun to take action before the Commission reported in 1909.

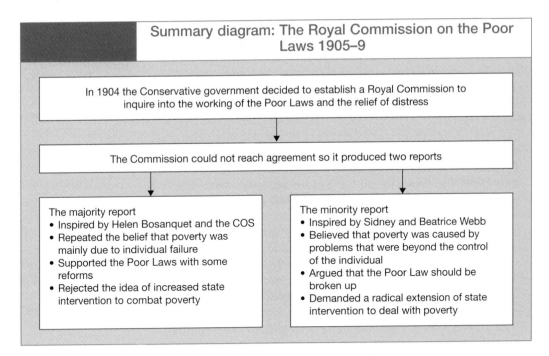

Summary diagram: The Royal Commission on the Poor Laws 1905–9

In 1904 the Conservative government decided to establish a Royal Commission to inquire into the working of the Poor Laws and the relief of distress

The Commission could not reach agreement so it produced two reports

The majority report
- Inspired by Helen Bosanquet and the COS
- Repeated the belief that poverty was mainly due to individual failure
- Supported the Poor Laws with some reforms
- Rejected the idea of increased state intervention to combat poverty

The minority report
- Inspired by Sidney and Beatrice Webb
- Believed that poverty was caused by problems that were beyond the control of the individual
- Argued that the Poor Law should be broken up
- Demanded a radical extension of state intervention to deal with poverty

3 | The Liberal Social Reforms

Key question
To what extent did the Liberal social reforms mark a significant break with nineteenth-century attitudes to poverty?

The Liberals did not come to power with a systematic programme of reform, and they were not working to a predetermined plan. Each of the Liberal welfare measures had its roots in particular concerns and circumstances. However, the reforms did address all the key areas of poverty identified in the reports and investigations of the previous decade, and it is useful to examine them with these areas in mind:

- poverty in childhood
- poverty and the elderly
- poverty due to low pay
- poverty as a results of illness
- poverty as a result of unemployment.

Poverty in childhood

Key question
To what extent did the Education and Children Acts mark a significant break with nineteenth-century attitudes to poverty?

The report of the Inter-Departmental Committee on Physical Deterioration of 1904 had drawn particular attention to poverty in childhood as a source of unfitness in adults. The Liberal government's first pieces of social legislation were a response to this concern, although the link was not a direct one. In many ways the legislation on children illustrates that change came as a result of pressure from a wide range of other groups, rather than just depending on the commitment of the Liberals.

Education (Provision of Meals) Act 1906

Key date
Education (Free School Meals) Act: 1906

This Act allowed local authorities to provide school meals for children who were in need. The Liberals had shown no urgency in this area but the introduction of a **private member's bill** proposing free school meals by the Labour MP William Wilson forced them to make their minds up. The government decided to adopt the measure. There was a major issue at stake because the opponents of free school meals argued that they undermined the role of the parent. A 1906 article in the *Spectator* magazine warned that:

> to feed a child is to give relief to its parents, and the effect must be to undermine their independence and self-reliance, and to give to their children an object-lesson in the evasion of responsibility which will never be forgotten, and which will bear fruit when they in turn become parents.

Not surprisingly the COS supported this position, with Helen Bosanquet maintaining that free school meals would have the effect of 'permanently demoralising large numbers of the population' and would lead to the break-up of the family as parents lost the incentive to provide for their offspring.

The 1906 Act set one precedent by overcoming these objections and allowing the state to take responsibility for something previously considered a family responsibility. It set another by not disenfranchising the parents of the children concerned. An important element in the stigmatisation of those claiming Poor Law relief had been the withdrawal of the claimant's right to vote, if he had one in the first place (women at this time had no right to vote in national elections, although they did have the vote in local politics). This was based on the notion that those who 'took' from the state rather than contributed to it were somehow less than full citizens. The government had now accepted that those in need who received benefits were entitled to retain their full rights as citizens.

Education (Medical Inspections) Act 1907

If the immediate pressure for free school meals had come from the emerging Labour Party, the inspiration for school medical inspections came from within the government's own civil service. Professor Oliver MacDonagh has argued that a central reason for the growth of state intervention was pressure from the professional bureaucracy employed by the state, which was always concerned to expand its own influence. This could be for reasons of empire building or a genuine desire to make things better.

The Education (Administrative Provisions) Act of 1907 is good evidence to support this theory. Sir Robert Morant, Permanent Secretary at the Board of Education, felt that his political masters were too cautious and decided that he would make things happen despite them. He buried the recommendations for school medical inspections in clause 13 of a complicated piece of legislation and MPs failed to pick up the significance of the measure when it was debated in Parliament. Once the Act was passed, Morant followed it up by issuing two administrative circulars to local education authorities regulating the operation of inspections and authorising them to provide medical treatment, as well as inspection.

Private member's bill
A bill introduced by a backbench MP rather than the government. If such a bill gets the support of a majority of MPs it can become a law.

Key term

Education (Medical Inspections) Act: 1907

Key date

Like the 1906 School Meals Act, the 1907 Act was not something that the Liberal government had planned. And also like the 1906 Act, the principle was contentious. State interference in the medical welfare of children was said to undermine the role of parents, in the same way that school meals did. Yet both measures had a major impact despite their opponents. Although the 1906 Act was permissive (local education authorities were not compelled to supply school meals), by 1914 over 14 million meals per annum were being provided for 158,000 children. In a similar way, the 1907 Act did not compel local authorities to set up clinics, but by 1914 most were providing some medical treatment for children.

Children Act 1908

Key date
Children Act: 1908

The Liberal government introduced the Children Act in 1908. It was heavily influenced by the lobbying of pressure groups like the National Society for the Prevention of Cruelty to Children. The Act brought together dozens of older pieces of legislation and added new measures:

- Penalties were imposed on parents who abused or neglected their children.
- Poor Law authorities were made responsible for visiting and supervising the victims of cruelty or neglect.
- Nursing and private children's homes were to be registered and inspected.
- Children under 14 were banned from public houses and it became illegal to sell cigarettes to those under 16.
- The legal system was also reformed to establish Juvenile Courts and separate children from adult criminals; this built on the 1907 decision to introduce borstals for young offenders.

As with the earlier Education Acts, the 1908 Children's Act represented a significant extension of the role of the state in the welfare of children.

Poverty and the elderly

Key question
To what extent did the 1908 Old Age Pensions Act mark a significant break with nineteenth-century attitudes to poverty?

The elderly man or woman, forced by poverty to live out his or her final years in the workhouse, was one of the most tragic images in the literature of turn of the century Britain. In fact, by the early 1900s most of the elderly relieved by the Poor Law were receiving outdoor relief, and even in the workhouses conditions were more relaxed. Nevertheless, the poverty of the elderly and the stigma of the Poor Law had provoked a generation of campaigners to look for alternative methods of helping the aged poor.

Key term
Contributory principle
Workers had to pay into the scheme before they were entitled to take benefits from it.

Early proposals

As early as 1878, Canon William Blackley had proposed a pension scheme based on the **contributory principle**: people would pay a regular weekly amount into a fund that would provide them with an income when they reached a certain age.

Joseph Chamberlain took up the cause in the 1890s and in 1898 a Treasury committee reported in favour of contributory pensions. Such a scheme faced two difficulties. First, many of the poor would not be able to afford the contributions; that, after all, was why the poorest were, in effect, excluded from membership of friendly societies (see page 77). Secondly, the friendly societies themselves were totally opposed to a contributory scheme, as it would represent competition for the limited savings of the working class. Governments were fearful of the political power of the friendly societies, so proposals for a contributory scheme made no headway.

An alternative scheme was put forward in the 1890s by campaigners led by Charles Booth. He believed in a non-contributory scheme: the elderly would receive pensions by right and the pensions would be financed through taxation. This was opposed by those, like the COS, who believed that thrift and self-help were the only keys to unlock the door of poverty. If pensions were available as a right, they asked, why should anyone bother to save for their old age? The second obstacle to non-contributory pensions was finance: the estimated cost in the 1890s was £16 million, more than the total expenditure on the Poor Law. Although a Select Committee of the House of Commons in 1899 recommended the introduction of non-contributory pensions, the drain on public finance caused by the Boer War scuppered this plan.

Support for old age pensions

By 1908 there was a broad consensus in favour of some form of old age pension. The Labour Party and the TUC had supported the campaign for Booth's pension scheme which was led by F.H. Stead. The friendly societies had come to realise that the drain on their reserves caused by elderly members claiming sickness benefit could be stopped by the introduction of state pensions. They favoured a non-contributory scheme so that there would be no new competition for working-class savings. Even the COS now accepted the need for pensions, although only contributory pensions were in accordance with their self-help principles. H.H. Asquith, the Liberal Chancellor of the Exchequer, had begun to investigate the possibility of state pensions in 1906, and in April 1907 the Cabinet agreed to a non-contributory scheme, which they introduced the following year.

> **Key date**
>
> Old Age Pensions Act: 1908

Old Age Pensions Act 1908

This Act was brought in by David Lloyd George, who had succeeded Asquith as Chancellor. Its main provisions were:

- Pensions were financed out of taxation – they were non-contributory.
- A pension of five shillings per week was to be paid to everyone over 70 who had an income of less than eight shillings per week from other sources.
- Married couples received seven shillings and six pence.

- Those with incomes of more than eight shillings were to receive a reduced pension on a sliding scale.
- Those with an income of more than 12 shillings per week got nothing.
- Anyone who had been imprisoned in the previous 10 years, or who had claimed poor relief in the last two, or who was a drunk, or who had habitually failed to find work, was also excluded.

There is no doubt that the old age pension was popular; the government had estimated some 500,000 pensioners at a cost of £6.5 million and were surprised that 650,000 actually claimed the pension in 1909, at a cost of £8 million. By 1915 the number of pensioners had risen to just under one million. By paying the pension through post offices the government succeeded in completely divorcing them from the Poor Law, thus revealing, in the words of Lloyd George, 'a mass of poverty and destitution which is too proud to wear the badge of pauperism'.

Criticisms

The payment of pensions as of right, removing the Poor Law stigma from welfare benefit, and the decision to finance a non-contributory scheme out of general taxation, can be seen as new departures in the way the state responded to poverty. On the other hand, the introduction of old age pensions can be seen as less than radical:

- First, the age at which the pension became available was very high. The setting of the age at 70 was harsh for people in their sixties who could no longer earn a living.
- Secondly, the amount itself was very meagre. Five shillings per week was only sufficient to top up an income. It was hardly enough to survive on by itself. Indeed, Churchill admitted that the government had, 'not pretended to carry the toiler to dry land. What we have done is to strap a lifebelt around him'. In fact the government has been criticised for changing little more than the name of the benefit. The proportion of people over 70 claiming the pension in 1909 was similar to the proportion claiming Poor Law relief before the Act. Moreover, the usual weekly Poor Law payment in the early years of the century was around five shillings – the same as the pension. This has led the historian Eric Midwinter to describe old age pensions as, 'in practice, the "nationalisation" of outdoor relief for poor people ... the scheme demonstrated little more than a transfer from local to central taxation.'
- Thirdly, a continuing belief in nineteenth century morality was betrayed by the removal of ex-offenders and the 'workshy' from those eligible for pensions. The notion of the 'deserving' and the 'undeserving' had not gone away. The historian Pat Thane calls the new benefit 'A pension for the very poor, the very respectable and the very old'.

This picture shows some of the first elderly people to collect their old age pensions from the post office. Removing old age pensions from any association with the Poor Law was designed to encourage the elderly not to feel ashamed about claiming benefit. This was a radical change as the authorities had been discouraging people from claiming poor relief since 1834.

Poverty due to low pay

In the nineteenth century governments had passed a number of Factory Acts dealing with issues such as child employment, hours of work and safety. However, the idea that they would legislate to set minimum wages was an intervention too far. The widespread belief was that wage rates could only be set by the laws of supply and demand. It was believed that any attempt by the state to interfere would cause bankruptcy for the firm concerned and unemployment for the workers. Yet Booth and Rowntree had both revealed that one of the major causes of poverty was the inadequacy of wages and this could not be ignored. In particular, conditions in the so-called **'sweated' trades** had been revealed as scandalous following a long campaign. The Report of the 1908 Select Committee on Home Work described the problem in detail: long hours, hard work, low wages and cramped and unhealthy conditions.

The result of these concerns was that the government did decide to intervene in the setting of some wages. The 1909 Trade Boards Act established minimum wages for 200,000 workers in the box-making, tailoring and lace-making industries. The

Key question
To what extent did the Trade Boards and Mines Acts mark a significant break with nineteenth-century attitudes to poverty?

Sweated trades
Low-paid hard work, often done at home and usually involving payment based on the amount of work done rather than the number of hours employed.

Key term

Key date

Trade Boards Act: 1909

minimum rates, both for those who were paid by the hour and for those who were paid according to their output ('piece' rates), were to be set by boards made up of employers' representatives, workers' representatives and civil servants. The government also intervened to set minimum wage levels for miners by the 1912 Mines Act. Though limited in scope and effect, these measures

THE SWEATER'S FURNACE: OR. THE REAL "CURSE" OF LABOUR.

small rooms, not more than nine or ten feet square, heated by a coke fire for the presser's irons, and at night lighted by flaring gas-jets, six, eight, ten, and even a dozen workers may be crowded . . . The stench and foul vapours about the place are very bad . . . As regards hours of labour, earnings, and sanitary surroundings, the condition of these people is more deplorable than that of any body of working men in any portion of the civilised or uncivilised world."—*See Lord Dunraven's Speech on the Sweating System.*

"*In the sweat of thy brow shalt thou eat thy bread!*"
What hideous echo from mocking lips
Rings through this den of despair and dread,
Where the hot fume mounts and the dank steam drips?
What devilish echo of words divine?
Oh, gold hath glitter and gauds are fine,
And Mammon swaggers and Mode sits high,
And their thrones are based on *this* human stye!

"That hole of sorrow," the last dark deep
Of DANTE's dream, may no longer keep

Its horrible eminence. Singers sweet
Of buds that burgeon and brooks that fleet [Spring]
Beneath the touch of the coming
Come here, cast eyes on this scene —and sing!
Sing, if the horror that grips your throat
Will leave you breath for one golden note;
Rave of March in a rhythmic rapture;
Rhapsodise of the coming of May,
Seek from the carolling lark to capture [lay
A lilt of joy that shall fire your
With a rural jubilance strong to drown
The maddened moan of these thralls of Town.

"All the circumstances of the trade, the hours of labour, the rate of remuneration, and the sanitary conditions under which the work is done are disgraceful . . . In the 'dens' of the Sweaters, as they are called, there is not the slightest attempt at decency. . . . In the vast majority of cases work is carried on under conditions in the highest degree filthy and unsanitary. In

The attack on the sweated trades: an 1888 *Punch* cartoon.

did mark a significant shift away from the nineteenth-century *laissez-faire* attitude that the government should not intervene in the setting of wages.

Poverty as a result of illness
The problem of poor health
One of the greatest fears in all human societies is the fear of ill-health. In turn of the century Britain, despite the public health reforms of the nineteenth century (see page 91), death rates remained high. This was particularly the case in poor areas. The infant mortality rate, which is regarded as a particularly sensitive measure of public health, had remained at 153 per thousand and showed little sign of reducing.

Lack of medical insurance
The concern about 'national efficiency' meant that the Liberals were well aware of these problems. Some six to seven million people had some form of medical insurance in the early 1900s. However, many people found it difficult to keep up regular payments and as a result let their policies lapse. Poor people who could not afford to insure themselves through friendly societies faced a major crisis when faced with the need for medical attention. This was compounded by the loss of income that would result from the illness of a wage earner.

Compulsory health insurance
Lloyd George and his New Liberal colleagues decided that their priority was not illness itself, but the poverty that resulted from illness. The cost of old age pensions convinced the Liberals that they would be unable to finance health protection directly from taxation. Lloyd George had visited Germany and been impressed with their social insurance scheme. Thus the Liberals decided to deal with the problem of poverty caused by ill-health through a system of compulsory health insurance.

Opposition
Even more than was the case with pensions, there were powerful vested interests opposed to any national health insurance plan:

- The medical profession, though anxious to escape from the contracts imposed on many doctors by the friendly societies, did not want to become state employees.
- The friendly societies themselves feared that a government insurance scheme would all but destroy the reason for their existence.
- The large commercial insurance companies such as the Prudential were worried about the profits they would lose as a result of state competition.
- Employers campaigned against both the cost and the time that any scheme would involve for them.
- Many workers themselves objected to the idea of compulsory deductions from their wages. Mindful of the experience of the

Key question
To what extent did the 1911 National Insurance Act mark a significant break with nineteenth-century attitudes to poverty?

workhouses, they were also wary of any extension of state interference in their lives.

The first part of the 1911 National Insurance Act attempted to reach a compromise that would satisfy this opposition:

- The administration of the scheme would be carried out by friendly societies, trade unions or commercial insurance companies approved by the government.
- The cost of insurance was to be divided between the parties involved: male workers would pay 4d per week into the insurance fund (3d for females), their employer 3d and the state 2d.
- In return, the insured worker would be entitled to free medical treatment by a doctor chosen from a panel organised by the local insurance commission.
- Men would also be entitled to 10s per week sick pay (7s 6d for women) for the first 26 weeks of sickness.
- Women would receive 30s maternity benefit.
- Disablement benefit of 5s per week was to be established, and sufferers from tuberculosis and certain other diseases would be entitled to free treatment in a sanatorium or other specialist institution.
- Insurance was to be compulsory for all workers between 16 and 70 earning under £160 per year. Employers would deduct the worker's contribution from his or her wages and purchase special stamps to the value of the contributions, which would be stuck on the worker's insurance card.

Of all the Liberal welfare reforms, national health insurance was the most ambitious, the most important and probably the most unpopular. The fact that workers were forced to contribute led to resentment. Although Lloyd George attempted to promote insurance by claiming that workers were getting '9d for 4d', poorer employees found that their wages had, in effect, been cut. Moreover, because everyone paid the same contribution regardless of income, the poorest workers lost the highest proportion of their earnings.

The Webbs described the worker's contribution as a **poll tax** and argued that the scheme should have been funded by an extra tax on the rich. Employers disliked the fact that they were also forced into the national insurance system and had to pay into it out of their profits. Nevertheless, despite these criticisms, by 1914 some 13 million workers were insured under the scheme. An important safety net for the alleviation of poverty caused by ill-health had been established.

Poverty as a result of unemployment

Two years into their administration, the Liberal government was confronted with an unemployment crisis. By 1908, 7.2 per cent of the workforce, or 800,000 workers, were out of employment.

Booth and Rowntree had already identified unemployment as an important cause of poverty, and now the Liberals were forced to do something about it. Louise Santer, born in 1894 near Hastings in Kent, remembered the unemployment of her father, who was a scaffolder,

> I can remember my father walking to Crowhurst in the snow drifts trying to get to work. There was nothing in them days…If you hadn't got work you got nothing. Us children, we often got no bread…Sometimes we couldn't go to school if it was wet because we got no shoes. We must have owed the baker and the grocer some money. They used to let us have credit, but we never could pay them.

The nineteenth-century reaction to unemployment had often been to blame individuals for their failure to find work and to deny that the state could do anything about the problem. If workers failed to help themselves the only alternatives were charity or the Poor Law.

By 1908 attitudes had begun to change, and the new thinking on unemployment was spelled out by William Beveridge in his 1909 book *Unemployment: A Problem of Industry*. Beveridge had been sub-warden at the Toynbee Hall settlement in East London from 1903 to 1907, where he had been influenced by Charles Booth. In 1908 Beveridge joined the Board of Trade as a civil servant and his views were an important influence on the Liberals.

Beveridge believed that unemployment was an inevitable result of the capitalist industrial system. He said that there were bound to be periods of depression when work could not be found, no matter how hard an individual looked for it. Rather than blame the individual, Beveridge believed that workers needed help to locate the work that was available and financial support if they still could not find employment. He also believed that the state could do something to create work in times of depression. These three elements were to form the basis of Liberal policy on unemployment.

Labour Exchanges

The 1909 Labour Exchanges Act was intended to promote the mobility of labour: in other words, to help the unemployed find the work that was available. In an age of limited communications, such an initiative was intended to relieve some of the hardship experienced by people searching for work. Under the Act, unemployed people would be able to go to a local Labour Exchange and be advised of the vacancies in their particular trade.

In order to encourage the unemployed to use them, both Beveridge and Churchill, the President of the Board of Trade, were keen to stress that the Labour Exchanges were separate and

Labour Exchanges
Act: 1909

Key date

distinct from the Poor Law. Eighty-three exchanges were opened in February 1910 and there were 430 by 1914. In that year two million workers registered at the Exchanges, which were finding 3000 jobs a day. But the Labour Exchanges were not a complete success. Three-quarters of those registered did not find new jobs through the exchanges. Trade unions also remained suspicious of the Exchanges, believing that they were being used by employers as a way of lowering wage rates.

Unemployment insurance

The second element in the Liberal answer to unemployment was a scheme to provide maintenance to those out of work. The Poor Law was no longer considered an appropriate way to deal with the unemployed and friendly society or trade union insurance schemes had failed to attract more than a minority of workers. The Liberals' solution was to establish a national unemployment insurance scheme incorporated in the same 1911 Act that introduced health insurance. The proposal was not to cover the whole workforce but just those trades that were particularly prone to seasonal or cyclical unemployment:

- Unemployment insurance was made compulsory for around 2.25 million workers in the building and construction, ironfounding, shipbuilding, mechanical engineering, vehicle construction and sawmilling industries.
- Employees had to pay 2.5d per week into the insurance fund and this was matched by 2.5d from their employer. The state contributed around 1.66d per week for each worker.
- Benefit of 7s per week was available to unemployed members of the scheme, and contributors were entitled to one week's benefit for every five contributions paid, up to a maximum of 15 weeks.
- Subsidies were also made available to support trade union insurance schemes which paid higher levels of benefit.

As with health insurance, the contributory nature of the unemployment scheme was attacked on the grounds of unfairness: a flat-rate contribution represented a higher proportion of a poor worker's income than that of someone who was better paid. To counter opposition to contributory benefits, Churchill had argued that the contribution principle was in fact essential. It would establish that workers had a right to benefit and at last remove issues of morality and blame from support for the unemployed. 'I do not like mixing up morality and mathematics' he said, and argued that those who contributed had a right to benefit even if they had lost their job deliberately. In fact Churchill was overruled on this matter and the 1911 Act stated that anyone 'who loses employment through misconduct or who voluntarily leaves his employment without just cause' would be excluded from benefit.

The scheme was only intended as a first step and it only covered a minority of workers. Some two-thirds of those insured in 1913 were skilled workers and this indicates that the scheme did little for the really poor. Nevertheless, from July 1913 to July 1914, 23 per cent of insured workers claimed benefit and this shows that unemployment insurance was meeting a need. The scheme marked another decisive break from the Poor Law treatment of unemployment and established the principle that maintenance of the unemployed was a responsibility of national government rather than a local matter.

Creating work

The third element in the Liberal response to unemployment was an attempt to create work in time of depression. Local job creation schemes had been a response to unemployment since the 1886 Chamberlain circular (see page 61) and the 1905 Unemployed Workmen Act had empowered distress committees to provide temporary relief work. The Liberal plan was to create a Development Fund that would stimulate employment through public works in time of depression. The fund, which was set up in 1909, also worked by promoting local initiatives, and in this sense it could be seen as a continuation of previous policies. However, the attempt by central government to intervene in the economic cycle was a radical break from nineteenth-century attitudes. For the following 70 years British governments were to accept that intervention to promote employment was both possible and necessary.

Summary diagram: The Liberal social reforms

Poverty in childhood

1906 Education Act – free school meals

1907 Education Act – school medical inspections

1908 Children Act – action on cruelty and neglect, inspection of private children's homes, age limits on alcohol and tobacco consumption, juvenile courts

Poverty and the elderly

1908 Old Age Pensions Act – non-contributory pensions for the over-70s on low incomes paid through post offices

Criticised because of the high age at which it could be claimed, the meagre amount that was paid and the Victorian morality which denied the pension to the 'undeserving'

But by 1915 nearly one million old people were receiving the pension

Poverty due to low pay

1909 Trade Boards Act – established minimum wages for 200,000 workers in sweated trades

1912 Mines Act – established a minimum wage for miners

Unemployment and ill-health

1911 National Insurance Act – compulsory contributory scheme for millions of workers. Benefits payable in the event of sickness or unemployment Opposed by many doctors, friendly societies and insurance companies so they were all incorporated into the administration of the scheme

1909 Development Fund – established to stimulate employment

1909 Labour Exchanges Act – intended to help unemployed workers to find work

4 | The Origins of the Welfare State?

Many historians have described the Liberal social reforms as representing the beginning of the welfare state. Derek Fraser in *The Evolution of the Welfare State* (1973) highlights national insurance in particular as representing 'the origins of the welfare state', and he concludes his chapter on Liberal social policy by asserting that, 'Whatever historical perspective is used, one cannot escape the conclusion that Liberal social policy before the First World War was at once at variance with the past and an anticipation of radical changes in the future.'

Key question
Can the Liberal social reforms be regarded as the beginning of the welfare state?

The term 'welfare state' is commonly understood to mean the system of social welfare established by the Labour government in 1945. The key elements of this system were:

- a comprehensive collection of benefits to compensate for loss of earnings due to unemployment, old age, sickness or widowhood
- free and universal health care and education
- central government responsibility for the promotion of full employment and a healthy environment.

It is clear that many of these elements echoed the initiatives of the Liberals before 1914: benefits outside the Poor Law were established and the government began to accept the need for central action to deal with unemployment. Moreover, the man whose report provided the inspiration for the welfare state in 1945, William Beveridge, was a key figure behind the Liberal reforms of 1908–14. In order to finance their reforms, Lloyd George made a significant attack on the rich in his 1909 'People's Budget'. The 1945 Labour government also sought to redistribute wealth from the rich to the poor through high taxes and high levels of public spending.

On the other hand, there were significant differences between the Liberal measures before the First World War and the Labour measures after the Second World War. The Liberals came to office without an overall strategy for the relief of poverty, and many of their reforms were little more than responses to pressing economic and political circumstances. Victorian moral attitudes were present in all the reforms, the financial value of benefits was limited, and many of the poor found that they remained outside the unemployment insurance net. The fact that health and unemployment insurance both relied on workers' own contributions was a significant difference from the 'cradle to grave' support offered in 1945, even though national insurance did continue in the welfare state.

Nevertheless, despite the lack of an overall plan, despite the persistence of some Victorian morality, and despite their limitations, it is probably fair to say that the Liberal reforms provided at least some of the foundations of the welfare state. Attitudes to poverty and welfare had undergone a fundamental shift.

Summary diagram: The origins of the welfare state?

Were the Liberal reforms the origins of the welfare state?

Yes:
- Benefits outside the Poor Law were established
- Government began to accept the need for central action to deal with unemployment
- The man whose report provided the inspiration for the welfare state in 1945, William Beveridge, was a key figure behind the Liberal reforms of 1908–14
- Welfare reforms financed partly through taxes on wealthier citizens

No:
- The Liberals came to office without an overall strategy for the relief of poverty, and many of their reforms were little more than responses to pressing economic and political circumstances
- Victorian moral attitudes were present in all the reforms
- The financial value of benefits was limited
- Many of the poor found that they remained outside the unemployment insurance net
- The fact that health and unemployment insurance both relied on workers' own contributions was a significant difference from the 'cradle to grave' support offered in 1945, even though national insurance did continue in the welfare state

Study Guide: AS Questions

In the style of Edexcel

(a) In what ways did the Liberal welfare reforms represent a new approach to dealing with the problem of poverty?

(b) Why, in the years 1908–12, did opposition to the Liberal governments' welfare reforms become widespread?

Source: adapted from Edexcel, June 2005

Exam tips

The cross-references are intended to take you straight to the material that will help you to answer the questions.

(a) A good introduction to an answer to this question might be to outline the new approaches to poverty referred to in the question:

- 'New' Liberalism
- a better understanding of the causes of poverty through the work of people like Rowntree
- concerns about 'national efficiency'
- a recognition that increased state intervention was necessary (pages 103–8).

You need to show how the major welfare reforms reflected these new approaches:

- The Old Age Pensions Act reflected the understanding of life-cycle poverty (page 97), and the fact that pensioners did not lose their right to vote, unlike those in receipt of poor relief, represented a new way of treating the poor.
- The 1906 School Meals legislation and the other welfare reforms affecting children were motivated in part by new concerns over national efficiency.
- The 1909 Trade Boards Act and other reforms regulating wage levels were a direct interference with the labour market that was, in part, a response to the growing political power of organised labour.
- Finally, the 1911 National Insurance Act represented a recognition that the state had to intervene to support people in times of sickness and unemployment and that this intervention could no longer be limited to the Poor Law (pages 118–22).

This is not a 'how far' or 'to what extent' question so it is not necessary to give the other side of the argument in detail, however in you conclusion you might mention how some aspects of the Liberal welfare reforms (such as the exclusion of certain categories of person from pension entitlement) were rooted in Victorian attitudes rather than 'new' approaches.

(b) The key to this answer is to identify the wide range of interests that opposed the Liberal reforms.

To get the higher level of marks for this answer you need to show how these forces of opposition became widespread and how they combined with each other. You could do this by looking at the opposition which was based on hostility to state intervention and how this increased as the Liberal reforms became more significant:

- Conservatives and property owners – did not want to pay for the cost of the reforms through higher taxation.
- Employers were against interference in wage setting and the cost and bureaucracy involved in paying their national insurance contributions.
- Friendly societies and industrial insurance companies feared that they would lose their business as a result of the 1911 National Insurance Act.
- Some workers disliked the growth of state interference and the compulsion that was involved in national insurance.
- Organisations such as the COS and their supporters believed that poverty could best be dealt with through voluntary effort and thought that the growth of state intervention was a positively bad thing.

You could then look at those opponents who became frustrated that the reforms had not gone far enough:

- Trade unions and the labour movement thought the reforms were inadequate. There were also allegations that Labour Exchanges were being used to force down wage levels.
- Fabian socialists like the Webbs also felt that the reforms had not gone far enough. They thought that national insurance should be financed through general taxation rather than compulsory contributions (page 119).

In your conclusion try to address the key word 'widespread'. You may feel that it was the scale of the reforms and the way that they were financed through higher taxation that caused much of the opposition to them.

In the style of OCR

Study the four sources on poverty and national efficiency, and then answer the sub-questions.

(a) **Study Sources B and C**

How far do these two sources differ as evidence for attitudes towards government responsibility for welfare?

(b) **Study all the sources**

Using all these sources and your own knowledge, examine the view that, in the period 1900–14, there was growing support for the need for state intervention in the problem of poverty and national efficiency.

Source A

From: Seebohm Rowntree, Poverty: A Study of Town Life, *1901. A factory owner and researcher of working-class life, who concluded that more than a quarter of the population of York were living in poverty, here explains its consequences.*

Let us clearly understand what 'bare physical efficiency' means. A family living on the poverty line must never go into the country unless they walk. The father cannot smoke tobacco and can drink no beer. The mother can never buy any clothes for herself. The children can have no pocket money for toys or sweets. If any of these rules is broken, the extra expenditure can only be met by limiting the diet and sacrificing physical efficiency.

Source B

From: Minority Report of the Royal Commission on the Poor Law and the Relief of Distress, 1909. A report by a minority of members of the Royal Commission suggests that the existing Poor Law should be replaced by a completely new welfare system.

The nation faces today, as it did in 1834, an ever-growing expenditure from public and private funds, resulting in a minimum of prevention and cure, the far-reaching demoralisation of character and the continuance of much unrelieved poverty. With regard to the relief of poverty, the Poor Law should now be included in a consistent welfare system. This should be based on recovering the cost from all who are able to pay, and exempting those who cannot do so.

Source C
From: Norman Pearson, The Idle Poor, *1911. A middle-class writer argues for a policy to control the idle poor.*

It is not to be feared that the habitual vagrant is seldom capable of being reformed. As a rule, he is not an ordinary person, but one who is a pauper in his blood and bones. Broadly speaking, paupers belong to inferior stock, and the community needs to be protected against them. Therefore the proper authorities should be given the power of segregating and detaining those who burden the present, and endanger the future, of our race.

Source D
From: R.C.K. Ensor, The Practical Case for a Legal Minimum Wage, *1912. A member of the Fabian Society puts the 'national efficiency' case for a minimum wage.*

If the labour unrest of these days indicates a disease in society, then the policy of a legally enforced minimum wage should appeal to moderate and far-seeing statesmen. We all know the findings of Mr Seebohm Rowntree. His figures probably understate the case today because the last decade has seen a steep rise in the cost of living. With low wages, physical efficiency is not maintained. The State should interfere in the matter of wages, just as it has with other problems which destroyed the nation's human resources.

Source: adapted from OCR, May 2002

Exam tips
The cross-references are intended to take you straight to the material that will help you to answer the questions.

(a) You are asked to compare the sources 'as evidence' so it is important to look at the provenance of the sources (i.e. their origins and authors) as well as their content. The minority report (Source B) called for increased government action on welfare and was heavily influenced by the Fabians Sidney and Beatrice Webb. As R.C.K. Ensor (Source D) is also a Fabian, and writing only three years later, you would expect him to have a similar viewpoint. Rowntree (Source A) was also sympathetic to social reform so his argument is likely to have common ground with

Sources B and D. You don't know much about Pearson (Source C), but the title of his book, 'The Idle Poor', suggests that he is probably critical of the poor and unlikely to support increased social welfare.

Regarding the content of the sources, there is a possible difference in the type of person each source is dealing with. Source B is referring to the general problem of poverty and the Poor Law. In Source C Pearson's target is more ambiguous – he starts by referring to the 'habitual vagrant', but soon targets 'paupers' in general.

Source B is concerned about the growing cost of poverty. The majority report does not believe that this expenditure is effective in relieving poverty. Pearson, in Source C, doesn't mention this. He sees paupers as almost a separate people, of 'inferior stock'. The minority report does refer to 'demoralisation of character', which may indicate some similarity between the sources in their attitude to the poor. However, while Source C sees paupers as a threat, who should be shut away from the rest of the community, Source B has a much more positive attitude, calling for a consistent welfare system financed by those who can afford to pay for it.

It is vital to address the issue of 'how far' the sources differ when answering this type of question, particularly in your conclusion. Looking at both provenance and content, do they mainly agree or mainly disagree?

(b) Good answers to this type of question will achieve a balance between using the evidence in the sources and employing your own knowledge. Rather than simply working your way through the sources, think about the question. What are the arguments for and against the view put forward in the question? You need to use the sources and your own knowledge as evidence on either side of the argument.

Growing support for state intervention is indicated by most of the sources. Source A is from Rowntree's survey and, although the extract does not contain an explicit call for more state intervention, the implication of his findings was that more had to be done (page 98). The minority report of the 1909 Royal Commission on the Poor Law (Source B) is more explicit in calling for 'a consistent welfare system', and this was to involve much more state intervention.

Making links between sources is always good, so you might want to make a connection between Sources B and D. The minority report was heavily influenced by Fabians Sidney and Beatrice Webb, so it is not surprising that the Fabian member in Source D wants state interference in wage rates.

From your own knowledge you can argue that the success of both the new Liberals and the Labour Party in the 1906 election indicate growing support for state intervention. The problem of unemployment and concerns about 'national efficiency' convinced many people that the state needed to take a more active role in providing welfare (pages 101–8).

You need to show that there is evidence on the other side of the argument. The majority report of the Royal Commission reflected a widespread opposition to any move beyond the new Poor Law (pages 109–10) and Source C reflects this more conservative attitude, although it should be noted that Pearson's proposals also involve action by 'the proper authorities'.

The majority report reflected the views of a large range of organisations, including charities and businesses like the industrial insurance societies, who did not want increased state intervention. You can also argue that the electoral evidence does not support the view that there was increased popular support for state intervention. The issues of poverty and welfare were not central in the 1906 General Election campaign and, in any case, many voters turned away from the Liberals in the two elections of 1910 (page 105).

You must come to an explicit judgement on the basis of the evidence – was there growing support for state intervention? If there was growing support, how significant was it?

Study Guide: Advanced Level Questions

In the style of AQA

Study the following source material and then answer the questions that follow.

Source A
From: The Majority Report, Royal Commission on Poor Laws, *1909.*

We feel that pauperism and distress can never be successfully combated by administration and expenditure. The causes of distress are not only economic and industrial; in their origin and character they are largely moral. Government by itself cannot correct or remove such influences. Something more is required. The co-operation … of the community at large, and especially of those sections of it which are well off is indispensable. There is evidence from many quarters to show that the weak part of our system is not want of public spirit or benevolence, or lack of funds, or of social workers … Its weakness is lack of organisation, of method, and confidence in those who administer the system.

Source B
From: The Minority Report, Royal Commission on Poor Laws, *1909.*

We find that these institutions (workhouses) have a depressing, degrading and positively injurious effect on the character of all classes of their inmates, tending to unfit them for the life of respectable citizenship.

We find that the task of dealing with unemployment is altogether beyond the capacity of authorities having jurisdiction over particular areas; and can be undertaken successfully only by a Department of the National Government under a Minister responsible to Parliament – a Minister for Labour.

No successful dealing with the problem is possible unless provision is made simultaneously for all the various sections of the unemployed by one and the same authority.

Source C
From: K. Laybourn, The Evolution of British Social Policy and the Welfare State, *1909.*

Unable, due to a variety of political, social and economic restraints, to implement either the Majority or the Minority Reports of the Poor Law Royal Commission, the Liberal governments opted for a compromise that was to prove of temporary duration. Driven by a commitment to new Liberal ideas, the concern for national efficiency and the hope of political advantage, the Liberal governments produced something which … became recognised as the foundations of the Welfare State.

(a) **Use Sources A and B and your own knowledge**
   To what extent do Sources A and B agree on the causes of, and the solutions to, the problem of the poor in the early twentieth century?
(b) **Use Sources A, B and C and your own knowledge**
   'The social legislation introduced by the Liberal governments 1906–1914 was limited by financial restraint and ignored the recommendations of contemporaries.' Assess the validity of this view.

Source: adapted from AQA, June 2003

Exam tips
The cross-references are intended to take you straight to the material that will help you to answer the questions.

(a) This question asks you to assess the extent to which the sources agree on two things: the causes of poverty and the solutions to the problem of poverty. The best strategy is probably to deal with the issues one at a time.
   As far as causes are concerned, Source A, although admitting that poverty can be caused by economic and social factors, strongly emphasises the moral failings of the poor as the most important element. In contrast, Source B explicitly blames the workhouse for demoralising the poor, and implicitly suggests that unemployment is beyond the power of the individual to control. You must directly address the issue of extent – in this

case there seems to be little agreement as to the causes of poverty.

There is an element of agreement between the sources on solutions to the extent that they both agree that the current system is failing. They both also see some role for the government. However, while Source A emphasises community action directed more efficiently, Source B is very clear in calling for greater government action, in particular, a national government department headed by a Minister of Labour. So again there is little agreement, with Source B advocating a state collectivist solution in contrast to the voluntary effort implied in Source A.

(b) In order to get high marks for your answer to this question you need to do several things:

- Deal with two issues – whether the Liberals ignored the recommendations of contemporaries and whether they were limited by financial restraint.
- Use both the sources and your own knowledge – this is essential.
- Respond to the question of how valid – you must come to a conclusion that explicitly answers this.

The sources both come from the Royal Commission on the Poor Laws and the majority and minority reports represent two distinct sets of recommendations. Source A implicitly suggests that the state should not get further involved in welfare provision, as it claims that government cannot solve the problems it describes. You need to expand on this and explain the broad position of the majority report – in favour of voluntary and charitable support for the poor underpinned by the deterrent Poor Law (pages 109–10). To an extent, you could argue that the Liberals did listen to these contemporary recommendations, because they did not abolish the Poor Law. On the other hand, old age pensions, national insurance and the regulation of certain wages through the 1909 Trades Board Act all went against the spirit of the majority report recommendations.

The minority report's recommendations were for much greater state intervention (page 110). To a certain extent the Liberal social reforms did respond to this demand – Source C (not a contemporary document but the views of an historian) goes as far as to say that they became recognised as the foundations of the welfare state. On the other hand, the Liberals did not go as far as the minority report wanted. For example, Source B calls for the establishment of a Ministry of Labour, and this is something the Liberals did not create.

The recommendations of other contemporaries were sometimes recognised as solutions by the Liberals, and sometimes not. For instance, Booth's plan for labour colonies (page 95) was not taken up by the Liberals, but they did broadly accept his proposals for old age pensions.

The issue of financial restraint can be illustrated by the terms of the 1908 Old Age Pensions Act (pages 114–15). The terms on which pensions were given could have been more generous, but the government was concerned about the financial implications, even the limitations on the availability of pensions could not prevent them from costing £8 million in 1909. The same argument could be advanced regarding national insurance, as the contributory system was a method of controlling government expenditure. On the other hand, for some Liberals this was an issue of principle rather than finance. There is evidence that government ministers believed that a non-contributory scheme might demoralise the workforce in the way that outdoor relief was alleged to have done in the past.

Make sure you write a concluding paragraph, which addresses both sides of the question, and comes to a clear decision on 'the validity of the view' in each case.

6

War, Depression and the Birth of the Welfare State 1914–48

POINTS TO CONSIDER

Changes in welfare provision in the first half of the twentieth century came about as a result of three things:

- First, the 1914–18 and 1939–45 wars had a huge impact on the way British society and economy were organised. They made people accustomed to a far higher level of state intervention than in the nineteenth century
- Secondly, as Britain became a democratic society, the pressure from below for social reform became a far more powerful influence on those in government
- Finally, the impact of a world depression and mass unemployment in the 1930s forced politicians to look at different ways of responding to this problem

This chapter focuses on three distinct periods:

- The First World War and its impact
- The interwar period 1919–39
- The Second World War and the birth of the welfare state 1939–48

Key dates

1914–18	First World War
1918	Representation of the People Act
1924	First Labour government
1925	Widows', Orphans' and Old Age Contributory Pensions Act
1926	General strike
1929	Poor Law reform/abolition
1929–31	Second Labour government
1939–45	Second World War
1942	Publication of the Beveridge Report
1945–51	Third Labour government
1948	Founding of the National Health Service

Key question
What was the impact of the First World War on British society?

Key date

First World War: 1914–18

Key terms

The Great War
The 1914–18 war. The empires of Britain, Russia and France fought against those of Germany, Austria-Hungary and Turkey. In 1917 the USA joined the war on the side of Britain and its allies.

Coalition government
A government made up of more than one political party.

1 | The First World War and its Impact

The war and politics

In August 1914 the Liberal government led by H.H. Asquith declared war on Germany. Despite predictions that it would be over by Christmas, **'the Great War'**, as it came to be known, lasted for four years and became the bloodiest conflict in history. For the first time rival nations pitted not just their armed forces but the entire resources of their societies and empires against one another.

The Liberal Party, even though it had introduced major welfare reforms such as national insurance and old age pensions, was still committed to a fundamentally *laissez-faire* approach to economy and society. It soon became clear, however, that this approach was unsustainable when faced with the demands of industrialised warfare. A much greater level of government intervention was required in order to mobilise Britain's people and resources to fight the war efficiently. For many Liberals this was too much and, by 1916, the party had split into two factions. Asquith was replaced by the more dynamic David Lloyd George as the head of a **coalition government**, which, since 1915, contained representatives from the Conservative and Labour parties as well as Liberals. The Liberals were never again to govern by themselves and this marked a fundamental shift in the balance of British politics.

Wartime economy and society

The First World War was an industrial war. Whole populations had to be mobilised for the war effort, in order to supply the massive amounts of weaponry and munitions required by the armies, navies and air forces of the combatants. Even before the end of Asquith's administration, the government had been forced to take drastic measures to fight the war. The 1914 Defence of the Realm Act (DORA) and its later amendments gave the government emergency powers to regulate many areas of British life that had been hitherto free of government interference:

- Controls were placed on trade, smashing the Liberals' cherished belief in free trade.
- Industries were directed to switch production to goods that were needed for the war effort.
- Railways were taken away from their private owners and placed under direct government control.
- The government imposed strict regulations on workers in key industries such as mining and munitions. For example, they were not allowed to change jobs without government permission.
- Newspapers were censored in order to protect the morale of citizens.
- Public-house opening hours were restricted in order to keep workers efficiently sober. Beer was watered down and drinkers were prohibited from buying alcohol for their companions.

In 1916 **conscription** was introduced. Young men were now obliged to join the armed forces whether they wanted to or not. By 1918, both prices of goods and private rents were under state control and food rationing had been introduced. Never before had government intervened so thoroughly in so many aspects of the life of the nation.

Despite the increase in government regulation and control, there was little improvement in welfare or the alleviation of poverty. Some limited measures were taken both for 'national efficiency' (see page 107) and to preserve the morale of the population:

see page 107

- In October 1914, family allowances were introduced for members of the armed forces.
- In 1915, pensions were introduced for the widows of those killed in the war.
- Regulations were introduced to safeguard and improve the welfare of munitions workers.
- In 1916, national insurance was extended to cover most workers.

But substantial reforms were postponed until after the war.

The consequences of the war

Over 750,000 British people were killed in the First World War and 1.6 million were wounded, but by 1918 Britain had emerged victorious. In four distinct ways the war had profound consequences for the future treatment of poverty.

The rise of Labour

Political developments during the war created the conditions where the demand for state welfare was to become much more compelling. In 1918 Parliament passed the Representation of the People Act. All working-class men and some women were given the right to vote for the first time and the electorate rose to 21 million people. Many of these new voters were poor or potentially poor and had a direct interest in supporting parties who were pledged to tackle poverty and improve welfare. The Labour Party (see page 102), which was committed to helping the working class, was now in an excellent position to seize political power. Labour's urban heartlands were the very places where the increase in the number of voters was most pronounced. More than this, the war had split the Liberal Party and so Labour had a tremendous opportunity to replace them as the main alternative to the Conservatives. Indeed, Labour went on to form its first government in 1924 and achieved power for a second time in 1929.

see page 102

Key term

Conscription
The compulsory enlistment of men into the armed forces.

Key dates

Representation of the People Act: 1918

First Labour government: 1924

Second Labour government: 1929–31

Russian Revolution
In 1917 the world's first Communist revolution took place when the Bolsheviks overthrew the dictatorial Tsarist monarchy. Some people believed that this would lead to a series of socialist revolutions throughout the industrialised world.

National debt
The total amount of money owed by a government.

Versailles Treaties
The peace treaties at the end of the First World War. Germany and her allies had their armed forces limited and their empires dismantled. Germany was forced to pay large amounts of money to France to compensate for wartime destruction.

State intervention

Important precedents had been established for greater state intervention during the war. If government control, rather than private enterprise, had been the best way to win the war, surely the same recipe would be best to deal with peacetime problems? Lloyd George certainly recognised that the war had created possibilities that had not existed before 1914. 'The whole state of society', he believed, 'is more or less molten and you can stamp upon that molten mass almost anything … the country will be prepared for bigger things immediately after the war.'

A better future

Thirdly, in order to keep the population loyal during the war, promises of a better future had been made. The government was seriously worried that the workers might turn against the war effort and the spectre of the **Russian Revolution** added to the fear of a revolution in Britain. Lloyd George had pledged that the government would build 'homes fit for heroes'. Even more conservative politicians accepted that improvements in welfare had to be made for the sake of social stability.

The cost of war

However, the fourth major consequence of the war created a major obstacle to possible improvements in state welfare. Victory in the war cost Britain dearly. In 1914 Britain was still the greatest trading nation on earth, but by 1918 much of that trade had been disrupted. Economic rivals such as the USA were major beneficiaries. Britain had borrowed heavily in order to fight the war so that the **national debt** had risen from £650 million at the start of the war to £7500 million at its end. The British Empire expanded to its greatest extent following the 1919 **Versailles Treaties**, but even this was a burden: in the early 1920s the cost to the British government of ruling Iraq was greater than the entire expenditure on health at home. These financial pressures were to put a severe limit on plans to improve state welfare provision despite the social and political pressure for change.

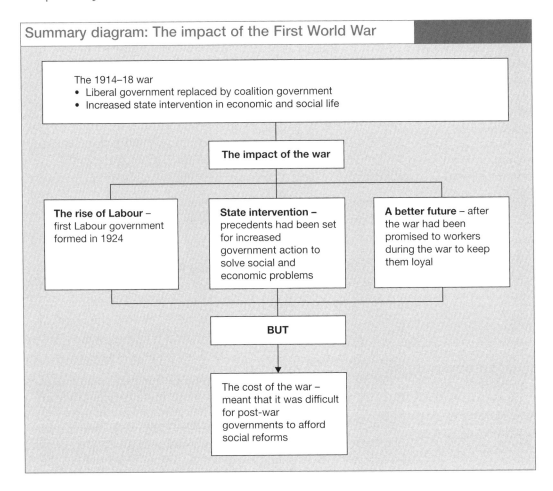

Summary diagram: The impact of the First World War

The 1914–18 war
- Liberal government replaced by coalition government
- Increased state intervention in economic and social life

The impact of the war

The rise of Labour – first Labour government formed in 1924

State intervention – precedents had been set for increased government action to solve social and economic problems

A better future – after the war had been promised to workers during the war to keep them loyal

BUT

The cost of the war – meant that it was difficult for post-war governments to afford social reforms

2 | The Interwar Period 1919–39

Key question
What problems did the interwar governments face in dealing with poverty and welfare?

During the 1920s and 1930s, Britain was governed by a variety of administrations (see Table 6.1). These governments were faced with similar problems, whatever their political persuasion. However, the depression after 1929 made the issue of unemployment dominant in the 1930s.

The housing crisis

Poor-quality housing had been one of the most obvious features of working-class poverty since the industrial revolution. There was some progress in the late nineteenth century when philanthropists, like George Peabody, started to build decent homes for working people at affordable rents. The state had also made some efforts to clear slums and provide the first council housing through the 1875 Artisans and Labourers' Dwellings Act and the 1890 Housing of the Working Classes Act. However these efforts only scratched the surface of the problem.

By 1918 there was an additional problem. Rents had been kept down through government controls introduced during the war. This, combined with rising building costs, made it unprofitable for private developers to build new working-class housing. The

Table 6.1: British governments of the interwar period

Dates	Government	Composition	Prime Minister
1918–22	National Government	Coalition of Conservatives and Liberals who followed Lloyd George	David Lloyd George
1922–4	Conservative	Conservative	Andrew Bonar Law (1922–3); Stanley Baldwin (1923–4)
1924	Labour	Labour **minority government** supported by Liberals	James Ramsay MacDonald
1924–9	Conservative	Conservative	Stanley Baldwin
1929–31	Labour	Labour minority government supported by Liberals	James Ramsay MacDonald
1931–40	National government	Conservative-dominated coalition which also included Liberals and Labour MPs who were loyal to MacDonald	James Ramsay MacDonald (1931–5); Stanley Baldwin (1935–7); Neville Chamberlain (1937–9)

Key term

Minority government
If a political party fails to win the majority of seats in the House of Commons it can still become the government with the temporary support of another political party.

only way that Lloyd George's promise of 'homes fit for heroes' could be delivered was through state-funded social housing.

Two important Acts of Parliament in the post-war years established council housing as a major solution to housing poverty. The 1919 Housing and Town Planning Act made it compulsory for local councils to deal with housing problems in their areas and provided government money to help them to build new housing. As a result 213,000 council homes were built between 1919 and 1922. However, it was at this point that the financial consequences of the war started to bite. The programme was scrapped as part of a series of cost-cutting measures and the minister responsible for housing, Christopher Addison, was sacked.

The 1924 Housing Act

Labour's success in the November 1923 General Election partly resulted from the failure of the post-war coalition government to maintain the housing programme. Labour's manifesto had promised to 'abolish the slums' and 'promptly build an adequate supply of new homes'. The 1924 Housing Act was probably the most important achievement of the short-lived 1924 Labour government. The Act revived the main features of its 1919 predecessor by again providing government subsidies to local councils for house building. By 1931, half a million homes had been constructed. This represented a substantial attack on the problem of poor housing and established the principle of state-funded council housing as the main solution to this problem.

Widows, orphans and the aged

One of the most important of the pre-war Liberal social reforms had been the 1908 Old Age Pensions Act, which introduced non-contributory pensions for people over 70 (see page 114). However, the scheme had a number of weaknesses:

Widows', Orphans' and Old Age Contributory Pensions Act: 1925

Poor Law reform/abolition: 1929

Key dates

- First, many workers did not live to 70. Those who did live that long were often unable to work through their sixties and so were forced to seek help from the Poor Law until they reached pensionable age.
- Secondly, the pension was means tested, which reduced the benefits available for pensioners who had a small additional income.
- Thirdly, there was no provision for the families of male workers who died. The surveys of Booth and Rowntree had identified death of the main wage earner as a major cause of poverty.

Minister of Health Neville Chamberlain's 1925 Widows', Orphans' and Old Age Contributory Pensions Act attempted to deal with these problems. Workers who were in the insurance scheme now paid a weekly contribution which was matched by their employer and topped up by the state. Pensions were no longer to be means tested and could be claimed from the age of 65. If an insured worker died, benefits were payable to his widow and children.

The Act was passed despite the opposition of the industrial insurance companies and friendly societies (see page 77), who believed that it represented state encroachment on their territory. These interests had been powerful enough to block the reform of the Poor Law in the first decade of the century. It is significant that in 1925 even a Conservative government was prepared to ignore their protests. The political pressure for extended state intervention was becoming stronger.

The dismantling of the Poor Law

The introduction of old age pensions and national insurance meant that many people faced with poverty were now assisted outside the Poor Law. However, for those outside the insurance schemes, the Poor Law remained the last resort and it still carried all the stigma and fear associated with the workhouse. Increased democracy after the First World War had a direct effect on the Poor Law, as socialist candidates stood for election to the boards of guardians. Once elected these left-wing guardians made it their mission to provide much more generous help to Poor Law applicants.

The most famous example of this movement came in Poplar, east London, where the future Labour Party leader George Lansbury highlighted the inadequacies of the Poor Law and

Key term

Poplarism
Used to describe
left-wing boards of
guardians, like
those in Poplar, east
London, who used
their position to
raise the levels of
relief and the
general conditions
provided for Poor
Law applicants.

provided higher levels of outdoor relief to the elderly and the
unemployed. Lansbury was eventually removed from his position
as a guardian by the Conservative government in 1926. But
'**Poplarism**' had a strong impact and even the Conservatives had
come to accept that the Poor Law was not a suitable welfare
system for the twentieth century. The 1929 Local Government Act
abolished the boards of guardians and transferred their powers to
local councils. Councils already had committees overseeing
services for children, the elderly and the sick and these took over
the work of the Poor Law in each area. New Public Assistance
Committees were established by each council to supervise benefits
for the able-bodied unemployed who were not covered by
national insurance. Finally, Poor Law medical facilities were
transferred to local councils. The Poor Law was not officially
abolished until 1948 but the result of the 1929 Act was that most
aspects of it were absorbed into the local government system.

Mass unemployment

The biggest social problem of the interwar period was
undoubtedly mass unemployment (see Table 6.2). Since the
industrial revolution unemployment had been a significant cause
of poverty but the unemployment of the 1920s and, particularly,
the 1930s was on a scale that threatened to shatter the entire
social and political structure. In Germany, mass unemployment
resulted in the collapse of democracy and the establishment of
Hitler's Nazi state. In Britain, there were also fears that mass
unemployment could lead to a fascist dictatorship or a
Communist revolution.

Table 6.2: Unemployment in Britain between the wars

Year	Number unemployed (millions)	Workforce unemployed (per cent)
1921	2.2	12.2
1922	1.9	10.8
1923	1.6	8.9
1924	1.4	7.9
1925	1.6	8.6
1926	1.8	9.6
1927	1.4	7.4
1928	1.5	8.2
1929	1.5	8.0
1930	2.4	12.3
1931	3.3	16.4
1932	3.4	17.0
1933	3.1	15.4
1934	2.6	12.9
1935	2.4	12.0
1936	2.1	10.2
1937	1.8	8.5
1938	2.2	10.1

Source: adapted from W.R. Garside, *British Unemployment
1919–1939*, Table 2, page 5.

Causes of unemployment

The immediate post-war problem of unemployment resulted from the structural weaknesses of the British economy. Many of Britain's industries, such as coal-mining, shipbuilding and textiles, were outdated and were facing heavy competition from rising new economies like the USA. The situation was already problematic before 1914 but the disruption of Britain's trade during the war had made things even worse. Throughout the 1920s unemployment did not fall below one million. But the **Wall Street Crash** of 1929, and subsequent world depression, led to workers being laid off on a huge scale. By 1932 there were 3.4 million unemployed, 17 per cent of the workforce, of whom nearly half a million were long-term unemployed. Officially this was defined as going a year without having three consecutive days in work.

Effects of unemployment

Unemployment caused tremendous physical and psychological suffering. Unemployment benefit was hardly enough to live on. Many families at the time reported that they could get through the weekend reasonably well fed, but struggled in mid-week as the money began to run out. As unemployed Nottinghamshire miner George Tomlinson recorded in 1937:

> Monday and Tuesday are not too bad. There is usually a bit of meat from the 'Sunday joint', and with a few potatoes and greens it is possible to make a decent meal or two. It is on Wednesday and Thursday that the real pinch comes.

As with poverty in the nineteenth century, careful budgeting was essential: any expenditure beyond the absolute necessities was likely to result in hunger. Often it was the women in unemployed families who would deprive themselves in order to feed their children and husband, who was seen as the bread-winner in the household. An inquiry by the **Pilgrim Trust** found that a third of the wives of unemployed men in Liverpool suffered from ill-health. Other investigations across the country reported similar findings. With long-term unemployment came a sense of frustration and loss of self-esteem. People were not only impoverished but felt rejected by society.

Unemployment policies

All governments in the 1920s and 1930s faced the same dilemma when confronted with the problem of mass unemployment. How could millions of people be maintained at some sort of basic level, whilst retaining incentives to work, and without a crippling financial cost to the state? In attempting to answer this question governments responded differently from their predecessors in two important ways.

First, it was recognised that attempting to relieve mass unemployment by the workhouse was no longer a practical or desirable option. In the aftermath of the 1926 **General Strike** the

Key terms

Wall Street Crash
In 1929 the price of shares on the New York stock exchange in Wall Street fell rapidly. Many investors went bankrupt and confidence drained from business. Companies started to reduce their workforces and many collapsed. The result was mass unemployment that spread throughout the industrialised world.

Pilgrim Trust
A charity that carried out studies into unemployment in the 1930s.

General Strike
In 1926 all the major trade unions went on strike in support of the miners, whose pay and conditions were being attacked by the coal owners. The strike ended without success.

Key date

General Strike: 1926

threat of the workhouse was used to intimidate striking coal miners. But, in general, outdoor relief was provided to uninsured workers, and the 1929 Local Government Act, in effect, abandoned the workhouse test. For most of the able-bodied unemployed between the wars, relief was given through national unemployment insurance benefits.

The second major change was in the way the national unemployment scheme was administered. The 1911 Act was strictly based on the insurance principle: the assumption was that the amount being paid into the scheme by insured workers, their employers and the state would be sufficient to cover the benefits paid to the unemployed. The problem with this assumption was that it was based on an average unemployment rate of 5.32 per cent and assumed that workers would only be unemployed for short periods. Benefits were only paid for the first 15 weeks of unemployment.

In the 1920s, the rate never fell below 10 per cent and much unemployment was long term. To make the scheme financially balance, governments had to choose between savage cuts in benefits, unaffordable increases in contributions or increased subsidies by the state. In the immediate post-war years the first two options were politically impossible so the third option was implemented.

The 1921 Unemployment Insurance Act allowed the long-term unemployed to claim **'uncovenanted' benefit** (known as extended benefit between 1924 and 1928) once their 15 weeks had expired. It also created a system of payments for dependants. Because this was financed by extra treasury payments, it broke with the idea of a balanced self-financing insurance system: there was potentially no limit to the amount of money governments would need to pour into the insurance fund.

In all, 18 Acts of Parliament were passed between 1920 and 1930 in order to shore up the system, with 'transitional' relief being introduced in 1927 for those who had paid no contributions into the scheme. For government the problem only got worse, with more and more money being required to subsidise the insurance fund, which by 1931 was £115 million in deficit. In that year, with the economy in crisis following the 1929 Crash, the Labour government was confronted with two reports recommending the options that had been rejected for the previous 12 years. Both the Royal Commission on Unemployment and the **May Committee** recommended cuts in benefits and increased contributions as the only way to balance the budget. As a result, in September 1931 benefits were reduced by 10 per cent, standard benefits were limited to 26 weeks and transitional benefits became dependent on a stringent 'means test'.

In 1934, following a decline in the number out of work, the **national government** restored the 10 per cent cut and replaced the local Public Assistance Committees (PACs) with centrally appointed and controlled Unemployment Assistance Boards (UABs). Welfare for the unemployed was now clearly seen as a national, state responsibility.

Key terms

Uncovenanted benefit
A payment made to unemployed workers who had exhausted their entitlement under the national insurance scheme.

May Committee
A group set up to look into the financial crisis faced by the government. The committee was dominated by bankers and, in August 1931, recommended large cuts in public expenditure.

National government
Many Labour ministers refused to go along with the cuts in unemployment benefit that the May Committee had recommended. In response, in August 1931, the Labour Prime Minister Ramsay MacDonald and a group of supporters joined with the Conservatives and some Liberals to form a coalition 'national' government.

I KNOW 3 TRADES
I SPEAK 3 LANGUAGES
FOUGHT FOR 3 YEARS
HAVE 3 CHILDREN
AND NO WORK FOR
3 MONTHS
BUT I ONLY WANT
ONE JOB

A man makes his own protest against unemployment in 1935.

The means test

For those on the receiving end of these policy twists and turns, the balancing of budgets was a much more personal and immediate matter. The terms on which benefit was offered came to be a cause of even more hatred. Governments had felt the need to put in place measures to replace the workhouse test with alternative ways of being 'tough' with claimants. In the 1920s the Not Genuinely Seeking Work Clause had forced workers to prove that they were actively looking for work, even in areas where there was clearly none to be found.

The means test was a step further. In assessing entitlement to benefit, the PACs and UABs took into consideration the income of everyone in the household, including children and elderly relatives. This inquisition could have a terrible impact on family life. In 1933, a skilled engineer, married for 20 years, wrote of the strain on his marriage caused by unemployment. His wife had managed to get a part-time job as a house-to-house saleswoman,

The Jarrow Crusade. In 1936 200 workers from the town of Jarrow, in north-east England, marched 300 miles to London to highlight the poverty their community was facing. Seventy per cent of Jarrow's workers were unemployed and facing extreme poverty. The march had little immediate effect but it became a powerful symbol of the problem of mass unemployment.

but under the means test the engineer knew that if he revealed his wife's earnings his benefits would be cut:

> If that happened, home life would become impossible. When, therefore, I was sent a form on which to give details of our total income I neglected to fill it up. For this I was suspended benefit for six weeks. This was the last straw. Quarrels broke out anew and bitter things were said. Eventually, after the most heartbreaking period of my life, both my wife and my son, who had just commenced to earn a few shillings, told me to get out, as I was living on them and taking the food they needed.

The Labour MP Aneurin Bevan, who fought for the rights of the unemployed both in Parliament and locally as a member of the Monmouthshire Public Assistance Committee, described the means test as 'a principle that eats like acid into the homes of the poor'. Labour **left-wingers** like Bevan, and groups like the National Unemployed Workers Union, organised widespread campaigns against the means test and the way the benefit regulations were interpreted. When Labour came to power in 1945, they would be determined to prevent mass unemployment from happening again.

Key term

Left-winger
A member of the more radical section of the Labour Party who wanted more socialist policies to extend state control of the economy and distribute wealth in favour of the working class.

Profile: Aneurin Bevan 1897–1960

1897 – Born in Tredegar, Monmouthshire
1910 – Became a coal miner at the age of 13. Soon joined the Labour Party and became active in the Miners' Union
1919 – Went to London on sponsorship to study at the Central Labour College
1921 – Returned to Wales. Unemployed but became an unpaid advisor in his local community
1925 – Appointed as a union official
1928 – Elected to Monmouthshire County Council
1929 – Elected MP for Ebbw Vale constituency
1936 – Member of group that founded the left-wing newspaper *Tribune*
1939 – Expelled from the Labour Party and then re-admitted
1942 – Became Editor of *Tribune*
1945 – Became Minister of Health
1951 – Became Minister of Labour
1951 – Resigned from government
1956 – Shadow Foreign Secretary
1959 – Became Deputy Leader of Labour Party
1960 – Died of cancer

Early life

Aneurin Bevan was born into a mining family in South Wales. One of 10 children, he experienced poverty in his early years and left school at the age of 13 to become a coal miner. He soon became politically active, joining both the Labour Party and the Miners' Union. He began studying in his spare time and at the end of the First World War, Bevan gained a scholarship to study Economics, Politics and History at the Central Labour College in London. Here he was impressed by the ideas of Karl Marx. On his return to Wales, the mine owners saw him as a potential troublemaker and he was unable to find work in the pits. After several years of unemployment Bevan was appointed in 1925 as a trade union official and he was a prominent local leader of the 1926 General Strike.

Political career

In 1928, Bevan was elected to Monmouthshire County Council and, in the following year, was elected MP for the constituency of Ebbw Vale. He opposed the policy of cuts pursued by the Labour government and was a fierce critic of Ramsay MacDonald's decision to leave the Labour Party in 1931 and form a coalition 'national' government with the Conservatives and Liberals.

Throughout the 1930s and early 1940s, Aneurin Bevan was one of the leading left-wing members of the Labour Party. He wanted to work with left-wing groups outside the Labour Party in order to fight the policies of the national government and he was briefly expelled from the Party in 1939 for pursuing this policy. His main pre-occupation in the 1930s was unemployment and the operation of the means test. He worked hard to defend his unemployed constituents against cuts in benefits imposed by the local PACs. In 1936, along with like-minded MPs, Bevan established the left-wing weekly newspaper *Tribune* and in 1942 he became *Tribune*'s Editor. He used this position to campaign for greater social reform.

In government
When Labour came to power in 1945, Bevan was appointed Minister of Health. In this important position he steered the National Health Service Act through Parliament and, between 1948 and 1951, he supervised the setting up of the NHS. In 1951 Bevan briefly became Minister of Labour but resigned from the government when the Cabinet decided to introduce charges for spectacles, dentures and medical prescriptions.

Later career
After his resignation, Bevan became the unofficial leader of Labour's left wing and a critic of the leadership. Labour had lost the general election of 1951 and lost again in 1955. Bevan was never again to be in government but, in his latter years, he became more reconciled to the party's leadership. He became Deputy Leader of the Labour Party in the year before his death.

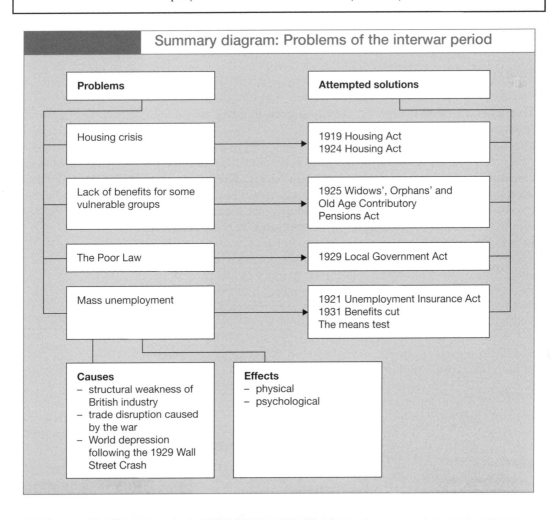

Summary diagram: Problems of the interwar period

Problems

Attempted solutions

Housing crisis → 1919 Housing Act / 1924 Housing Act

Lack of benefits for some vulnerable groups → 1925 Widows', Orphans' and Old Age Contributory Pensions Act

The Poor Law → 1929 Local Government Act

Mass unemployment → 1921 Unemployment Insurance Act / 1931 Benefits cut / The means test

Causes
- structural weakness of British industry
- trade disruption caused by the war
- World depression following the 1929 Wall Street Crash

Effects
- physical
- psychological

3 | The Second World War and the Birth of the Welfare State 1939–48

Second World War: 1939–45

Key date

The 1939–45 war had a profound impact on the provision of welfare in Britain. The war changed attitudes within Britain and led to the election of the first majority Labour government. This government was committed to improving welfare for Britain's population.

The Second World War and British politics

In 1939 the Conservative-dominated national coalition government declared war, following Nazi Germany's invasion of Poland. To many the war was the product of the failed foreign policy of **appeasement** pursued by the Conservatives.

Within a year Neville Chamberlain had been replaced as Prime Minister by Winston Churchill, one of the few Conservatives who had opposed appeasement. Churchill brought some of the leading Labour politicians into his wartime coalition cabinet – Clement Atlee as Deputy Prime Minister, Herbert Morrison as Home Secretary and Ernest Bevin as Minister of Labour and National Service. In the dark days of 1940, Britain stood alone against the might of Nazi Germany. But, with the USA and the USSR entering the war in 1941 as Britain's allies, the tide gradually turned and by 1945 British, US and Soviet troops had occupied Berlin. The involvement of leading Labour politicians in successful wartime government was an important factor in Labour's election victory in 1945.

Key question
What was the impact of the Second World War on British politics?

Appeasement
The foreign policy pursued by British governments in the 1930s that aimed to avoid war by making concessions to the demands of the German and Italian dictators Hitler and Mussolini.

Key term

The impact of the war on welfare provision
A sense of community

The Second World War had an impact on welfare provision in a variety of ways. As in the 1914–18 conflict, the government was forced to intervene much more directly in social and economic affairs in order to mobilise the nation's total resources to fight the war. Industries came under direct state control, food and essential supplies were rationed and men were conscripted into the armed forces. The sense of sharing a common experience was especially felt through food rationing, which was applied to rich and poor alike. This collectivist response to the emergency of war proved successful. Many people became convinced that a more thoroughly planned, state-directed solution to peacetime problems such as poverty and unemployment might be effective.

The promise of a better world after the war was also an important ingredient in the journalism and film making designed to keep up wartime morale. As **J.B. Priestley** commented in one of his Sunday evening *Postscripts* broadcasts heard by millions in 1940, 'We're actually changing over from the property view to the sense of community, which simply means we realise we're all in the same boat'. For Priestley, as with other left-wingers who now found themselves in positions of influence, 'the sense of community' meant a much greater role for government in welfare provision.

Key question
What was the impact of the Second World War on ideas about poverty and welfare?

J.B. Priestley
A playwright, novelist and left-wing commentator whose broadcasts on the BBC in 1940 were listened to by an estimated 40 per cent of the population.

Key term

Key date

Publication of the
Beveridge Report:
1942

Evacuation

One of the things that certainly put Britons from different social classes in the same houses, if not in the same boat, was the evacuation policy which began in 1939. The general belief that 'the bomber would always get through' resulted in the voluntary removal of children and pregnant women from high-risk target areas to safer countryside areas. Some 827,000 unaccompanied school-age children were evacuated in the early years of the war, along with 524,000 mothers with very young children and several thousand pregnant women.

Inevitably, the evacuees came from poor inner-city areas, and the middle-class families, with whom they were billeted were horrified at their condition and insanitary habits. They were particularly scandalised by the fact that many of the evacuees suffered from vermin such as head lice. One of the early myths of the Second World War home front was that the evacuees received a universally warm welcome from the families with whom they were placed. This showed that everyone was 'pulling together'. In fact the subsequent testimonies of many evacuees showed that they were often treated as second-class citizens and many returned to the cities to face German bombs in preference to their unhappy lives in the countryside. Nevertheless, the experience of the evacuation, even if they didn't particularly like it, did bring home to many comfortably well-off British families the reality of inner-city poverty in a unique way. This undoubtedly made many usually conservative people more willing to accept post-war proposals for the reform of the welfare system.

The Beveridge Report

The Beveridge Report of 1942 was the clearest expression of the new and more radical approach to poverty and welfare that had developed in the early years of the war. Commissioned by the Labour Minister for Reconstruction, Arthur Greenwood, the report set out a vision of a 'welfare state' that would provide for all citizens 'from the cradle to the grave'. Previous Poor Law and unemployment policies had been preoccupied with distinguishing between the deserving and the undeserving and achieving a balanced budget. The Beveridge Report had a much more generous attitude towards the poor, concentrating on providing universal benefits on the basis of need. It also proposed that the power of the state should be used to provide full employment. Beveridge outlined the principles of his plan:

> The first principle is that any proposals for the future, while they should use to the full the experience gathered in the past, should not be restricted by consideration of sectional interests established in the obtaining of that experience. Now, when the war is abolishing landmarks of every kind, is the opportunity for using experience in a clear field. A revolutionary moment in the world's history is a time for revolutions, not for patching.
>
> The second principle is that organisation of social insurance should be treated as one part only of a comprehensive policy of

social progress. Social insurance fully developed may provide income security; it is an attack upon Want. But Want is one only of five giants on the road of reconstruction and in some ways the easiest to attack. The others are Disease, Ignorance, Squalor and Idleness.

The report proposed a system of social insurance based on **flat-rate** contributions. Payments would be made to those in need without a means test. Family allowances would be available to all, again without a means test. The 'giant' of disease was to be tackled by means of a universal health service. The report sold over 600,000 copies – a remarkable number considering this was wartime. Opinion polls at the time suggested that nine out of ten people were in favour of Beveridge's proposals.

Flat-rate
In a flat-rate system everybody pays the same contribution or receives the same benefit.

Key term

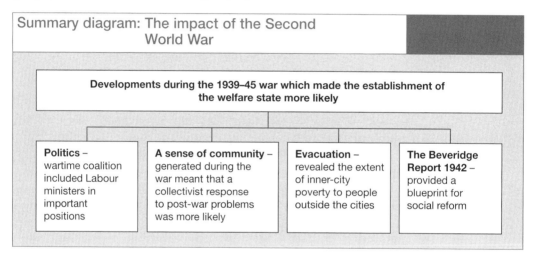

Summary diagram: The impact of the Second World War

Developments during the 1939–45 war which made the establishment of the welfare state more likely

| Politics – wartime coalition included Labour ministers in important positions | A sense of community – generated during the war meant that a collectivist response to post-war problems was more likely | Evacuation – revealed the extent of inner-city poverty to people outside the cities | The Beveridge Report 1942 – provided a blueprint for social reform |

4 | The Achievements of the Labour Government

Labour's victory

In the 1945 General Election the Labour Party achieved a remarkable victory, winning 394 seats in parliament with 48 per cent of the vote. In their election manifesto, *Let Us Face the Future*, Labour had promised:

- to increase government control over industry
- to establish a National Health Service
- to extend social insurance
- to pursue a policy of full employment.

These things were popular with voters, who wanted to live in a better society, having survived the trauma of war. Despite the popular respect for Churchill's wartime leadership, his party was unpopular, being identified with both the depression of the 1930s and the failed policy of appeasement. Moreover, despite Churchill's acceptance of the need for welfare reform, his wartime

Key question
How did the Labour government establish the 'welfare state'?

Third Labour government: 1945–51

Key date

A Labour Party general election poster from 1945. The poster was intended to encourage women to discuss the election and Labour's proposals with their husbands, fathers and sons who were still serving in the armed forces. The poster clearly associates the war against the dictators with the 'battle' for a better Britain. Another key labour slogan in the election was 'and now, win the peace'.

administration had been criticised for failing to act on the Beveridge proposals in the years since 1942. Churchill's ill-judged attack on Labour during the election campaign, when he warned that a socialist government would be forced to employ **Gestapo-like** methods to enforce their policies, helped to alienate moderate voters, who had spent the last five years fighting the Nazis, and respected the role that the Labour Party had played in that struggle. The votes of the armed forces were a significant factor in Labour's victory.

Labour's achievements

Labour's achievements in building a welfare state based on Beveridge's plan were impressive, especially considering the damage that the war had inflicted on the economy. Two initiatives in the last days of the wartime coalition aimed to combat the problems of ignorance and idleness:

- The 1944 Education Act for the first time established the principle of universal free secondary education for all children and the Labour government ensured that this was implemented.
- The 1944 **white paper** on employment policy officially set out the idea that the state should use public spending as a means to prevent unemployment by both stimulating the economy and employing people directly. The Labour government accepted this proposal and post-war government spending was

Key terms

Gestapo-like
The Gestapo were the secret state police in Hitler's Germany. They were notorious for their brutal treatment of opponents.

White paper
A government policy proposal.

explicitly used to give people jobs, rather than pay them to be unemployed.

Founding of the National Health Service: 1948

Key date

The government also produced new legislation to deal with Beveridge's other 'giants on the road to reconstruction'. In terms of welfare, a new and comprehensive 'cradle to grave' social insurance system was established through four Acts of Parliament:

- *Family allowances*. The 1945 Family Allowances Act provided a universal flat rate five shilling per child payment for second and subsequent children. This was an entitlement for all families, whatever their income, and was financed directly by the state – no contributions were necessary.
- *Industrial injuries*. The 1946 National Insurance (Industrial Injuries) Act established benefits for the victims of accidents at work or illness caused by work (e.g. respiratory diseases suffered by coal miners). This was to be financed from the national insurance fund.
- *National insurance*. The 1946 National Insurance Act was the centrepiece of the social insurance legislation. The Act brought together unemployment and sickness benefits, old-age pensions, maternity and widows' benefits, guardians' allowances for orphans and death grants to cover funeral expenses. All these were now flat-rate benefits provided in return for flat-rate contributions on a weekly basis. The standard payment for sickness, unemployment and old-age was set at 26s per week, which was a significant increase from the previous level of benefit. Additional payments were made for dependants.
- *National Assistance Board*. Finally, the 1948 National Assistance Act established a National Assistance Board, which was to provide means-tested benefits for people who had no entitlement to insurance benefits or for whom the benefits were insufficient. The Board replaced the local Public Assistance Committees and the Act explicitly abolished the remaining aspects of the Poor Law. Beveridge himself was opposed to national assistance as it was non-contributory.

Together these four Acts provided a social security system that was designed to provide a safety net against destitution for the whole population. It would replace the Poor Law, the industrial insurance societies and the previous unemployment benefit regime. A total of 50 million leaflets were distributed to every home to publicise the new system, which was formally launched in July 1948.

The National Health Service

The Labour government's most ambitious project, the National Health Service (NHS), was also launched in July 1948. Before the war, medical treatment had been provided in a wide variety of ways. Doctors were independent and charged for their services, although some of these costs could be covered by the national insurance scheme, as well as the industrial and private insurance companies. Hospitals were sometimes private, sometimes voluntary (i.e charities) and the former Poor Law hospitals were administered by local authorities. The result of this patchwork was that the quality and quantity of health care varied from one area to another and many people could not afford to pay for the medical attention they needed.

The aim of the 1946 National Health Service Act was to provide free health care for all citizens through a national system. This Act was opposed by a number of interests:

- The Conservatives opposed it on the grounds that it would be too costly.
- The main organisation representing doctors, the British Medical Association (BMA), objected that they would lose their independence (and their opportunity to make money) if they became salaried employees of the state.
- Hospital consultants (senior medical specialists) also feared that they would lose their ability to charge for private patients under the new system.

Aneurin Bevan, Labour's Minister of Health, tackled this opposition in two ways. First, all the existing hospitals were nationalised (taken over by the state) but the old teaching hospitals, such as St Thomas's and Barts in London, were allowed to retain a level of independence through their own boards of governors. Moreover, the consultants would be allowed to continue their lucrative private work on top of their NHS work. Secondly, the general practitioners did not become salaried officials but instead were paid a sum of money for every patient on their NHS list. All citizens were entitled to join a list. So everyone could now see a local doctor for free and be treated for free, or be referred for free treatment at an NHS hospital. Compared to the previous situation, where ill-health had been a major cause of poverty for large sections of the population, this was a massive improvement in the provision of welfare in the UK.

The reforms of the Labour government were in part radical extensions of the role of the state and, in part, evolutionary developments built on previous legislation. The scale of the reforms gives a good idea of their impact on British society: 25 million people were issued with national insurance numbers under the social insurance system and there were over 200 million NHS prescriptions for medicine in 1951.

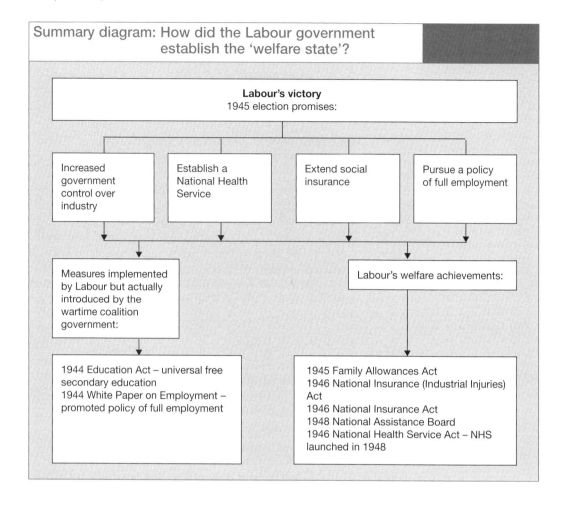

Summary diagram: How did the Labour government establish the 'welfare state'?

Labour's victory
1945 election promises:

- Increased government control over industry
- Establish a National Health Service
- Extend social insurance
- Pursue a policy of full employment

Measures implemented by Labour but actually introduced by the wartime coalition government:

Labour's welfare achievements:

1944 Education Act – universal free secondary education
1944 White Paper on Employment – promoted policy of full employment

1945 Family Allowances Act
1946 National Insurance (Industrial Injuries) Act
1946 National Insurance Act
1948 National Assistance Board
1946 National Health Service Act – NHS launched in 1948

Study Guide: Advanced Level Question

In the style of OCR

How far is the creation of the welfare state by 1948 explained by pressure from the working class?

Source: OCR, January 2005

Exam tips

The cross-references are intended to take you straight to the material that will help you to answer the question.

Any question beginning 'how far' or 'to what extent' requires you to compare one factor against a range of others and come to a balanced judgement. In this case the question is concerned with causation: why was the welfare state created by 1948? Was it just because of pressure from the working class or did other factors play a part? Because this question is from the 'synoptic themes' paper it is important for you to show patterns of continuity, development and change over a long period.

- You need to show how working-class pressure for social reform developed over a long period. For example, you can point out that the growth of a mass electorate in the late nineteenth century began to force politicians to consider increased state intervention. The Liberals were responding to political pressure when they introduced the social reforms of 1906–14 (pages 103–4). During the interwar period this working-class political pressure continued but it was only in 1945–48 that it resulted in the establishment of the welfare state.
- On the other hand, it can be argued that other concerns led to greater state intervention, for example the concerns about 'national efficiency' (pages 107–8). Again, you need to trace this through the whole period – you may think that it was a more important influence in some periods than others.
- You need to examine the circumstances that led to the election of the Labour Party in 1945 and the subsequent creation of the welfare state. Clearly working-class pressure had a part to play, but the wartime experience of many British citizens of all classes led them to accept the need for an expansion of state welfare (pages 148–50).
- You need to show the relationship between all these factors.
- In your conclusion, based on the evidence you have produced, you must come to a balanced judgement. You may conclude that working-class pressure was the dominant factor in the creation of the welfare state or you may conclude that it was one of a range of factors, not necessarily the dominant one.

7 Conclusion: Change and Continuity

POINTS TO CONSIDER

This final chapter draws together some of the major themes in the book. The main themes are:

- The different explanations of why welfare policies changed over the period
- Key turning points in the history of welfare policy 1815–1948
- What had changed?
- Historians' interpretations of the history of poverty and welfare

Key dates

1834–1929	Period of the new Poor Law
1906–14	Period of the Liberal welfare reforms
1919–39	Interwar period dominated by unemployment
1945–51	Establishment of the 'welfare state' by the Labour government

1 | Why Did Welfare Policies Change?

Government policies change in response to pressures from society and changing attitudes. The development of state welfare policies in the period 1815–1948 was shaped by a number of such influences:

Key question
How can the changes in state welfare policies over the period 1815–1948 be explained?

- Changing attitudes about the nature of poverty and the role of the state.
- The political pressure of middle-class ratepayers and voters and the demands of the working class.
- The pressure of prevailing economic circumstances.

Changing attitudes about the nature of poverty and the role of the state

At the start of the nineteenth century, the dominant attitudes towards the treatment of poverty were changing. The paternalism of the old Poor Law was giving way to a harsher view of the poor, which concentrated on individual moral failure. This view, clearly expressed in the 1834 Report of the Royal Commission on the Poor Laws, blamed the poor for their own poverty and resulted in

Key question
How far was the changing role of the state a result of changing social attitudes towards poverty?

the harshness of the new Poor Law. For the next half century this attitude towards poverty and welfare was underpinned by the individualist philosophy of self-help.

Self-help

The idea that people should help themselves, rather than rely on the state for welfare, was the basis of the 1834 Poor Law Amendment Act. People were forced to make other arrangements for dealing with poverty if they wanted to avoid the workhouse. In 1859 Samuel Smiles' book *Self-Help* was published. The book was a best seller. This suggests that the idea of self-help had become widely accepted. In some ways the idea of self-help could be seen as a justification of the capitalist system, which had allowed individuals to accumulate wealth with little regard for their more unfortunate neighbours. For the prosperous Victorian middle classes the idea of self-help was convenient:

- It suggested that their own position was morally justified because anyone, no matter how humble, could help himself to rise up to a position of prosperity.
- It also absolved the middle classes from the duty of funding the poor through higher taxes, because it implied that poverty was the fault of the individual and only their own efforts could relieve their condition.

In *Self-Help*, Samuel Smiles wrote that government support for the poor inevitably made people dependent on the state. So, while the idea of self-help dominated, it was unlikely that any government would be prepared to extend the role of the state in welfare provision, because politicians believed that any extension of state welfare would demoralise the nation. Self-help was closely associated with the doctrine of free trade – the idea that government should not impose any tariffs or duties on imports or exports. Both beliefs underpinned the notion of the small state: mid-Victorian governments tried to confine themselves to a minimum amount of intervention in the economy and otherwise left individuals, businesses and voluntary organisations to get on with things with little interference.

Booth and Rowntree

Attitudes towards poverty and welfare did begin to change in the late nineteenth century with the writings of social investigators, such as Booth and Rowntree. Gradually, a significant number of politicians and opinion-formers began to accept that poverty was caused by problems beyond the control of the individual and that state welfare was the only way in which these problems could be adequately addressed. Even groups committed to individualism, like the Charity Organisation Society (COS), came to accept that poverty was more than just a matter of individual moral failure. If poverty was often caused by forces beyond the control of the individual, it followed that the victims of these forces should not be treated though they were guilty of a crime.

The fundamental principle of the new Poor Law had been to stigmatise paupers, the implication being that they were to blame for their own situation. Clearly, the new attitudes meant that the new Poor Law was no longer an appropriate way to deal with the poor. Thus, all the social reforms of the Edwardian period sought to provide welfare outside the Poor Law and on terms that did not humiliate and stigmatise the poor. The decision to pay old age pensions through post offices was the clearest statement that attitudes had changed; where once the elderly had been discouraged from claiming welfare, now they were positively encouraged.

However, although the Liberal social reforms of 1906–14 marked a significant shift in attitudes towards poverty and welfare, they also contained some of the old Victorian attitudes:

- the voluntary and private insurance societies retained a privileged role
- the contributory insurance principle dominated
- the Poor Law itself remained in force.

Radical ideas

More radical attitudes were expressed in the minority report of the 1909 Royal Commission into the Poor Laws. The minority report was heavily influenced by the beliefs of Sidney and Beatrice Webb and George Lansbury, all members of the newly formed Labour Party. Labour's programme was strongly influenced by socialism – the idea that the state had a central role in organising society and the economy in a much more egalitarian way, in order to redistribute money from the rich to the poor.

Although Labour would have to wait until 1945 before it could implement some of these policies, ideas about the role of the state were radically changed by the experience of the First World War. In order to mobilise society's resources to fight the first fully industrialised and globalised total war, the government was forced to take a much more active role in the organisation of the economy and society. The Liberals were even forced to abandon their long-held policy of free trade. The result was that when the war ended in 1918, it was impossible to return to Victorian notions of poverty, welfare and the state.

The interwar period saw the gradual fading away of the Poor Law and its replacement with a series of unemployment acts, which put the role of the state firmly at the centre of welfare provision, even if there were major debates as to the level at which benefit should be set.

The 1945 Labour government

By 1945, attitudes had changed even more radically. The Second World War had further entrenched the central role of the state in the life of the nation. The shared experiences of the war, the sense that it was a war for democracy, and the bitter memories of the depression of the 1930s, together created a broad consensus.

There was a general agreement that more needed to be done to provide comprehensive and universal welfare on the basis of need, rather than moral judgements. The welfare state established by the post-war Labour government represented these new ideas about poverty, welfare and the role of the state.

Key question
How far did the state change its policies towards the relief of poverty as a result of popular pressure?

The political pressure of middle-class ratepayers and voters and the demands of the working class

Another way of looking at the development of welfare policy is to see it as the product of social influences on government. Throughout this period, politicians needed to respond to pressure from voters and, as the electorate expanded so they were required to modify their positions.

1815–50

In the early nineteenth century the electorate was very small and politics was dominated by the interests of landowners. However, the 1832 Reform Act extended the right to vote to the growing middle class, whose wealth tended to come from trade and industry rather than land. The 1834 Poor Law Amendment Act was clearly a response to social pressures, although historians disagree as to whose interests were being addressed.

The newly enfranchised middle classes were certainly keen to see a reduction in the rates that they paid and this was one of the aims of the Act. Some factory owners saw the new Poor Law as a way of keeping down wages.

However, there is also evidence that landowners wanted the Act. The 'Swing' riots of the 1830s were a major cause for concern. Some landowners believed that the workhouse system would enable them to reassert their control over their discontented rural populations.

In this period the working class and poor did not have a vote so in many respects politicians could ignore their concerns – this is why the harsh new Poor Law could be established without much opposition in Parliament. However, popular protest did have the power to influence the detailed operation of the system at a local level. Opposition to the new Poor Law, particularly in the north of England, delayed the building of new workhouses. In some areas the workhouse test was applied less rigorously because guardians feared the reaction of the local population.

1850–1914

In the second half of the nineteenth century, the interests of middle-class property owners continued to exert pressure on both Liberal and Conservative governments to keep public spending to a minimum level. So, although there were new laws improving public health and education in the 1870s, there were no advances in state welfare outside the Poor Law in this period. At a local level, boards of guardians represented the middle classes and were under continuous pressure to keep the rates low. This was normally associated with a restriction on outdoor relief. Charity, rather than increased state provision, was widely seen as the appropriate response to poverty, and charity, as prescribed by groups like the COS, was a powerful way for the Victorian middle classes to assert their authority over the poor.

By the late nineteenth century things were beginning to change. The Reform Acts of 1867, 1872, 1883, 1884 and 1885 had given working-class voters a much more significant voice in Parliamentary elections. The Local Government Act of 1894 also widened the social composition of the boards of guardians. All this meant that there was pressure to improve Poor Law conditions and provide more extensive state welfare. New Liberalism was partly a response to these new electoral conditions, as was the birth of the Labour Party in 1900. The architects of the Liberal social reforms of 1906–14 sometimes explicitly justified their proposals by arguing that, without welfare reform, the working class would turn to socialism.

1914–45

During the First World War, Prime Minister David Lloyd George had to promise a fairer post-war Britain in order to keep working-class loyalty. One aspect of this fairer world was to be an increase in social welfare, particularly better housing, and another was the extension of the franchise to all working men. The 1918 Representation of the People Act gave the vote to all men and some women and this laid the basis for much more pressure for improved state welfare. The debates about the level of unemployment benefit, which dominated domestic politics in the late 1920s and 1930s, to some extent reflected the need for all political parties to consider the working-class vote. The election of a majority Labour government in 1945, committed to comprehensive welfare reform, was to a great extent the triumph of working-class interests, even though many middle-class voters were now also prepared to support Labour's programme.

The pressure of prevailing economic circumstances
The nineteenth century

Changing politics and changing ideas can, in many ways, be seen as reflections of changing economic realities. In the aftermath of the Napoleonic wars, the British economy in the early 1820s experienced low prices, low wages and high unemployment in rural areas. The new Poor Law could be seen in part as a response to these economic conditions, as local ratepayers attempted to protect themselves against the rising burden of outdoor relief. In general, for the next half century, the new Poor Law regime was a way of shielding the Victorian middle classes from the consequences of rapid economic change.

Industrialisation created the wealth for factory owners and traders on which mid-Victorian prosperity was based. But industrialisation was inevitably accompanied by massive economic dislocation, as older methods of manufacturing, such as handloom weaving, were replaced by more efficient factories. The workers who were made unemployed as a result of these changes had to be looked after somehow, and the new Poor Law was

Key question
How far was the changing role of the state a result of the changing economic pressures on governments?

designed to maintain them at the cheapest possible cost. Even when the British economy ran into more significant problems, in the 1880s and 1890s, and unemployment became more permanent and noticeable, there were no significant improvements in relief for the able-bodied unemployed.

The Liberal social reforms

The Liberal social reforms of the period 1906–14 were financed by an increase in taxation on the rich, but this was not the only reason for increased state expenditure. The government was already being forced to increase public spending due to the expansion of the military, as Britain became increasingly concerned about the threat from rival nations. Despite the protests of landowners against Lloyd George's radical 'People's budget' of 1909, and the opposition of employers to the 1911 National Insurance Act, the Edwardian period was one of relative economic prosperity and the higher taxes were affordable.

The interwar period

In the interwar period, Britain's economy once again went through a period of rapid and uncomfortable change. The 1914–18 war had weakened Britain's economy:

- there was a huge increase in the national debt
- trade was disrupted
- many of Britain's major industries, such as shipbuilding and coal mining, found themselves outdated.

The global collapse in trade, following the 1929 Wall Street Crash, tipped this already weak economy into depression and with this came mass unemployment. Middle-class employers and property owners were even more reluctant to pay for the costs of increased welfare. The government responded to the economic situation by making cuts in unemployment benefit. In 1931 the second Labour government collapsed as a result of these economic pressures.

The 1945 Labour government

After the Second World War, the national debt stood at record levels, and the economy had been completely disrupted. However, such was the strength of support for welfare reform that not even this unpromising economic situation could frustrate Labour's plans for a welfare state. In many ways, this demonstrates that although welfare policy can be shaped by economic circumstances, it is not necessarily determined by them if there is the political will to reform.

Summary diagram: Why did welfare policies change?

	Changing attitudes about the nature of poverty and the role of the state	The political pressure of middle-class ratepayers and voters and the demands of the working class	The pressure of prevailing economic circumstances
First half of nineteenth century (1815–50)	Attitudes behind 1834 Poor Law Amendment Act emphasised individual responsibility	Middle-class ratepayers wanted to cut the cost of the Poor Law. But popular protest against the new Poor Law frustrated the attempt to abolish outdoor relief	Rapid economic growth and the establishment of a free-market capitalist system assisted by the new Poor Law, which controlled relief expenditure and helped to keep wages low
Second half of nineteenth century (1850–1900)	Individualist attitudes underlying the principle of self-help and promoted by groups like the COS challenged by the findings of Booth and Rowntree	Middle-class voters and ratepayers still wanted to keep welfare costs low. But there was increasing pressure for social reform from newly enfranchised working-class voters	Economic problems in the 1880s and 1890s resulted in high levels of unemployment. The Poor Law was inadequate to deal with this
1900–14	New Liberalism and the growth of socialism led to an extension of the role of the state in welfare provision	The rise of Labour and the need to appease working-class voters was a factor in the Liberal social reforms	Increasing international economic competition led to concerns about 'national efficiency'. Liberal social reforms were a response to this
1914–50	Increased acceptance that the state should be the main provider of welfare, e.g. 1942 Beveridge Report	The establishment of full democracy increased the power of working-class voters, culminating in the election of the first majority Labour government in 1945	Weakened British economy and world depression led to welfare cuts in 1930s. However, post-war welfare state established despite serious economic problems

2 | Turning Points?

Key question
Were there key turning points in the development of welfare policies between 1815 and 1948?

Historians sometimes argue that a particular event or development was crucial in changing policy, or establishing a new approach to a problem. Other events, while important, may just accelerate an existing trend, or confirm changes that had already been set in train. Seven key points can be identified as potential turning points in the development of state welfare and the treatment of poverty in this period:

- The 1834 Poor Law Amendment Act
- The writings of the late nineteenth-century social investigators
- The minority report of the Royal Commission on the Poor Laws, 1909
- The Liberal social reforms 1906–14
- The First World War 1914–18
- The social legislation of the interwar period
- The Beveridge Report 1942
- The establishment of the welfare state.

The 1834 Poor Law Amendment Act

Key question
How far was the 1834 Poor Law Amendment Act a turning point in the provision of state welfare in Britain?

It is hard to argue that the new Poor Law did not mark a significant turning point in the history of British welfare provision. Before the 1834 Act, Poor Law provision varied from place to place, and there was no central authority responsible for regulating the operation of the laws. Outdoor relief was widespread and was often used as a way to subsidise wages during times of cyclical or seasonal unemployment. Workhouses were also variable in quality and in the type of support they provided.

The 1834 Act attempted to change radically the way the Poor Law operated. The main features of the new Poor Law were:

- the establishment of a central commission to which local boards of guardians were responsible
- the amalgamation of parishes into Poor Law unions and the building of a new workhouse in each union
- the commission established rigorous and detailed instructions about life in the workhouse
- most importantly, the new workhouses were to be deterrent institutions: life in the workhouse was designed to be so unpleasant that only the most desperate would consider entering it
- outdoor relief was to be denied to the able-bodied poor.

The aim of all this was to keep the cost of the Poor Law down and to force the poor to become more independent and individually responsible.

The new Poor Law was the main form of state welfare until the Liberal social reforms of 1906–14. Expenditure was kept under control and, to an extent, central authority was maintained even when the commission was replaced by, first, the Poor Law Board in 1847, and then the Local Government Board in 1871. Deterrent workhouses were established in every part of England, even though there was fierce resistance in some areas. However, outdoor relief for the able-bodied was never fully abolished, despite the best efforts of the central authority. But the Act did create a climate of fear, which meant that many poor people avoided any contact with the Poor Law authorities. This was a significant change.

The writings of the late nineteenth-century social investigators

Key question
How far were the writings of the late nineteenth-century social investigators a turning point in the understanding of poverty and welfare in Britain?

The 'discovery' of poverty in the late nineteenth century resulted in a significant change in the way it was viewed. In the middle decades of the nineteenth century, the commonly held view was that poverty was the fault of the individual and that it was up to the individual to dig themselves out of their situation. The doctrines of self-help and *laissez-faire*, along with the culture of the deterrent workhouse, had combined to establish this consensus. Samuel Smiles had written that 'help from without is often enfeebling in its effects' and whatever help was available was given under the strictest of conditions. The Charity Organisation Society was influential in upholding this individualist approach, and the Poor Law was deliberately constructed so as to discourage applications from anyone other than the most needy.

The writings of the social investigators in the latter part of the nineteenth century challenged the doctrine of individual responsibility and *laissez-faire*. In his book, *Life and Labour of the People in London*, Charles Booth attacked the prevailing views about poverty. Through a careful statistical argument, he demonstrated that poverty was caused by circumstances beyond the control of the individual, and that some 30 per cent of the London population lived in poverty. If poverty was not the moral responsibility of the individual then, Booth argued, the state should take a bigger role in providing welfare for the poor. His findings were supported by those of Seebohm Rowntree, whose 1901 book *Poverty: A Study of Town Life* painted a similar picture to that of Booth. Rowntree developed the concepts of life-cycle poverty and the poverty line, both of which again suggested that the state should do more to help the poor.

To the extent that the work of Booth and Rowntree began a reassessment of the nature of poverty, and the role of the state, their investigations do represent a turning point in attitudes. At a practical level, their writings also influenced New Liberalism at the turn of the century and so had an important part to play in the social reforms of 1906–14. On the other hand, their conclusions were resisted: Booth's ideas for state-financed old age pensions were rejected by the Royal Commission on the Aged Poor in 1894. Booth was also a member of the Royal Commission on the Poor Laws (1905–9) and made an unsuccessful attempt to reconcile the majority and minority factions on the Commission, before he retired due to ill-health. However, his own position was that the Poor Laws should be improved rather than abolished, a position out of step with his more radical colleagues.

Key question
How far was the 1909 minority report of the Royal Commission on the Poor Laws a turning point in the provision of state welfare in Britain?

The minority report of the Royal Commission on the Poor Laws 1909

The Royal Commission on the Poor Laws and Relief of Distress was set up in the final days of a Conservative government in 1904. The majority of the commissioners, heavily influenced by the ideas of the COS, proposed that the restriction on outdoor relief to the able-bodied be retained. In other words, they held fast to the key principle of the 1834 Act. They reasserted the view that poverty was 'largely moral' in its origins. They did accept that the boards of guardians were outdated, and should be replaced by Public Assistance Committees, which would be made up of local elected councillors and members of local charities. But, in many respects, the majority report reflected orthodox Victorian attitudes to poverty and the role of the state.

A minority of members of the Royal Commission dissented from these views and produced their own report. This provided a different analysis of the causes of poverty, and suggested far more radical action to deal with it. According to the report's authors, led by the Fabian socialists Sidney and Beatrice Webb, poverty was fundamentally economic, rather than moral, in character. The Poor Laws were irredeemably associated with an outdated concept of individual blame and should be abolished. The report proposed a central Ministry of Labour to deal with all aspects of unemployment, including training, benefits and public works schemes. Specialist committees in local councils would deal with issues of child poverty, the elderly and the sick and disabled.

The minority report clearly represented a sharp break from the orthodox thinking represented by the majority report. The proposal, that the state should take responsibility for unemployment and job creation, through a central ministry, was a policy that was adopted by post-war governments, and the proposals for specialist committees anticipated some aspects of the 1945 welfare state.

On the other hand, the minority report still saw the delivery of these services as a local matter, so to that extent its proposals were more limited than those of the Beveridge Report. Moreover, the minority report led to little in the way of immediate action. The failure to reach any compromise with the majority meant that the Liberal government pretty much ignored the Royal Commission altogether when framing its own reforms. The Poor Laws were not abolished until 1929. However, the central belief of the Fabians was 'the inevitability of **gradualism**', so the Webbs were perhaps unsurprised to find themselves influencing long-term change, rather than creating an immediate turning point.

Key term

Gradualism
The idea that change can be achieved piece by piece over a period of time.

The Liberal social reforms 1906–14

Apart from the distress committees set up by the Unemployed Workmen Act of 1905, nearly all state relief to the poor, before the Liberal reforms, was provided through the Poor Law. One of the main motives behind the new Poor Law was the determination to keep down the cost of welfare by restricting outdoor relief. The essence of the new Poor Law was the idea that the origins of poverty lay in moral failure. Relief in the workhouse was seen as a social stigma, and those in receipt of relief were seen as less than full citizens. Those who had the right to vote lost that right on entering the workhouse.

The Liberal government of 1906–14 did not abolish the Poor Laws. However, it did introduce a variety of measures, which provided significant amounts of welfare outside the Poor Law system:

Key question
How far were the Liberal social reforms of 1906–14 a turning point in the provision of state welfare in Britain?

- The Education Acts of 1906 and 1907 introduced free school meals and medical inspections for schoolchildren.
- Non-contributory old age pensions were introduced in 1908 to the over-70s.
- The 1909 Trade Boards Act and the 1912 Mines Act established statutory minimum wages in a variety of industries.
- The 1911 National Insurance Act provided financial support for the sick and the unemployed, on a contributory insurance basis.

The Liberal social reforms of 1906–14 marked a significant break with the nineteenth-century Poor Law regime in a number of ways:

- First, they re-established the right to receive 'outdoor relief' that the Poor Law had attempted to restrict since 1834. By 1915, a million pensioners were collecting pensions and 13 million workers were covered by national insurance.
- Secondly, the reforms established the principle that relief should be given without the stigmatisation of the workhouse system. Those in receipt of benefit no longer lost their right to vote.
- Thirdly, the reforms represented an acceptance that national government had a responsibility for dealing with the causes of poverty. In particular, unemployment and the level of unemployment benefit became a central issue for all governments from this point onwards.

Limitations of the reforms

Some historians have seen in the Liberal measures the origins of the welfare state. However, there was no coherent plan underpinning the reforms and they had many limitations. The financial value of the benefits provided was limited and many workers remained outside the insurance net. Some Victorian attitudes still persisted. Ex-offenders and old people who were branded 'workshy' were denied the pension. Even though the Liberals deliberately avoided the Poor Law when establishing their welfare systems, the Law itself was not abolished. The spectre of the workhouse continued to be a powerful symbol throughout the land. Despite a general relaxation in conditions, some paupers were still picking oakum in the 1920s. The Poor Law was not abolished until 1929 and, even then, it took a long time to transfer its responsibilities to other bodies.

Take-up of state welfare remained relatively low and this had to do with the nature of the Liberal social reforms themselves. The Poor Law, for all its faults, had been a universal system. Anyone in need could apply for help, even though they were discouraged from so doing. While old age pensions were more or less universal, they were subject to a strict means test. An elderly person who had a weekly income of over 12s per week got nothing.

National insurance was limited by design. Health insurance was provided for all manual workers, but not their families. The workers themselves could be excluded from the scheme if they were considered 'bad risks'. As late as 1938, National Health Insurance still only covered 42 per cent of the population. Unemployment insurance was more restrictive, with only workers in a limited number of trades participating in the scheme. Although the coverage for the unemployed was eventually extended, the insurance principle continued to restrict entitlement to benefits.

Unlike the Poor Law, which preceded them, and the welfare state which followed them, the Liberal measures did not represent a welfare system open to all. Nevertheless, it is hard to argue against the view that the Liberal social reforms did mark a turning point in the relief of poverty.

The First World War 1914–18

Key question
How far was the 1914–18 First World War a turning point in the relationship between the state and the poor in Britain?

The First World War marked a turning point in many aspects of British and world affairs. The sheer scale of the conflict, and the need to mobilise the whole population to fight it, inevitably entailed massive changes to the relationship between state and society. Before the war, the Liberal government had implemented a series of significant social reforms, which extended the role of the state in the relief of poverty. On the other hand, the Liberals had not challenged many aspects of the *laissez-faire* economy. The Liberals had continued to accept the view that state intervention should be kept to a minimum, and they held on to the doctrine of free trade as a fundamental belief.

During the war, the government was forced to take a much more interventionist approach. The 1914 Defence of the Realm Act (DORA) brought in censorship of newspapers and gave the government power to control production, transport and the direction of labour. Controls were placed on trade and, in 1915, duties were placed on some imports, ending free trade. In 1916, conscription was introduced, and by 1918 the government was controlling both domestic rents and prices in the shops. In the first years of the war, benefits were introduced for families of those in the armed forces, and in 1916 national insurance was extended to cover most workers.

Short-term impact

It is hard to argue that the First World War was a turning point in terms of its immediate impact on state welfare. Allowances to soldiers' families and the extension of the national insurance scheme were developments of existing policies and responses to immediate circumstances, rather than a radical break with the past. No significant new welfare measures were introduced during the war.

Long-term impact

The war did have major long-term significance for the future relationship between poverty and the state in a number of ways.

- First, the 1918 Representation of the People Act extended the right to vote in parliamentary elections to all men and some women (in 1929 this was extended to all women). This meant that, for the first time, all those who were in poverty, or feared that one day they might be, had a voice in the political system. The Labour Party now had a real opportunity to gain power, and Conservative governments also had to consider these new voters when deciding on their welfare policies. All this made it very likely, if not inevitable, that the role of the state in the provision of welfare would increase.
- Secondly, the war had set a precedent for massive state intervention in social and economic affairs. As Britain had been successful in the war it was difficult to argue for a return to the *laissez-faire* policies of the Victorian era. Again, this made increased state provision of welfare much more likely.
- Finally, in order to keep the loyalty of the working class during the war, the government had been forced to promise a much fairer society after the war. Although the specifics were vague, this represented a decisive shift in the terms of debate about welfare, which again meant that a return to Victorian policies was most unlikely.

The social legislation of the interwar period

Interwar unemployment legislation dominated the political agenda and some historians have identified the welfare measures of the 1920s and 1930s as a turning point in state welfare policy. At the end of the First World War, social policy essentially remained as the Liberals had left it in 1914. Contributory insurance schemes were in place to support some workers facing sickness or unemployment and means-tested old age pensions were available for the elderly.

Key question
How far was the social legislation of the 1920s and 1930s a turning point in the way the state provided welfare in Britain?

Limitations of the Liberal reforms

It is important to realise how many people were *not* covered by the Liberal social reforms. Despite efforts to expand national insurance, in 1918 only four million workers out of a workforce of 14 million were covered by the unemployment insurance scheme, and people in their sixties, those who had more than a small income, and those deemed unsuitable because of past behaviour, were excluded from the old age pension. For all those outside the scope of the Liberal measures, the Poor Law still represented the last resort.

Interwar legislation

The legislation of the interwar period was not a coherent plan to tackle poverty, but rather, a series of responses made, in particular, to the problem of unemployment. However, a number of important measures were passed that are significant in the history of welfare provision.

- First, the 1925 Widows', Orphans' and Old Age Contributory Pensions Act replaced the non-contributory pensions of the 1908 Act with a contributory benefit grafted on to the national insurance scheme. The scheme was also extended to cover dependants.
- Secondly, the 1929 Local Government Act transferred the running of Poor Law services, benefits and institutions to local councils.
- Thirdly, the various Unemployment Acts of the period attempted to deal with the reality of permanent mass unemployment. The Acts attempted to balance the contributions to the national insurance scheme with the level of benefits to unemployed workers, while at the same time providing support to those who were outside the scheme or who had exhausted their entitlement to benefits.

Significance of the legislation

The provision of state welfare in Britain changed significantly between 1918 and 1939. The effective removal of unemployment from the Poor Law, and the abolition of the boards of guardians, had reduced the fear of the workhouse and, to some extent, changed the nature of welfare provision. A range of welfare services for children, the sick and the elderly was now being provided by local authorities, through the Poor Law institutions, but without the deliberate humiliations of the nineteenth-century culture of less eligibility. In a similar way, in 1937 the Unemployment Assistance Board was given authority to provide benefit for unemployed workers who had made no contributions. This signified an acceptance by the state that support for the unemployed had to be comprehensive and not tied to the insurance principle.

Limitations of the legislation

On the other hand, throughout the 1920s and 1930s unemployed workers were subject to a means test and investigation into whether they were 'genuinely seeking work'. The inquisitorial nature of these investigations was a source of great resentment at the time. Up to half the applicants for what were known as 'transitional benefits' had either their claims rejected or their benefits reduced. As late as 1938, national health insurance still only covered 42 per cent of the population. So although some historians have claimed that by 1939 Britain's welfare services were amongst the most comprehensive in the world, there were still many gaps.

The Beveridge Report 1942

The welfare state established by the 1945–51 Labour government is generally recognised as representing a crucial development in welfare provision. Indeed, the term 'welfare state' represented a new conception of how the state should relate to the people. Labour's programme was to a great extent based on the report of William Beveridge published in 1942. This report on 'Social Insurance and Allied Services' was a response to the problems of poverty that existed in Britain at the start of the Second World War:

Key question
How far was the 1942 Beveridge Report a turning point for state welfare in Britain?

- continuing poverty for a significant number of people
- mass unemployment
- insurance nets that failed to protect the whole population
- benefits that were too low
- a patchwork of services that varied from area to area.

Beveridge's proposals

The Beveridge Report set out to attack what it described as the 'five giants' on the road to reconstruction: want, squalor, disease, ignorance and idleness. Beveridge proposed that the social security system should cover the whole population. Benefits should be available to support people facing any of the crises that could disrupt their normal income: unemployment, sickness, disability, the birth of children, death of the wage earner or old age. These benefits should be set at a level that was adequate to provide the means to live. Beveridge argued that pre-war benefits had not been set at such a level. Beveridge also proposed:

- a national health system to look after anyone who was sick
- direct government spending to keep employment levels high
- that the new system should be organised on a national basis.

The welfare state

The 'welfare state' established by the Labour government after 1945 was heavily influenced by Beveridge's proposals. Apart from action to promote employment, provide more council housing and reform education, the government established a 'cradle to grave' welfare system through the following:

- The 1945 Family Allowances Act, which provided a universal flat rate 5s per child payment for second and subsequent children.
- The 1946 National Insurance (Industrial Injuries) Act, which established benefits for the victims of accidents at work or illness caused by work (e.g. respiratory diseases suffered by coal miners).
- The 1946 National Insurance Act, which was the centrepiece of the social insurance legislation. The Act brought together

unemployment and sickness benefits, old age pensions, maternity and widows' benefits, guardians' allowances for orphans and death grants to cover funeral expenses.

- The 1948 National Assistance Act, which established a National Assistance Board to provide means-tested benefits for people who had no entitlement to insurance benefits, or for whom the benefits were insufficient.
- The National Health Service, which was launched in July 1948.

The new welfare state was a radical turning point in that the state took responsibility at a national level, to provide social security for the whole population. This meant that not only the poorest sections of society, but everyone could benefit from welfare provision, particularly family allowances and the National Health Service. Some historians have argued that there were continuities between the welfare state and the systems that preceded it: Beveridge was a Liberal, rather than a socialist, and contributory benefits remained at the heart of the system. However, it is hard to argue convincingly against the view that the Beveridge Report was a major turning point in the development of state welfare provision.

Summary diagram: Key turning points in the development of welfare policies between 1815 and 1948

The 1834 Poor Law Amendment Act

Before the 1834 Act:	The 1834 Act:	After 1834:
• Poor Law provision varied from place to place • No central authority • Outdoor relief was widespread and was often used as a way to subsidise wages • Workhouses were variable in quality and in the type of support they provided	• Established a central commission to which local boards of guardians were responsible • Amalgamated parishes into Poor Law unions and built a new workhouse in each union • The Commission laid down rigorous and detailed instructions about life in the workhouse • Resulted in new workhouses becoming deterrent institutions • Outdoor relief was to be denied to the able-bodied poor	• Expenditure was kept under control • Central authority was maintained • Deterrent workhouses were established in every part of England • A climate of fear was created, which meant that many poor people avoided any contact with the Poor Law authorities However: • Outdoor relief for the able-bodied was never fully abolished

The writings of the late nineteenth-century social investigators

Before Booth and Rowntree – the dominant ideas about poverty were that it was the fault of the individual and support from the state should be limited and conditional	The writings of Booth and Rowntree revealed that poverty was widespread and often not the result of individual failure	Following the writings of Booth and Rowntree, governments were more willing to extend state involvement in social welfare, e.g. the Liberal social reforms of 1906–14

Summary diagram: Key turning points in the development of welfare policies between 1815 and 1948 (continued)

The minority report of the Royal Commission on the Poor Laws 1909

Before the report • The dominant ideas about poverty were still that it was the fault of the individual and support from the state should be limited and conditional • These views were being challenged to some extent by the Liberal government which was increasing state provision through measures like the Old Age Pensions Act	The minority report of the Royal Commission provided a different analysis of the causes of poverty, and suggested far more radical action to deal with it: • Poverty was fundamentally economic, rather than moral, in character • The Poor Laws should be abolished • A central Ministry of Labour should be established to deal with all aspects of unemployment • Specialist committees in local councils would deal with issues of child poverty, the elderly and the sick and disabled	After the report: • Post-war governments did take responsibility for unemployment and job creation, through a central ministry • The 1945 welfare state reflected many of the report's recommendations **But** • The Report led to little in the way of immediate action • The Liberal government pretty much ignored the Royal Commission altogether when framing its own reforms • The Poor Laws were not abolished until 1929

The Liberal social reforms 1906–14

Before the Liberal reforms • Nearly all state relief to the poor was provided through the Poor Law • The idea that the origins of poverty lay in moral failure still dominated policy • Relief in the workhouse was seen as a social stigma	The Liberal government of 1906–14 did not abolish the Poor Laws. However, it did introduce a variety of measures, which provided significant amounts of welfare outside the Poor Law system: • The Education Acts of 1906 and 1907 • Old Age Pensions Act 1908 • The 1909 Trade Boards Act and the 1912 Mines Act • The 1911 National Insurance Act	The Liberal social reforms of 1906–14 marked a significant break with the nineteenth-century Poor Law regime in a number of ways: • First, they re-established the right to receive 'outdoor relief' that the Poor Law had attempted to restrict since 1834 • Secondly, the reforms established the principle that relief should be given without the stigmatisation of the workhouse system • Thirdly, the reforms represented an acceptance that national government had a responsibility for dealing with the causes of poverty **But** • The financial value of the benefits provided was limited and many workers remained outside the insurance net • Some Victorian attitudes still persisted • The Poor Law itself was not abolished • Take-up of state welfare remained relatively low

Summary diagram: Key turning points in the development of welfare policies between 1815 and 1948 (continued)

The First World War, 1914–18

Before the war:
- The Liberal government had implemented a series of significant social reforms, which extended the role of the state in the relief of poverty
- On the other hand, the Liberals had not challenged many aspects of the *laissez-faire* economy
- The Liberals had continued to accept the view that state intervention should be kept to a minimum, and they held on to the doctrine of free trade as a fundamental belief

During the war, the government was forced to take a much more interventionist approach:
- The 1914 Defence of the Realm Act (DORA)
- Controls were placed on trade, and, in 1915, duties were placed on some imports, ending free trade
- In 1916, conscription was introduced
- By 1918 the government was controlling both domestic rents and prices in the shops
- In the first years of the war, benefits were introduced for families of those in the armed forces, and in 1916 National Insurance was extended to cover most workers

After the War
The war did have major long-term significance for the future relationship between poverty and the state in a number of ways:
- First, the 1918 Representation of the People Act extended the right to vote in parliamentary elections to all men and some women (in 1929 this was extended to all women). All this made it very likely, if not inevitable, that the role of the state in the provision of welfare would increase
- Secondly, the war had set a precedent for massive state intervention in social and economic affairs
- Finally, in order to keep the loyalty of the working class during the war, the government had been forced to promise a much fairer society after the war

The unemployment legislation of the interwar period

Before the interwar legislation:
- Contributory insurance schemes were in place to support some workers facing sickness or unemployment and means-tested old age pensions were available for the elderly

But
- In 1918 only four million workers out of a workforce of 14 million were covered by the unemployment insurance scheme
- People in their 60s, those who had more than a small income and those deemed unsuitable because of past behaviour, were excluded from the old age pension
- For all those outside the scope of the Liberal measures, the Poor Law still represented the last resort

The legislation of the interwar period was not a coherent plan to tackle poverty, but rather a series of responses made to specific problems:
- The 1925 Widows', Orphans' and Old Age Contributory Pensions Act
- The 1929 Local Government Act transferred the running of Poor Law services, benefits and institutions to local councils
- The various unemployment acts of the period

Impact of the legislation:
- The Poor Law was effectively abolished
- A range of welfare services for children, the sick and the elderly were provided by local authorities
- The 1937 the Unemployment Assistance Board was given authority to provide benefit for unemployed workers who had made no contributions

But
- The means test was a source of great resentment
- Up to half the applicants for what were known as 'transitional benefits' had either their claims rejected, or their benefits reduced
- As late as 1938, National Health Insurance still only covered 42 per cent of the population

Summary diagram: Key turning points in the development of welfare policies between 1815 and 1948 (continued)

The Beveridge report 1942

Problems before the report:	Beveridge's proposals	The 'welfare state' established
• Continuing poverty for a significant number of people • Mass unemployment • Insurance nets which failed to protect the whole population • Benefits that were too low • A patchwork of services that varied from area to area	• A social security system to cover the whole population • Benefits available to support people facing any of the crises that could disrupt their normal income • Benefits should be set at a level that was adequate to provide the means to live • A national health system to look after anyone who was sick. • Direct government spending to keep employment levels high	by the Labour government after 1945 was heavily influenced by Beveridge's proposals: • The 1945 Family Allowances Act • The 1946 National Insurance (Industrial Injuries) Act • The 1946 National Insurance Act • The 1948 National Assistance Act • The National Health Service, which was launched in July 1948

3 | What Had Changed?

Key question
How far had poverty been reduced in this period?

Despite the attempts to treat poverty in a more sympathetic way, it is clear that the level of poverty had diminished little by 1914. The surveys at the end of the nineteenth century suggested that around a third of the population were living in poverty, with 10 per cent living in 'primary' poverty (insufficient income for the maintenance of mere physical efficiency). In some respects conditions for working people were better than they had been in the 1830s:

- Legislation on factory conditions, public health and education had provided some protection against exploitation, disease and ignorance.
- Thirteen-year-old children in state schools between 1900 and 1910 weighed on average nearly three kilograms more than children working in factories in the 1820s.
- The second half of the nineteenth century had also witnessed a significant rise in real wages for the working-class as a whole.

The fall in the death rate was also an indication that conditions had improved, although mortality rates continued to demonstrate the relative poverty of the working class. In 1911, infant mortality amongst the middle and upper classes was 76.4 per thousand but 132.5 per thousand for working-class children. In a similar way, Oxbridge undergraduates in 1914 were on average taller and heavier than working-class army conscripts in the 1914–18 war.

The social reforms of the pre-war Liberal government had no opportunity to make a major dent in the extent of poverty before the Great War, but they (and the legislation of the 1920s that developed from them) began to make a difference in the longer term. When Rowntree conducted a follow-up survey in the 1930s, he found that the percentage living in 'primary poverty' had fallen from 9.9 per cent to 3.9 per cent. Considering that the survey was conducted in the depths of the 1930s depression, this does indicate a noticeable improvement. Rowntree himself acknowledged this progress, even though the same survey showed that a further 20 per cent continued to experience 'secondary' poverty.

In a similar way Labour's post-war welfare state had begun to have an impact by the 1950s. Rowntree carried out a third survey of poverty in York which was published in 1951. His claims that the percentage of working-class individuals who were living in poverty (primary or secondary) had now fallen to 4.64 per cent have been challenged as inaccurate, but even the critics of his statistical methods acknowledge that the post-war welfare measures had reduced poverty, even though they had not eliminated it.

Key question
What are the different ways in which historians have interpreted the development of poverty and welfare in the nineteenth and twentieth centuries?

4 | Welfare and Historians

The 'Whig' interpretation

Historians are products of the age in which they live, and their interpretations have reflected changing contemporary attitudes to poverty and welfare. In the period after the Second World War the welfare state (see pages 151–3) was established. Historical writing in the 1960s and 1970s reflected the public consensus in support of the welfare state at this time. Historians such as D. Roberts (*The Victorian Origins of the British Welfare State*, 1960), B.B. Gilbert (*The Evolution of National Insurance in Great Britain: The Origins of the Welfare State*, 1966) and Derek Fraser (*The Evolution of the British Welfare State*, 1973) wrote books the very titles of which proclaimed a line of development leading from the Poor Law and the Liberal social reforms to the welfare state of the later twentieth century.

Such an interpretation has been criticised as a 'Whig' view of history. This is the school of historical thought that identifies lines of historical progress in the development of society. It is generally an optimistic view, which sees society's progress as a positive thing, each development building on its predecessor to create better social and institutional arrangements. In the view of these historians, society learnt from the mistakes of the Poor Law and the inadequacies of individualism and created a collectivist and universal welfare system that was much better than its predecessors. The support for the welfare state across the political spectrum in the period 1945–75 convinced these historians that their analysis was correct.

The collapse of the consensus in support of the welfare state in the last quarter of the twentieth century led to something of a re-appraisal. Fraser, in his postscript to the 1984 edition of *The Evolution of the British Welfare State*, acknowledged that things now looked rather different from the way they had seemed 10 years earlier:

We can now perhaps trace, more clearly than would have been possible in 1973, the whole life cycle of the welfare idea. It germinated in the social thought of late Victorian liberalism, reached its infancy in the collectivism of pre- and post-Great War statism, matured in the **universalism** of the 1940s and flowered in full bloom in the consensus and affluence of the 1950s and 1960s. By the 1980s it was in its decline, like the faded rose of autumn.

'Postmodernist' interpretations

The uncertainty about the future and value of the welfare state in the late twentieth century resulted in historians questioning the 'Whig' interpretation. If the welfare state was under threat, perhaps, they suggested, its coming about was not as inevitable and clearly signposted as had previously been thought. Historians in the 1980s and 1990s were, in any case, beginning to question the validity of grand explanations of historical development.

These **'postmodernist'** interpretations emphasised the untidy and discontinuous nature of history and stressed the importance of chance and accident in the development of social institutions. This type of analysis also allowed historians to concentrate on areas of history that had received little attention in the 'big' accounts of the development of poverty and welfare. For example, **feminist historians** began to examine the effect of welfare reforms on women, while others drew attention to the significance of women's informal family, friendship and neighbourhood networks in providing welfare in their own communities. In her book *Growing Up Poor* (1996), Anna Davin has charted the history of children in poor communities in the period 1870–1914, a hitherto neglected subject.

The conservative reaction

Another response to the contemporary 'crisis' of the welfare state has been a conservative reaction against the welfare state. This view stresses the positive elements in the Victorian approach to poverty and sees the seeds of late twentieth-century problems in the abandonment of these Victorian values. Gertrude Himmelfarb, in *The Idea of Poverty* (1984) and *Poverty and Compassion* (1991), is perhaps the best example of this approach. Professor Himmelfarb, particularly in her 1991 work, attempts to rescue the late Victorian middle classes from their critics by emphasising the value of morality in addressing the problems of poverty. She highlights the widespread Victorian view, held, she claims, by the working classes as well as the middle class, that individual moral responsibility was the key factor in improving the lives of the poor. Other historians had charted the transition from a moralistic view of welfare provision, sorting the deserving from the undeserving, to an objective view, dealing with categories of need, as representing social progress. Himmelfarb takes the opposite view and implies that the abandonment of morality, as a central element in welfare policy, has been a prime cause of the failure of the modern welfare state.

Marxist interpretations

While conservatives such as Himmelfarb argue that the state went too far in the direction of welfare provision for all, left-wing

Key terms

Universalism
The idea that benefits and welfare provision, like the NHS, should be available to everyone.

Postmodernist
The view that criticises grand theories and explanations.

Feminist historians
Believe that women's role in history has been neglected and seek to interpret the past from a woman's perspective.

Key terms

Marxist
The belief that all societies are divided into classes based on the economy of that society. For Marx, the struggle between these classes was the dynamic factor that explained historical development.

Historiography
The study of historians' interpretations of the past.

interpretations have stressed the inadequacy of welfare and the persistence of poverty. **Marxist** and left-wing interpretations of poverty and welfare have traditionally emphasised that both are reflections of the class structure of society. Poverty, according to this view, is an inevitable consequence of capitalism. For example, unemployment is something that suits capitalists because it helps to keep wages at a lower level than they would be if everyone had a job. Employers can always tell their workers that if they do not accept their pay and conditions there will be someone out of work available to replace them.

Historians who have examined the provision of welfare from a Marxist perspective have generally taken the view that neither philanthropists nor the state genuinely want to get rid of poverty. Both are reflections of the class system and are interested only in preserving capitalism. Welfare, according to this perspective, is provided only as a concession to workers, in order to keep their loyalty to a system against which they would otherwise rebel. For example, while observers like Thomas Malthus had argued for the complete abolition of poor laws, politicians realised that without some provision for the poor there might be a revolution. In a similar way, leading Liberals like Churchill were quite explicit in their hope that welfare measures would discourage voters from looking towards socialist alternatives.

Marxist **historiography** hit something of a crisis in the late twentieth century. Marxism's prediction, that capitalism would eventually collapse and be replaced by a socialist system run for the benefit of the workers, seemed to suffer a major blow with the collapse of the East European communist states in the late 1980s and early 1990s. Communist China also began to embrace capitalism. Even left-wing historians, who had seen these totalitarian states as distortions of true socialism, were shocked by the failure of socialist politics in Western Europe and the triumph of free market capitalism under leaders like Margaret Thatcher. Marxists of an older generation like E.P. Thompson and Eric Hobsbawm continued to defend their interpretations, but few historians in the last decades of the twentieth century or the start of the twenty-first were prepared to develop their ideas in a convincing way. Nevertheless, as we have seen, contemporary attitudes have an important influence on historical perspective. A crisis of capitalism and a resurgence of left-wing politics could lead to a revival of the view that poverty might yet be abolished as society finds a better way to run its affairs.

Some key books in the debate:
Derek Fraser, *The Evolution of the British Welfare State* (1973).
B.B. Gilbert, *The Evolution of National Insurance in Great Britain: The Origins of the Welfare State* (1966).
Gertrude Himmelfarb, *The Idea of Poverty* (1984) and *Poverty and Compassion* (1991).
D. Roberts, *The Victorian Origins of the British Welfare State* (1960).

Summary diagram: Historical interpretations of poverty and welfare

Historical interpretations of poverty and welfare

The 'Whig' interpretation	'Postmodernist' interpretations	The Conservative reaction	Marxist interpretations
• Identifies lines of historical progress in the development of society • Society learnt from the mistakes of the Poor Law and the inadequacies of individualism and created a collectivist and universal welfare system, which was much better than its predecessors	• Untidy and discontinuous nature of history • Stresses the importance of chance and accident in the development of social institutions • 'Big' explanations do not work	Stresses the positive elements in the Victorian approach to poverty and sows the seeds of late twentieth-century problems in the abandonment of these Victorian values	• Poverty is an inevitable consequence of capitalism • Welfare provided only as a concession to workers, in order to keep their loyalty to a system against which they would otherwise rebel

Study Guide: Advanced Level Questions

In the style of Edexcel

1. How far do you agree that prevailing ideas about the proper role of the state were the key factor determining what provision was made for the poor in the period 1830–1939?

Source: adapted from Edexcel, June 2004

Exam tips

The cross-references are intended to take you straight to the material that will help you to answer the questions.

In order to get a good mark for this type of question, it is essential that you cover a period of 100 years. It is also vital that you are analytical in your approach. Simply describing welfare changes between 1830 and 1939 is not sufficient. You need to compare the impact of prevailing ideas against other factors that may have determined the provision of the poor, e.g. political pressure or prevailing economic circumstances. When planning your answer, it is worth thinking about the period as a succession of eras. In each era you can compare prevailing ideas with other factors.

Era	Prevailing ideas about the proper role the state	Other factors determining provision for the poor
c1830–90	Belief in a small state and fear of the effects of 'dependency'. Ideas of *laissez-faire* and self-help; influence of COS (pages 75–84)	Pressure to reduce poor rates; fear of rural discontent; need to separate the deserving and undeserving poor (pages 21–3)
c1890–1918	Rowntree; New Liberalism; minority report of Royal Commission on the Poor Laws – all argued for growing state intervention (pages 95–110)	Electoral pressure of the working class; national efficiency question (pages 101–8)
c1918–39	Acceptance of increased state intervention by governments (pages 138–43)	Economic constraints, especially in 1930s (pages 141–7)

It is vital that you leave yourself time for an adequate conclusion, where you come to a considered judgement based on the evidence you have produced:

- Were prevailing ideas about the role of the state always the dominant factor?
- Was another factor, such as political pressure, always dominant?

You may come to the view that different factors determined welfare provision in different eras.

2. How far does the nature of state provision for the poor over the period 1830–1939 demonstrate continuity rather than change in government approaches to dealing with the problem of poverty?

Exam tips

The cross-references are intended to take you straight to the material that will help you to answer the questions.

In order to get a good mark for this type of question, it is again essential that you cover a period of 100 years and that you are analytical in your approach. There are two ways you could approach the question:

- One way is to go through the whole period explaining how things changed in each era but also how some things remained the same. For example, in the era 1830–90, governments maintained the central importance of the Poor Law in the way they dealt with poverty. This is evidence for continuity. In the period 1890–1918, increased state intervention shows that government approaches were changing. However, continuity is demonstrated by the fact that the governments of this era did not abolish the Poor Law.

Era	Continuity	Change
c1830–90 – era of the new Poor Law	New Poor Law the dominant form of state assistance (pages 37–65)	Some easing of workhouse conditions e.g. for the elderly, and improved medical provision (pages 60–5)
c1890–1918 – era of the Liberal social reforms	Failure to abolish the Poor Law; limitations of the Liberal reforms (page 124)	Growing state intervention; some attitudes beginning to change, e.g. conditions for the payment of old age pensions (pages 111–25)
c1918–1939 – era of debate over state unemployment payments	Cuts in unemployment benefit; policies such as the 'Not Genuinely Seeking Work' clause and the means test (pages 144–7) – all these things reflected an attitude that wanted to limit state support and emphasise the division between 'deserving' and 'undeserving'	Acceptance of increased state intervention by governments; effective abolition of the Poor Law (pages 138–43)

- An alternative is to go through the period showing how there were elements of continuity and then repeat the process showing the elements of change.
- In either case you need to establish some criteria for judging how change can be identified. In this case the criteria could include the degree of state intervention or the attitude of the state to the poor.
- In the end you must come to a judgement – do the aspects of change outweigh the elements of continuity or is continuity the dominant theme?

In the style of OCR

'The **most** important turning point in the treatment of the poor from 1834 to 1948 was the introduction of national insurance in 1911.' How far do you agree with this statement?

Source: OCR, January 2005

Exam tips

The cross-references are intended to take you straight to the material that will help you to answer the question.

You will need to outline briefly what the 1911 National Insurance Act was, but do not spend too much time describing the Act (pages 118–20). You will get higher marks for analysis rather than description.

In order to make a judgement about the significance of any historical turning point, it is necessary to compare the situation before the turning point with the situation after it. You are required to cover a 100-year period in your answer, so some detail is required in your descriptions of the situation, both before and after 1911:

- Before 1911, despite the introduction of the Old Age Pensions Act in 1908 by the Liberals, state welfare was dominated by the new Poor Law.
- After 1911, it could be argued that an alternative to the Poor Law had been created for many poor people who were protected by the insurance net.
- On the other hand, national insurance had some serious limitations, which might undermine claims that it was the most significant turning point.
- You need to compare the 1911 Act to other rival turning points. If you are not convinced that it is the most important, you should put forward an alternative (pages 163–71) and demonstrate why you believe it to be more significant. If you are convinced that it is the most important turning point, you need to explain why it is more important than, for example, the Beveridge Report of 1942 (pages 149–150).

Glossary

1870 Education Act   This Act set up local education boards to build schools in areas were there where not enough voluntary schools. The Act established the principle that every child had the right to an elementary education.

Appeasement   The foreign policy pursued by British governments in the 1930s that aimed to avoid war by making concessions to the demands of the German and Italian dictators Hitler and Mussolini.

Bashaws   A Bashaw was an authoritarian military governor in the Turkish Empire and a popular symbol of tyrannical rule.

Bastilles   Named after the infamous prison fortress in Paris that was seen as a symbol of injustice and tyranny. At the start of the French Revolution in 1789 the prison was stormed and the prisoners released.

Boer War   Fought in South Africa from 1899 to 1902, after a dispute between settlers of Dutch origin ('Boers') and the British Empire.

Capitalist market system   An economy where businesses and individuals trade without interference from the state. Ownership of land and businesses is concentrated in the hands of a relatively small class of people whose control of resources makes them wealthy. Also known as the free market system.

Casualised work   Irregular work, often with no guarantee of employment from day to day.

Charles Darwin   A naturalist most famous for developing the theory of evolution in his 1859 book *The Origin of Species by Means of Natural Selection*.

Chartism   A mass campaign for political reform in the 1830s and 1840s. The six points of the 'Charter' included the right to vote for all men and payment of MPs so that working men could stand for Parliament. Despite huge support, the movement was unsuccessful and faded away in the 1850s.

Coalition government   A government made up of more than one political party.

Conscription   The compulsory enlistment of men into the armed forces.

Constitutional crisis   A political confrontation relating to the rules under which the country is governed.

Contributory principle   Workers had to pay into the scheme before they were entitled to take benefits from it.

Demoralisation   In the nineteenth century this term was used to describe the condition of workers who allegedly had no incentive to find work because they were being provided for by the Poor Law. They had become dependent on the state.

Endowed charities   Charities whose founders had specified which groups should receive money from their fund.

Enfranchise   The franchise is the right to vote. If you are given the right to vote you become enfranchised.

Evangelical Tories   The Tories were one of the major political groups in Parliament in the 1830s. Evangelical Tories were those who were influenced by their Christian principles to take action against the evils of society.

Executive powers   The authority to enforce laws.

Fabian Society   A group of left-wing intellectuals in the late nineteenth century who went on to become founding members of the Labour Party.

Feminist historians Believe that women's role in history has been neglected and seek to interpret the past from a woman's perspective.

Flat-rate In a flat-rate system everybody pays the same contribution or receives the same benefit.

Free market An economic system where businesses and individuals trade without interference from the state. Also known as capitalism.

French Revolution In 1789 there was a violent revolution in France in which King Louis XVI and his aristocratic supporters were overthrown and subsequently executed.

Friendly societies These began when groups of neighbours, friends or workmates decided to form an association to protect themselves in time of need. Each member would contribute a certain amount of money each week and in return they would be entitled to payments from the funds if they found themselves in need due to sickness, unemployment or bereavement.

General Strike In 1926 all the major trade unions went on strike in support of the miners, whose pay and conditions were being attacked by the coal owners. The strike ended without success.

Gestapo-like The Gestapo were the secret state police in Hitler's Germany. They were notorious for their brutal treatment of opponents.

'Gladstonian' Liberalism Policies associated with the late-nineteenth-century Liberal leader William Gladstone who, though a reformer in many areas, believed in low taxation and a minimal, *laissez-faire* role for the state.

Gradualism The idea that change can be achieved piece by piece over a period of time.

Great Depression Used to describe the British economy from 1873 to 1896. It was characterised by a fall in prices and profits and a rise in unemployment.

Great Exhibition of 1851 Held at the Crystal Palace in London, this was a showcase for the achievements of British industry and empire.

Hegemony If an idea has gained hegemony it has achieved a position of authority and dominance.

Historiography The study of historians' interpretations of the past.

Indigent Someone who is unable to earn enough to live on through no fault of their own.

Industrial revolution The process by which powered machinery was introduced in Britain in the late eighteenth and early nineteenth centuries. Factories were built and the population began to shift from the countryside to the growing towns and cities.

Inflation A general rise in the level of prices.

J.B. Priestley A playwright, novelist and left-wing commentator whose broadcasts on the BBC in 1940 were listened to by an estimated 40 per cent of the population.

Labour Party Known as the Labour Representation Committee until 1906. Labour was formed in 1900 as a political party to represent the working class. It was financed and supported by the trade unions who hoped that it would result in parliamentary action in favour of working people.

Laissez-faire Literally means 'let it be'. The idea that the state should not get involved in economic or social issues but leave them for individuals and businesses to sort out.

Lancashire 'cotton famine' The US civil war (1861–5) resulted in a disruption of the supply of raw cotton. Lancashire textile mills were forced to lay off their workers when they ran out of supplies.

Left-winger A member of the more radical section of the Labour Party who wanted more socialist policies to extend state control of the economy and distribute wealth in favour of the working class.

Legislative powers   The power to make laws.

Marxist   The belief that all societies are divided into classes based on the economy of that society. For Marx, the struggle between these classes was the dynamic factor that explained historical development.

May Committee   A group set up to look into the financial crisis faced by the government. The committee was dominated by bankers and, in August 1931, recommended large cuts in public expenditure.

Mere physical efficiency   The bare minimum necessary for survival.

Minority government   If a political party fails to win the majority of seats in the House of Commons it can still become the government with the temporary support of another political party.

National debt   The total amount of money owed by a government.

National efficiency   Used by politicians around 1900 to describe the population's ability to compete in the world, both economically and militarily.

National government   Many Labour ministers refused to go along with the cuts in unemployment benefit that the May Committee had recommended. In response, in August 1931, the Labour Prime Minister Ramsay MacDonald and a group of supporters joined with the Conservatives and some Liberals to form a coalition 'national' government.

Outdoor relief   Financial support for people living in their own homes rather than the workhouse.

Parish   The smallest unit of local government.

Paternalist   Where an institution rules in what it regards as the best interests of the

people but without consulting them about this – kindly but oppressive rule.

'Peers versus people'   Used to describe the electoral conflicts of 1910 between the Conservatives, who had a majority in the House of Lords, and the Liberals, who had a majority in the House of Commons.

Philanthropy   Philanthropists were relatively wealthy people who used their money to provide for poor people, for example through setting up housing schemes.

Pilgrim Trust   A charity that carried out studies into unemployment in the 1930s.

Poll tax   A tax where every person pays the same amount, regardless of their income or wealth.

Poplarism   Used to describe left-wing boards of guardians, like those in Poplar, east London, who used their position to raise the levels of relief and the general conditions provided for Poor Law applicants.

Postmodernist   The view that criticises grand theories and explanations.

Poverty line   The amount of income necessary to live at a basic level.

Principle of less eligibility   The idea that the poor would not choose to go to the workhouse if they had any alternative because workhouse conditions were so unattractive.

Private member's bill   A bill introduced by a backbench MP rather than the government. If such a bill gets the support of a majority of MPs it can become a law.

Progressive   Favouring social reform and greater democracy.

Protectionism   The policy of imposing taxes on imports to make them expensive relative to home-produced goods.

Public Works Commissioners   A government-appointed body that had the power to grant loans for building projects.

Rateable value   How much a property was worth for the purpose of assessing the rates that should be paid on it.

Ratepayers   Property owners who paid rates, a tax on property used to finance local government spending.

Riot Act   The 1715 Riot Act made local magistrates responsible for the control of unruly citizens. If a crowd of more than 12 people did not disperse after the Riot Act was read to them the magistrate could order their arrest.

Russian Revolution   In 1917 the world's first Communist revolution took place when the Bolsheviks overthrew the dictatorial Tsarist monarchy. Some people believed that this would lead to a series of socialist revolutions throughout the industrialised world.

Salvation Army   Religious group formed in 1878 with the aim of reviving Christianity in British cities and helping the poor.

Select Committee   A group of MPs who investigate a particular issue.

Select vestries   Small committees that could specialise in Poor Law administration and employ salaried assistant overseers to supervise it.

Social authoritarianism   The imposition of values and ways of living on people regardless of what those people wanted.

Social Democratic Federation   A political party whose policies were influenced by the revolutionary ideas of Karl Marx.

Socialism   The belief that state control of essential services and resources can be used to redistribute wealth from the rich to the poor to create a fairer society.

Socialist   A believer in socialism. Socialism is the idea that society should be much more equal and that equality can be achieved through collective control of industry and resources, either through the state or through co-operatives.

Somerset House   The London headquarters of the Poor Law Commission.

Sweated trades   Low-paid hard work, often done at home and usually involving payment based on the amount of work done rather than the number of hours employed.

Taff Vale judgement   A legal decision in 1901 that effectively prevented trade unions from ever going on strike because the costs in damages would bankrupt them.

Ten Hour Movement   A campaign in the 1830s whose aim was to see legislation passed imposing a maximum 10-hour working day in factories.

The Great War   The 1914–18 war. The empires of Britain, Russia and France fought against those of Germany, Austria-Hungary and Turkey. In 1917 the USA joined the war on the side of Britain and its allies.

Trade unions   These were formed by groups of workers to negotiate better wages and conditions with their employers. Like friendly societies, trade unions also provided benefits for members who were in need.

Trades Union Congress   The association that brings together the major British trade unions.

Typhoid   A bacterial infection often contracted through drinking contaminated water. It was a widespread killer in the nineteenth century.

Uncovenanted benefit   A payment made to unemployed workers who had exhausted their entitlement under the national insurance scheme.

Universalism   The idea that benefits and welfare provision, like the NHS, should be available to everyone.

Utilitarianism   The idea that all institutions should be tested to see whether they produced 'the greatest happiness for the greatest number' and that institutions should be reformed if they failed to pass this test of utility (usefulness).

Versailles Treaties   The peace treaties at the end of the First World War. Germany and her allies had their armed forces limited and their empires dismantled. Germany was forced to pay large amounts of money to France to compensate for wartime destruction.

Voluntary schools   Schools that were set up and run by religious societies.

Wall Street Crash   In 1929 the price of shares on the New York stock exchange in Wall Street fell rapidly. Many investors went bankrupt and confidence drained from business. Companies started to reduce their workforces and many collapsed. The result was mass unemployment that spread throughout the industrialised world.

Welfare state   Established by the Labour government after 1945, the aim of the welfare state was to provide support to everyone who needed it from 'the cradle to the grave'. Benefits were to be provided by central government and included a National Health Service.

White paper   A government policy proposal.

Working-class radicals   Workers who believed that the government should be more democratic and do much more to support their class.

Yeomanry   A reserve volunteer force that could be used to suppress public disorder and to assist the regular army in the event of invasion or insurrection.

Index